THE PARTICIPATORY JOURNALISM
OF MICHAEL HERR, NORMAN MAILER, HUNTER S. THOMPSON, AND JOAN DIDION

Creating New Reporting Styles

THE PARTICIPATORY JOURNALISM OF MICHAEL HERR, NORMAN MAILER, HUNTER S. THOMPSON, AND JOAN DIDION

Creating New Reporting Styles

Jason Mosser

With a Preface by
Philip Sipiora

The Edwin Mellen Press
Lewiston•Queenston•Lampeter

Library of Congress Cataloging-in-Publication Data

Mosser, Jason.
  The participatory journalism of Michael Herr, Norman Mailer, Hunter
S. Thompson, and Joan Didion : creating new reporting styles / Jason
Mosser ; with a preface by Philip Sipiora.
     p. cm.
  Includes bibliographical references and index.
  ISBN-13: 978-0-7734-2599-6 (hardcover)
  ISBN-10: 0-7734-2599-3 (hardcover)
  1. Reportage literature. American--History and criticism. 2. American
prose literature--20th century--History and criticism. 3. Journalism--
United States--History--20th century. 4. Herr, Michael--Criticism and
interpretation. 5. Mailer, Norman--Criticism and interpretation. 6.
Thompson, Hunter S.--Criticism and interpretation. 7. Didion, Joan--
Criticism and interpretation. I. Title.
  PS366.R44.M86 2012
  818'.540309--dc23
                                    2012003606
hors série.

A CIP catalog record for this book is available from the British Library.

The Edwin Mellen Press   The Edwin Mellen Press
        Box 450   Box 67
  Lewiston, New York   Queenston, Ontario
   USA 14092-0450   CANADA L0S 1L0

              The Edwin Mellen Press, Ltd.
              Lampeter, Ceredigion, Wales
              UNITED KINGDOM SA48 7DY

          Printed in the United States of America

This book is dedicated to the members of my original dissertation committee, especially Dr. Hubert McAlexander and Dr. Christy Desmet. I would also like to dedicate the book to all my friends and colleagues who have expressed interest in and support for this project.

Table of Contents

Preface

The New Journalism has been around for nearly two generations and the surface topography of its celebrity proponents is well known. However, there has been relatively little theoretical exploration of the some of the more complicated theoretical nuances of the movement in its various practices. Jason Mosser's emphasis on the "participatory" nature of New Journalism calls attention to the fact that it is a more public, discernibly creative genre of public, reportorial discourse than has been recognized.

Any extensive analysis of a genre of discourse takes place, *a priori*, observing an overriding imperative to demonstrate that the characteristics of the genre add up to a definable, defensible system of language. The systematics of explanatory discourse have changed little since Aristotle's time. Mosser gently massages the tradition of genre explanation in offering an analysis that is probing and interrogative rather than declamatory and probative. His work attempts to contextualize the conditions that make possible a new form of expression that is both reportorial and creative, with a marked emphasis on the creative. Mosser contextualizes his subject in deftly probing the contributions of Capote, Wolfe, Thompson, Herr, Mailer, and Didion.

Over the past few decades, there has been a movement in some disciplines to locate invention within the metaphorical tradition. Hayden White, for example, argues that there is a powerful metaphorical basis in historiography, a tropical sensibility or philosophy of analysis that profitably functions as a foundation for writing history—a way of "seeing the world" that is inextricably intertwined with generic perspectives: tragedy, comedy, and so forth. Paul de Man, influential literary critic, has examined the theoretical/metaphorical architecture of all language,

i

especially discourse that traditionally has been considered non-metaphorical (logic and the sciences, for examples). For Mosser, too, metaphor is a kind of epistemology and this quality of insight, as well as risk-taking, is refreshing in the domain of journalism.

This study examines the work of its major proponents in terms of how their language is driven by a complex weave of figuration and grammar. Mosser's analysis invokes the pioneering work of Kenneth Burke and Mikhail Bakhtin (particularly the use and implications of heteroglossia), but that influence in no way detracts from the originality of Mosser's probing perceptions into the maze of discourse generally referred to as New Journalism. A core principle of Mosser's impressive work is the attitude he reveals in his approach to such diverse journalists. Mosser provides detailed, rigorous, tentative, conditional inductions and deductions that are strengthened by his discernibly non-dogmatic approach. Mosser is an explorer and inquirer who is inter- and intradisciplinary, an approach that serves him and his readers well. His designation of journalists as "narrators" is indicative of this multi-disciplinary sensibility and provides a hint of his respect for the power of literary narrative in narrative journalism.

The focused treatment of Michael Herr's *Dispatches*, particularly as gestures of anaphora, chiasmus, epanaphora, epizeuxis, and conduplicato, come together in a sophisticated synthesis of figuration and grammar, a terrain that is emphatically rhetorical and highly individualized. As Mosser argues, "Dispatches is partly about its own language, certainly, but its primary subject is not the writing of the text itself. Its real subject is the war in Vietnam." This description calls attention to the overall historical emphasis of journalistic discourse, possible only (ironically) through a rich tapestry figuration, normally the antithesis of stable reference of most discourses. Mosser demonstrates, with agility and power, how language becomes more alive, passionate, and charged with meaning though the power of metaphor.

The treatment of Norman Mailer and his complex tapestry of fiction/nonfiction brings forth an analysis that is impressively precise in its execution. Mosser places a primary emphasis on authorial voice and its role in shaping historical meaning: " "I would argue that one of Mailer's functions as a participant in the event, and one of his purposes as narrator, is to act as a catalytic agent to set the drama in motion." Indeed, as Mailer scholars well know, any rigorous study of Mailer's work requires a study of the man himself and the ways he embeds himself, through voice(s) (particularly the personification of history). A key to reading Mailer, according to Mosser, is to hone in on the technical representations of his protagonists as they are locked in cosmic battles. Mosser's analysis of Mailer's style is fueled by Mailer's obsession with literary language in nonliterary forms--without formal structure, emphatically figural, and explicitly and self-consciously aesthetic. It is reasonable to posit that Mosser has redefined the Mailerian journalistic aesthetic through his pervasive examination of patterns of literary language. Mosser's analysis incorporates ancient rhetorical movements such as the concept of *kairos* (special time) in noting Mailer's concern for the importance of the exigencies of time, time that is urgent rather than temporal. Mailer's values are reflected in the designation of time as opportunity, special moment(s) in which choices of action (or inaction) lead to dramatic consequences.

Mosser's treatment of Hunter Thompson engages in a rigorous treatment of rhetorical and linguistic characteristics that inform Thompson's style of journalism. In particular, Mosser is concerned with Thompson's fetish for aggressive speculation in

iii

locating the chaos of contemporary existence as calling for a special kind of journalism, a kind of reporting that has discursive weaponry sufficient to deal with the turbulence of the times and the cynicism and sinister nature of the dominant culture. The challenge of twentieth-century (and beyond) angst calls for a playful style, which represents significant change from the traditions and conventions of the past. What is particularly original about Mosser's respective treatments is his ability to modify his theoretical template according to the circumstances and styles of his subjects. (Indeed, Mosser shows a sensitivity to the importance of his own *kairos*.) Thompson is not Mailer, however, and each writer requires a unique set of tools for systematic analysis, which Mosser sagely supplies. His attention to Thompson's reliance of parataxis reveals that techniques such as these are far more than journalistic or literary mechanisms. They are tools for discovering and conveying "reality," and in that sense are accurately characterized as epistemological strategies, no small gesture.

The exploration of Joan Didion's journalism brings the influence of discourse theorists Burke and Bakhtin together in a dramatic closing. Mosser perceptively examines Didion's concern for what Burke called the rhetorical scene: the context of an occasion infused with the attitudes and beliefs of participants. Didion posits the arbitrariness of meaning itself and her journalism is rife with illustrations of the impossibility of establishing stable meaning by means of the journalistic enterprise. Mosser analyzes style, particularly Didion's use of appositives and dependent clauses, to dramatize the insertion of various subtexts as part of the essential context of her reporting. These subtexts, as in the work of Mailer, are often in opposition to one another, thus creating a cauldron of energy that gives birth to powerful perspectives that are enhanced by the rhythms of asyndeton and isocolon. Chiasmus (reversal of word order) is the residue of Didion's new style, which in turns calls into question the sort of logical progressions that traditional journalism "reports." There is an element of meta-journalism in play also, as with Mailer, that announces a concern for the reporting of stable fact. Indeed, the auto-reflections of new journalists such as Didion call attention to the problematics of making sense of experience. As Mosser notes, "Didion creates a sense of disorientation." The result is an open-endedness that permeates her writing with, always and already, an emphasis on the dialectical struggle of ideas in conflict.

What is the primary contribution of this book? I think that it is Mosser's indefatigable spirit of interrogation. His analysis does not pretend to demonstrate a thesis, at least in the traditional sense of the concept. Yet he meticulously examines dozens of rhetorical, figural, and grammatical gestures in the works of America's great journalists of the past half century. Mosser's theoretical template is broad and deep, but it is neither formulaic nor reductive. His critique is the beginning of a technical odyssey that reminds us that the most rigorous analysis of language sometimes concludes that powerful, articulate, and creative language often defies categorization, yet it is by the deft strategy of categorization that we come to know what we do not know with confidence.

Dr. Philip Sipiora
Professor
University of South Florida

Acknowledgments

I would like to acknowledge Dr. Christopher Bloss, Dr. Michael Fournier, and Dr. Christine Heilman for their help in preparing this manuscript. I would also like to thank The Norman Mailer Society and The International Association of Literary Journalism Studies for their support of my work.

Chapter One:

Participatory New Journalism

Genre: New Journalism

The mid-1960s saw the emergence of New Journalism, an experimental literary movement embraced by writers as diverse as Tom Wolfe, Truman Capote, Norman Mailer, Hunter S. Thompson, Joan Didion, and Michael Herr, among others.[1] Whether New Journalism is really new is debatable. The practice of literary journalism dates at least as far back as Defoe's *Journal of the Plague Year* in the eighteenth century; more modern precursors range from London and Crane in the nineteenth century to Orwell and Hemingway in the early twentieth; and in later decades writers like A.J. Liebling, Lillian Ross, John Hersey, and others were writing elegant journalistic pieces for magazines like *The New Yorker*.[2] Clearly, then, New Journalism has historical

---

[1] Some of the other writers Tom Wolfe anthologizes as practitioners of New Journalism are Gay Talese, Joe Ezsterhaus, Terry Southern, Rex Reed, Richard Goldstein, Robert Christgau, George Plimpton, John Gregory Dunne, Gary Wills, and Joe McGinnis, but there are others. See Tom Wolfe and E.W. Johnson, eds., *The New Journalism* (New York: Harper & Row, 1973).

[2] Thomas B. Connery, ed., *A Sourcebook of Literary Journalism: Representative Writers in an Emerging Genre*, NY: Greenwood Press, 1992; Tom Wolfe, preface, *The New Journalism* (New York: Harper & Row, 1973);

precedents, but in contrast to the standard journalistic practice of the 1960s, the new attitudes and techniques Tom Wolfe and other young reporters brought to their work did revitalize the relatively neglected genre of literary journalism. Wolfe has vividly recounted his early days as a reporter for the New York *Herald Tribune* when, in the spirit of the times, he, Jimmy Breslin, Dick Schaap and others were challenging the journalistic status quo.[3] Journalists and critics have attempted to apply other labels—literary journalism, advocacy journalism, alternative journalism—that may be more descriptive than New Journalism, but the latter phrase has become the canonical term for American literary journalism of the 1960s and 70s.[4]

Whether New Journalism is really journalism has been more controversial. As a hybrid of news writing and creative writing, New Journalism presented a challenge to conventional journalistic practice by attempting to break down the traditional

---

Norman Sims, ed., *Literary Journalism in the Twentieth Century* (New York: Oxford UP, 1990); Kevin Kerrane and Ben Yagoda, eds., *The Art of Fact: A Historical Anthology* (NY: Simon & Schuster, 1997); and John C. Hartsock, *A History of Literary Journalism: The Emergence of a Modern Narrative Form* (Amherst: U. of Massachusetts Press, 2000). Articles on the history of the form include Jay Jensen, "The New Journalism in Historical Perspective." *Journalism History* 1.2 (1974): 37, 66; Joseph Webb, "Historical Perspectives on the New Journalism." *Journalism History* 1.2 (1974): 38-42, 60; George Hough, "How New?" Journal of Popular Culture 9 (1975): 114-123; and Jack Newfield, "Is There a New Journalism?" in Ronald Weber, ed., *Reporter as Artist: A New Look at the New Journalism Controversy.* NY: Hastings House, 1974. Four anthologies that situate New Journalism in an historical context are Nicolaus Mills, comp., *The New Journalism: A Historical Anthology*, NY: McGraw-Hill, 1974; Norman Sims, ed., *The Literary Journalists: The New Art of Personal Reportage*, (NY: Ballantine Books, 1984); Norman Sims and Mark Kramer, eds., *Literary Journalism: A New Collection of the Best American Nonfiction*, (NY: Ballantine Books, 1995); and Norman Sims, ed., *True Stories: A Century of Literary Journalism* (Evanston, IL: Northwestern UP, 2007).
[3] Wolfe, 3-36.
[4] Hartsock, 3-4.

2

barriers between fiction and journalism. In an early essay on the emerging form, James Murphy defines New Journalism as an "artistic, creative, literary reporting form with three basic traits: dramatic literary techniques; intensive reporting; and reporting of generally acknowledged subjectivity."[5] Tom Wolfe states in the preface to his 1973 anthology of New Journalistic writing that what distinguished the hybrid form from conventional journalism was the New Journalists' adoption of fictional techniques like scene by scene construction, realistic dialogue, selective point of view, and symbolic details.[6] I will argue that the texts under consideration here are journalistic because their rhetorical purpose is to report on historically verifiable, contemporary events. At the same time, some critics have refused to grant these texts their status as journalism, primarily on the grounds of their experimental techniques and lack of objectivity.[7] Other critics reject labels like New Journalism or literary journalism that confer upon certain kinds of journalistic writing a privileged status. Phyllis Frus, for example, objects to this categorization, arguing that "Designating narratives as 'literary' places them within an objectivist and essentialist framework that inevitably affects our readings of these works: it implies some aesthetic judgment and tends to remove the text from historical or political analysis."[8] The key words here are "implies" and "tends" which suggest that reading a text for its political content precludes reading it for aesthetic appreciation. Like so many critics writing on New Journalism, Frus gets locked into false either/or alternatives in her thinking about generic

---

[5] Murphy, 16.

[6] Wolfe, 31-32.

[7] R. Thomas Berger, "Literary Notions and Utilitarian Reality," *Style* 16:4 (1982): 452-457; Herbert Gold, "Epidemic First Personism" *Atlantic* August 1971: 85-87; John Hersey, "The Legend on the License" *Yale Review* 70:1 (Autumn 1980): 1-25.

[8] Frus, x.

categories. Literature, the argument runs, is an aesthetic object, unrelated to the real world and read primarily for appreciation; journalism is a factual medium read for information only, not for an aesthetic experience. However, New Journalistic texts may be analyzed for their informative, thematic, *and* aesthetic values all at once. I will argue that New Journalism's social and political content and its aesthetic form are, indeed, inseparable.

Critics writing on New Journalism have tended to lump the writers together based on their use of traditional novelistic techniques, elements these works certainly share, but sharper distinctions need to be made to account for the different narrative and stylistic approaches these individual writers have adopted. When texts as radically different in approach as Truman Capote's *In Cold Blood*, Tom Wolfe's *The Electric Kool-Aid Acid Test*, and Hunter S. Thompson's *Hell's Angels* first appeared in the mid- to late-1960s, they established that whatever New Journalism was, it resisted easy categorization. Capote approached his subject much like a realistic novelist, fusing journalistic research and novelistic techniques to recreate the drama of a multiple murder. As narrator, he occasionally adopts the point of view of a given character; however, like the conventional realist, Capote maintains the detached, objective perspective of a third-person narrator. Yet, like all literary journalists, Capote falls short of complete objectivity. In an interview with journalist George Plimpton, Capote stated that it was necessary for him to omit a great deal of material from the vast research he compiled on the Clutter case, and omission is always subjective, selecting some facts over others; he has further conceded that "one can always manipulate."[9] In *Acid Test*, Wolfe similarly provides his readers with interior views of his subjects, Ken Kesey's Merry Pranksters and their early experiments with

---

[9] Plimpton, 196-99.

LSD, but he adopts a stance of authorial detachment, appearing only briefly as a character in his own text. Employing a narrative device he calls the "Hectoring Narrator," a mocking, ironic voice that addresses characters directly but without the first person pronoun, Wolfe as reporter attempts to distance himself from his subject.[10] Nevertheless, his narrative voice betrays the inherent subjectivity of his texts. Wolfe claimed that his texts were mimetic representations of the thoughts, words, and actions of the participants in his narratives, but as Wilfrid Sheed has discerned, even though Wolfe "maintains that he finds a language proper to each subject…this language is surprisingly similar"; Sheed argues that the truths Wolfe uncovers are not so much those inherent in his subjects but "Wolfe-truths."[11] Despite the rhetorical stance of objectivity and detachment Capote and Wolfe claimed to achieve, Daniel Lehman argues that "all nonfiction narrators are homodiegetic [existing as characters in their texts] in that their access to characters and information has to be negotiated within the boundaries of previously occurring events, thus making them characters (even if unnamed) in the stories they tell."[12] Wolfe admitted as much when he said "I seldom use the first person anymore, because whether you know it or not, you've turned yourself into a character."[13] In the context of the literary and journalistic scenes of the mid-1960s, Wolfe's promotion of the kinds of reporting he and other writers were producing at the time reveals his artistic and political agenda. As Lehman writes, "Wolfe was fending off another more politically engaged form of New Journalism. From the left of the 1960s had arisen the challenge of a committed form of writing that, while it differed from Wolfe's,

---

[10] Wolfe, 17.
[11] Sheed, 295.
[12] Lehman, 50.
[13] Wolfe, 57.

represented just as deep a rupture in the mid-century American practice of corporate 'objective' [...] journalism."[14] Nat Hentoff and other young reporters began calling for a new "advocacy" journalism that openly acknowledged the reporters' personal biases and allegiances.[15] In *Objectivity and the News*, Dan Schiller observes that during the 1960s a new generation of journalists "called for a more active journalism, a 'participant' journalism skeptical of official accounts of public affairs."[16] The implication of this call for a more personally engaged journalism was that all reporting was to some degree subjective and that the mainstream media's claim to objectivity was a falsehood, a pretense of neutrality that allowed the government, corporations, and the military-industrial complex to manipulate the media through official statements and press releases. Jack Newfield has compared mainstream reporting of the student protests at Columbia University in the 1960s with underground media coverage and exposed the media's "bias in the direction of authority" that consistently privileged official sources over first-hand accounts in alternative newspapers.[17]

Unlike Capote and Wolfe, Thompson staked no claim to detachment or objectivity in his reporting. When he gained access to the inner circle of the Hell's Angels motorcycle gang, he wrote his account largely in the first person, creating a narrative persona who also became an important character in the story. At one point in the text, he even maintains that "I had become so involved in the outlaw scene that I was no longer sure whether I was doing research on the Hell's Angels or being slowly absorbed by them."[18]

---

[14] Lehman, 80.
[15] Hentoff, 53.
[16] Schiller, 160.
[17] Newfield, 59.
[18] Thompson, *Hell's Angels*, 46.

Later, he admits that "I was so firmly identified with the Angels that I saw no point in trying to edge back to neutrality."[19] William McKeen argues that Thompson "does not want to be the distanced observer that Wolfe can be, or to stand back to have the novelist's manipulative stance, as Capote did."[20] Differentiating himself from Wolfe, Thompson said this:

> See, Wolfe is not a participant. He's a hell of a reporter. But being part of the story is critical to me. Because that's where I get my interest in it. Wolfe gets his interest from backing off. And I get my interest from the adrenalin that comes from being that close.... When Wolfe did that book on Kesey, he wasn't there for a lot of it. He recreated it ... I can't do that. It's too much damn work. It's easier to be there. Maybe it's more of a risk.[21]

Even though both writers are categorized as New Journalists, then, Thompson's remarks make it clear that he and Wolfe adopt fundamentally different strategies. Thompson's autobiographical approach, shared in their own ways by the other New Journalists in this study, is the one in which I am most interested. In considering the autobiographical context of these texts, I am performing a variation on what Lehman calls an "outside in" reading of nonfiction texts in which "we read what we can discover about the author's outside presence in history against the narrative stance that [he or she] constructs ... inside the text ... to read nonfiction narrative over the edge of text and experience."[22] As a genre, autobiography is a narrative about key events in the life of the writer, mixing memory, introspection, and analysis of

---

[19] Thompson, *Hell's Angels*, 143.
[20] McKeen, *Thompson*, 33.
[21] McKeen, 33.
[22] Lehman, 76.

both the writer's life and the times in which he or she lived. Autobiographical narratives are sometimes unreliable, unverifiable, even fictional. Autobiography differs from memoir in that the latter tends to focus on incidents from a particular period— not so much a single event—of a person's life; the two genres further differ in that memoir is more personal, emphasizing the individual's self in the process of personal or spiritual development. In critical discourse about New Journalism, the debate has primarily focused on how the writers negotiate the boundaries between journalism and fiction, specifically the novel, but New Journalism's autobiographical elements have received relatively scant attention.[23] Autobiography allows us to make useful distinctions between the writers whose work falls in to the category of New Journalism and to create a sub-category of New Journalism based on the narrator's direct participation in the narrative. At the same time, the critical approach I have adopted is not primarily biographical. My purpose is not to interpret these texts based on information about the writers' formative life experiences; rather, my primary concern is with the way they employ stylistic techniques to construct their rhetorical personae and to dramatize their personal participation in historical events.

---

[23] Malini Johar Schueller, *The Politics of Voice: Liberalism and Social Criticism from Franklin to Kingston* (Albany, NY: State University of New York Press, 1992); James N. Stull, *Literary Selves: Autobiography and Contemporary American* Nonfiction (Westport, CT: Greenwood Press, 1993); Gordon O. Taylor, *Chapters of Experience: Studies in Twentieth Century American Autobiography* (NY: St. Martin's Press, 1983); David T. Humphries, *Different Dispatches: Journalism in American Modernist Prose* (NY: Routledge, 2006); Albert E. Stone, *Autobiographical Occasions and Original Acts: Versions of American Identity from Henry Adams to Nate Shaw.* (Philadelphia: University of Pennsylvania Press, 1982); and Robert A. Lee, *First Person Singular: Studies in American Autobiography,* NY: St. Martin's, 1988.

Of course, as John Hartsock notes, in a work of literary journalism "the degree of involvement by the author is relative."[24] In the course of Capote's extensive primary research in rural Kansas, the scene of the murders in *In Cold Blood*, he certainly did become personally involved with his subjects, especially—as dramatized by two recent biopics, *Infamous* and *Capote*—with convicted murderer Perry Smith.[25] Similarly, Wolfe spent a great deal of time with Kesey and the Pranksters, occasionally entering the narrative in the first person, but for the most part both he and Capote attempt to efface their presence by placing themselves in the background, making themselves all but invisible. The key difference between Thompson's participatory approach and the approaches adopted by Capote and Wolfe is that the narrative persona in their works does not appear—despite the writers' extensive first-hand research of sources—as the focus of the narrative. The narrative distance that Capote and Wolfe create presupposes an attitude of detachment and objectivity that is largely missing from the work of Thompson and the other writers in this study. Through style and characterization, each participatory New Journalist creates a rhetorical persona, a controlling consciousness whose observations and reactions to historical events, based on direct participation, guide the readers' understanding. Unlike the speaker in a lyric poem or the narrator of a conventional work of fiction, little distance separates the real-life literary figures I will discuss from their personae, for several reasons. First, with the exception of Norman Mailer, who in *The Armies of the Night* writes about himself in third-person, becoming his own protagonist, these texts all feature an "I," a first-person

---

[24] Harstock, 200.

[25] *Capote*, Dir. Bennett Miller. Perf. Philip Seymour Hoffman and Catherine Keener, 2005; and *Infamous*, Dir. Douglas McGrath. Perf. Toby Jones and Sandra Bullock.

narrator whose direct participation is explicitly acknowledged. Next, the unique epistemological status of nonfiction texts, grounded in the actual, historically-verifiable world, virtually negates any distinction between writer and narrator. Finally, like Capote and Wolfe, Mailer, Thompson, and Didion have achieved a degree of notoriety that makes it difficult for readers to read their texts without referring to what they know about these writers through their public, media-created images. Accordingly, throughout this study I will refer to these writers as themselves and as "the narrator" interchangeably.

Journalist as Participant

The texts I have chosen to analyze are, in order, Michael Herr's *Dispatches*, Norman Mailer's *The Armies of the Night*, Thompson's *Fear and Loathing: On the Campaign Trail '72,* and Joan Didion's *Salvador* and *Miami*. Three out of the four writers I will discuss have relatively well-known public personae. Michael Herr is the exception to the other more familiar literary figures discussed in this book, but *Dispatches* offers us an opportunity to examine how a previously unknown self can be constructed through style. The self that Herr displays is a representative of the 1960s countercultural consciousness and postmodern sensibility. Toby Herzog writes that "Herr wasn't … naïve about the ethos of Vietnam: the politics; the Catch-22 mentality of the military bureaucracy; and the drugs, language, and protest of the late-1960s culture transported to the soldiers in Vietnam" and that he "came prepared to give his readers a perspective of the war they would not receive from traditional journalism."[26] As a young reporter in Vietnam in 1967, Herr's war experience was a rite of passage in which a hyper-intelligent, hyper-self-conscious young man from the American middle class plunged heroically headlong into the

---

[26] Herzog, 78.

heart of darkness that was the war in Vietnam and survived, though damaged—as were so many veterans and correspondents from the war—to write his account. Unlike the other writers in this study, Herr has chosen to live a more reclusive life, maintaining a relatively low profile, and little biographical information on his life is available.[27]

The other writers have created public selves not just through their writing but through live and televised appearances, newspaper and magazine articles, biographies and dust jacket photographs, as well as through parody and caricature. Thus, "Stormin' Norman" Mailer, a self-proclaimed "nice Jewish boy from Brooklyn," Harvard graduate, and World War II veteran, achieved both fame and infamy as the *enfant terrible* of the American novel after the publication of *The Naked and the Dead*, as a TV personality on talk shows, as a mayoral candidate in New York City, as an experimental filmmaker, as the champion of convicted murderers Gilmore and Abbot (the latter with unfortunate consequences), as a foe of feminism, as a public brawler, as the man who stabbed his second wife, and most notoriously, as an egomaniac and self-promoter. As Michael Lennon writes, "Mailer is Proteus. Perhaps no career in American literature has been at once so brilliant, varied, controversial, improvisational, public, productive, lengthy and misunderstood."[28] Further, Mailer was widely regarded as a leading leftist intellectual and chronicler of his time. Assessing Mailer's persona, Alan Petigny writes that

> by the late 1960s Norman Mailer was a cultural
> icon, widely seen as an irreverent rebel with a

[27] Arthur J. Kaul, ed., *American Literary Journalists*, 1945-1995, Detroit: Gale Research, 1997.

[28] Lennon, xi.

progressive vision. Mailer's scathing critique of
social conformity, his championing of
existentialism, his warm support for the civil rights
movement, and his opposition to the war in
Vietnam made it clear that he was no friend to
conservatism.[29]

Of course, the private lives of these writers can be and often are
quite different from their public selves, and this was evidently true
in Mailer's case, but what readers might know, believe, or expect
from these writers will always inform their reading, especially of
nonfiction.

Hunter S. Thompson was another cultural icon, the original
"outlaw" or Gonzo journalist, a former Freak Party candidate for
sheriff of Aspen, Colorado, the young reporter who rode with and
was ultimately stomped by the Hell's Angels. Best known for *Fear
and Loathing in Las Vegas*, required reading for anyone interested
in the 1960s drug culture, Thompson acquired a legendary
reputation as a consumer of copious quantities of illicit substances
with a penchant for paranoia, violence, and invective. Marc
Weingarten refers to Thompson's tough-guy persona when he
writes, "No story was worthy for Thompson unless he could
immerse himself, body and soul, and come out on the other side
with a piece of writing tinctured with his own blood and sweat."[30]
Thompson is known not just through his role as author but through
his portrayals by Bill Murray in *Where the Buffalo Roam* and
Johnny Depp in the film adaptation of *Fear and Loathing in Las
Vegas*; he is also known as the prototype for the character Dr.
Duke in Gary Trudeau's *Doonsebury* comic strip.[31] A recent

---

[29] Petigny, 185.
[30] Weingarten, 124.
[31] *Where the Buffalo Roam*. Dir. Art Linson. Perf. Bill Murray and
Peter Boyle. Universal Pictures, 1980; and *Fear and Loathing in Las Vegas*. Dir.

documentary, *Gonzo: The Life and Work of Dr. Hunter S. Thompson*, was released in 2008.[32] Thompson's persona is prone to play pranks on the characters in his narratives, including adopting disguises and skipping out on hotel bills, and to goof on his readers as well, diverting them with digressions and satirical fabrications. Yet, another side of Thompson's persona is his dark, prophetic vision, informed by his Southern Christian background, inscribed in his texts with allusions to the books of *Jeremiah* and *Revelations*. I should add that since I first wrote this book as my dissertation back in the early 1990s, two of its subjects, Hunter S. Thompson and Norman Mailer, are no longer living. Thompson committed suicide in 2005; Mailer succumbed to cancer in 2007. The lives and exploits of both literary figures have been recorded in numerous official and unofficial biographies.[33]

Of all these writers, Didion's public persona is the most enigmatic. The daughter of a generations-old family in

---

Terry Gilliam. Perf. Johnny Depp and Benicio Del Torro. Fear and Loathing LLC, 1998.

[32] *Gonzo: The Life and Work of Dr. Hunter S. Thompson*, Dir. Alex Gibney. Perf. Hunter S. Thompson and Johnny Depp, 2008.

[33] Biographies of Mailer include Mary Dearborn, *Mailer: A Biography* (Boston: Houghton Mifflin, 1999); J. Michael Lennon and Donna Pedro Lennon, *Norman Mailer: Works and Days* (Shavertown, PA: Sligo Press, 2000); Peter Manso, *Mailer: His Life and Times* (NY: Simon and Schuster, 1985); Hillary Mills, *Mailer: A Biography* (NY: Empire Books, 1982); and Carl E. Rollyson, *The Lives of Norman Mailer* (NY: Paragon House, 1991). Biographies of Thompson include E. Jean Carroll, *Hunter: The Strange and Savage Life of Hunter S. Thompson* (NY: Penguin, 1993); Paul Perry, *Fear and Loathing: The Strange and Terrible Saga of Hunter S. Thompson* (NY: Thunder's Mouth Press, 2004); Jann Wenner and Corey Seymour, *Gonzo: The Life of Hunter S. Thompson* (NY: Little, Brown, 2007); and Peter O. Whitmer, *When the Going Gets Weird: The Twisted Life and Times of Hunter S. Thompson; A Very Unauthorized Biography* (NY: Hyperion, 1993). Personal memoirs of Thompson include Michael Cleverly and Bob Braudis, *The Kitchen Readings: Untold Stories of Hunter S. Thompson*, NY: Harper, 2008; Ralph Steadman, *The Joke's Over: Bruised Memories: Hunter S. Thompson and Me*, Orlando, FL: Harcourt, 2006.

Sacramento, CA, Didion attended Berkeley, married the writer John Gregory Dunne—whose death she writes about in *The Year of Magical Thinking*—and has worked as a journalist, novelist, and occasional screenwriter. In the title essay from her collection *The White Album*, she cites a psychiatric report that diagnoses her as "*a personality in process of deterioration with abundant signs of failing defenses and increasing inability of the ego to mediate the world of reality.*"[34] Viewed from an archetypal perspective, Didion's neuroses and psychoses suggest a connection between emotional pathology and creativity that paradoxically provides extraordinary clarity of vision and prescience of place. Her probing self-analysis can be seen as her enactment of the Delphic oracle's admonition to "Know Thyself." The effect of Didion's narratives, particularly of her journalism of the 1980s and 1990s, is often oracular as well. Juan Corradi captures the inscrutable mysteriousness of Didion's *Salvador* when he writes:

> Joan Didion's phrases bring forth the peculiar state of hypnotic abeyance that is the essence of terror. She achieves this effect through the careful notation of detail and the unabashed watchfulness over language. She refuses both analysis and synthesis, she rejects abstractions and eschews conclusions. Instead, she reports on these as discursive operations performed by near and distant actors while they seek to mask, or neutralize, or routinize a truth that is everywhere in evidence but impossible to face; objective and abject, like a corpse.[35]

The opacity of these texts sometimes requires her readers to process complex syntax, to ask questions along with the writer, and

---

[34] Didion, 14.
[35] Corradi, 161.

to experience moments of insight, sometimes luminous, often dark and disturbing. Like the other New Journalists in this study, Didion insists on directly witnessing the events she describes and on calling attention to political violence, propaganda, and oppression wherever she finds it. In her essay "On Morality," she argues emphatically in favor of what she calls "wagon train morality," the social contract that binds us to ensure our survival, and this moral imperative informs her journalism.[36]

A consideration of the biographical and autobiographical facts about a writer's life is consistent with the method of textual analysis Kenneth Burke sets forth in *A Grammar of Motives*, based on the Pentad: act, agent, agency, scene, and purpose.[37] Such an analysis will require us to read for what we can discover about the agents who perform actions, the actions themselves, the agencies or means through which actions are performed, the scene of actions, and the purpose for the actions. Equally important is the sixth term Burke added, forming a sextet: the attitude with which actions are performed. Clearly, the most important agents are the writers themselves, the protagonists of their own narratives, and the actions they perform are two-fold: (1) their direct participation in the events they narrate and (2) their adoption of what Burke, in *The Philosophy of Literary Form*, calls stylistic "strategies" to construct rhetorical personae through which they seek identification with readers (1).[38] To appreciate the importance of immediate experience as a rhetorical strategy, we can look to the example set by George Orwell, whose book-length journalism, *Homage to Catalonia* and *The Road to Wigan Pier*, set a new standard for participatory journalism. Richard Filloy argues that Orwell's reliance on personal experience and development of his

---

[36] Didion, 158.
[37] Burke, *Grammar*, xv-xxiii.
[38] Burke, *Philosophy*, 1.

15

rhetorical ethos is his "chief means of persuasion," claiming that for Orwell, "immediacy of experience is a kind of shorthand induction," i.e., it functions as anecdotal evidence which may be more persuasive than second-hand accounts or facts gathered through research.[39] Filloy explains, in Burkean terms, that the "writer's character, insofar as it is the means by which the reader and writer are shown to be 'consubstantial,' is basic to persuasion."[40] At the same time, the journalists themselves are not the only characters in these narratives; their texts are populated by a wide variety of other participants in the events, from American soldiers in Vietnam to El Salvadoran guerillas.

When we consider these writers' real historical situations and the elements of the communications triangle, involving writer, subject, and reader, we need to add readers to the list of dramatic personae.[41] Implicit in this relationship is the notion that these narratives are not only rhetorical but political. In these New Journalistic texts, politics, as defined by John J. Pauly, indicates "that realm of symbolic confrontation in which groups of citizens organize, enact, and negotiate their relationships with one another. Through ... writing, publishing, and reading, groups come to imagine one another and thus to constitute the very forms of public life."[42] In his well-documented analysis of New Journalism as a social phenomenon, Pauly identifies the radical new form of writing as "a politics of cultural style ... a social act that was conducted in particular venues and elicited commentaries that symbolically positioned opposing groups."[43] Many of these New Journalistic texts were originally published and mass-marketed in

---

[39] Filloy, 54-55.
[40] Hebidge, 2.
[41] Lindemann, 12.
[42] Pauly, 111.
[43] Pauly, 116.

16

major American magazines like *Esquire*, *Harper's*, and *Rolling Stone*, and in that respect they too became part of the overall scene as they were read and discussed by contemporary readers whose understanding of certain real life events was informed by these writers' narratives. Readers brought what they knew about writers and events to the text, especially with regard to actual events they might have experienced, directly or indirectly, and they participated in the construction of meaning. Despite the position of the New Journalist as central consciousness, then, the historical cultural context of these works suggests that the story they tell is never merely a personal one. As John Hollowell observes, "many of the important events of the sixties were *collective* experiences— mass political protests, urban riots, the war in Vietnam."[44] The New Journalist always acts against a broad historical background. The texts I will examine here are stylistic strategies for dealing with real-life situations like the war in Vietnam or the 1972 U.S. presidential campaign. The scene of these narratives, of course, changes from event to event and from text to text, but all of these writers began producing journalistic texts in the 1960s or 1970s, a period of tumultuous change and conflict within American society embodied by events like the civil rights movement, the war in Vietnam, the sexual revolution, the feminist movement, and the emergence of the counterculture and campus radicalism, and their texts alternately embody the upheavals and the uncertainties of the era. Their responses range from Mailer's identification with yippie radicals during an anti-Vietnam War march on the Pentagon in *The Armies of the Night* to Didion's deep ambivalence toward San Francisco's Haight-Ashbury hippie scene in her essay "Slouching Toward Bethlehem." Of course, Didion's book-length journalistic works *Salvador* and *Miami* appeared during the 1980s, the

---

[44] Hollowell, 14.

conservative Reagan years, and those texts reflect the reactionary political atmosphere of the era.

By becoming directly involved with his or her subject, these New Journalists assume roles analogous to that of a sociologist or anthropologist, viewing society as a text to be read and interpreted. In "Sociology and New Journalism," Thomas Meisenhelder compares the New Journalists' methodology to that of the Chicago school of sociology in the 1920s and 1930s. Among the shared techniques Meisenhelder mentions are "field work," observational research, and a dedication to viewing the social life of a group from inside that group.[45] As one of the technical innovations the New Journalists brought to reporting, Wolfe identifies the recording of "status details":

> the recording of everyday gestures, habits, manners, customs, styles of furniture, clothing, decoration, styles of traveling, eating, keeping house, modes of behaving ... plus the various looks, glances, poses, styles of walking and other symbolic details that might exist within a scene. Symbolic of what? Symbolic, generally, of people's *status* life, using that term in the broad sense of the entire pattern of behavior and possessions through which people express their position in the world.[46]

These "status details" are precisely the kind of phenomena on which a sociologist or anthropologist would choose to focus. David Eason finds that "much of the New Journalism focused on the alternative reality of the counterculture of the 1960s, and the perspective of the reporter is much like that of an ethnographer

---

[45] Meisenhelder, 467.
[46] Wolfe, 31-33.

confronted with a different culture."[47] Much New Journalism can indeed be read as ethnography, the "thick description" (to borrow Clifford Geertz's term) of a particular subculture,[48] and as Richard Hebdige observes, "tensions between dominant and subordinate groups [are] reflected in the surfaces of subculture."[49] Eason draws a further distinction between what he calls ethnographic realism and cultural phenomenology, and he suggests that the participatory journalistic approach these writers adopt, placing themselves in the center of their narratives, makes them, in effect, cultural phenomenologists:

Whereas ethnographic realism, like other forms of journalism, reveals the act of observing to be a means to get the story, cultural phenomenology reveals observing to be a vital part of the story. Observing is not merely a means to understand the world but an object of analysis ... Ethnographic realism represents style as a communicational technique whose function is to reveal a story that exists 'out there' in real life. Cultural phenomenology represents style as an epistemological strategy that constructs as well as reveals reality.[50]

Politicized New Journalism

During the 1960s, many Americans were either fascinated, repelled, or baffled by the behavior of various emergent and subordinate subcultures: hippies, yippies, radicals, feminists, and Black Panthers, among others. As John Hellmann explains, Americans in the 1960s were confronted by "a plethora of lifestyles and subcultures, each with a different set of assumptions and behavior patterns. Moreover, these 'societies' were highly

---

[47] Eason, 146.
[48] Geertz, 3-30.
[49] Hebdige, 2.
[50] Eason, 57, 59.

19

unstable: one could not be sure what a certain mode of dress, for instance, signified about the character or class of an individual."[51] New Journalists attempted to satisfy the public's curiosity (and their own) about emergent subcultures by detailed descriptions of their dress and behavior. In *The Armies of the Night*, for example, Norman Mailer describes the highly eclectic forms of dress and unconventional behavior of the countercultural participants in the march on the Pentagon.[52] To some degree, all New Journalists employ a reportorial method Tom Wolfe calls "Saturation Reporting" that clearly resembles that of the sociologist or anthropologist.[53] Wolfe says these writers

> developed the habit of staying with the people they were writing about for days at a time, weeks in some cases. They had to gather all the material the conventional journalist was after—and then keep going. It seemed all important to *be there* when dramatic scenes took place, to get the dialogue, the gestures, the facial expressions, the details of the environment. The idea was to give the full objective description, plus something that readers had always had to go to novels and short stories for: namely, the subjective or emotional life of the characters.[54]

The groups with which the New Journalists tend to spend the most time are marginalized, emergent, and subordinated subcultures, such as the late-60s counter-culture, or, in Didion's case in *Miami,* Miami Cubans, groups who, in Richard Hebdige's words, "are alternately dismissed, denounced and canonized ... treated as

---

[51] Hellmann, 9.
[52] Mailer, 108-09.
[53] Wolfe, 52.
[54] Wolfe, 51.

threats to the public order."[55] Generally, the writers' sympathies and allegiances lie with the efforts of emergent groups to assert their identity or seize political power. Because the New Journalists experience the feeling of alienation from the dominant culture common to twentieth-century literary artists, they understandably identify with marginalized groups within their own society. Writing of Thompson's journalism, in particular, Hartsock asserts that his radical approach "represents ... to borrow from post-colonial criticism, the colonial Other writing back to the Empire [which] is forced to see a side of itself that only the marginalized Other can provide."[56] This is, perhaps, even more true in Didion's case in the sense that her narrative persona in *Miami* and *Salvador* clearly aligns her with marginalized Hispanic populations. Hartsock contends that Didion opposes support for the right-wing government in El Salvador precisely because her subjectivity experienced to some degree what she perceived as the subjective terror of an entire society by the government's shadowy death squads. The issue is not whether she feels it completely but whether as part of her narrative ambition she can narrow the gulf to feel what a distanced object could not provide.[57] As literary artists and reporters, however, outsiders in relation to the groups they write about, these writers become even more marginalized than their subjects. Unable to unquestioningly adopt a political ideology, or assimilate into an alien culture, these New Journalists are often left with individual perceptions as the only guide to meaning. Their marginalization offers them a certain degree of detachment, despite their involvement and identification with emergent subcultures.

The consideration of society as text extends beyond the dress and behavior of cultural subgroups to the written texts a

---

[55] Hebidge, 2.
[56] Harstock, 200.
[57] Harstock, 201.

society produces. The other participants who appear in New Journalistic texts are actual public and private figures whose discourse on events the New Journalists appropriate for their own rhetorical purposes. New Journalistic texts display the quality Mikhail Bakhtin calls "heteroglossia," meaning *another's speech in another's language*, serving to express authorial intentions but in a refracted way. Such speech constitutes a type of

> *double-voiced discourse*. It serves two speakers at the same time and expresses simultaneously two different intentions: the direct intention of the character who is speaking, and the refracted intention of the author. In such discourse there are two voices, two meanings and two expressions. And all the while these two voices are dialogically interrelated.[58]

Often, the voices featured in a New Journalistic text are those of its antagonist, the corporate media. The New Journalists under consideration here incorporate the discourse of the dominant culture into their own texts in order to deconstruct its claims to objectivity and authority. By confronting the enemy on its own territory, these New Journalists practice a form of rhetorical sabotage. Frank Lentricchia maintains that a revolutionary culture must situate itself firmly on the terrain of its capitalist antagonist, must not attempt a dramatic leap beyond capitalism in one explosive rupturing movement of release, must work its way cunningly within it, using, appropriating, even speaking through its key mechanisms of repression.[59]

By assimilating fragments from the texts of corporate journalism into their own texts, these New Journalists parody that

---

[58] Bakhtin, 324.
[59] Lentricchia, 22-23.

alien discourse and contradict it as well, thus undermining its authority. Many of the voices heard in New Journalistic texts are those of marginalized groups whose viewpoints are generally suppressed by the establishment press. Newfield observed during the 1960s that "Insurgent movements are ... distorted [in media accounts] because they tend to get covered only in terms of confrontations and personalities rather than in the context of issues, ideas or historical background."[60] The dominant culture attempts, despite its claims to the contrary, to suppress conflicting points of view by silencing or assimilating them in order to create the impression that no alternative or oppositional culture in fact exists. Frank Lentricchia argues, however, that "Ruling culture does not define the whole of culture, though it tries to, and it is the task of the oppositional critic to re-read culture so as to amplify and strategically position the marginalized voices of the ruled, exploited, oppressed and excluded."[61] By incorporating marginalized voices into their texts, New Journalists further undermine the authority of establishment discourse, which claims that its one voice speaks for the many. In *Miami*, for example, Joan Didion allows the Cuban-American community, seemingly assimilated but effectively marginalized by the dominant Anglo power structure, to tell its own story. The voices featured in *Miami* are often Spanish voices which stubbornly challenge the Anglo culture's claim to cultural and political hegemony.

These historical events, like all historical phenomena, come to us in the form of signs. Voloshinov maintains that "Individual consciousness is not the architect of the ideological superstructure, but only a tenant lodging in the social edifice of ideological signs."[62] Voloshinov's metaphor suggests, for my purposes, that

---

[60] Newfield, 57.
[61] Lentricchia, 22-23.
[62] Voloshinov, 13.

New Journalists live, work, and think inside an "edifice" already constructed by social discourse. Performing the role of social critics, a role implicit in the rhetorical contract that both journalists and realistic novelists enter into with their readers, they critique the way various individuals and groups use language for their own ends. As Frank Lentricchia argues, "the substance, the very ontology of ideology ... is revealed to us *textually* and therefore must be grasped (read) and attacked (reread, rewritten) in that dimension."[63] New Journalists are attuned to the fact that social reality is a collective narrative that we write in the process of creating or recreating ourselves. William Dowling maintains that narrative is "not so much a literary form or structure as an epistemological category.... This is not to make the conventional claim that we make up stories about the world to understand it, but the much more radical claim that the world comes to us in the shape of stories."[64] In a sense, then, New Journalistic texts are running commentaries on the master historical narrative. The historical narratives that the New Journalists comment upon, like their texts, are open-ended. The narrative structures of their texts demonstrate, according to Frederic Jameson, that "our relationship to a historical fact is not a fixed, static one, but rather one that constantly expands and contracts according to a dialectical adjustment of our distance and of the point of view we take of our own situation."[65] These four New Journalists frankly acknowledge that their distance or lack of distance from the events they describe informs, in a relative way, their understanding. Further, the open-ended structure of these narratives suggests that while the writers' participation in events may come to an end, the historical situations to which their texts refer are ongoing. As Chris Anderson argues,

---

[63] Lentricchia, 22-23.
[64] Dowling, 95.
[65] Jameson, 394.

in "dramatistic" narratives like these, "the conclusions are always presented as tentative."[66] These writers refuse to impose an artificial sense of closure on historical narratives, the future developments and consequences of which are unknown, and in that sense they deflect attention from their own texts to the ongoing historical narratives which have not yet reached their conclusion. At the end of *Dispatches*, for example, we find Michael Herr and the soldiers who fought in Vietnam still attempting to come to terms with their experience. These New Journalists' view of history is never static but dynamic, and therefore we may say that they regard history as a dialectical process. As defined by Lentricchia, dialectics is "a theory of the discursive movement of social and political history ... of the emergent process of a liberating discourse."[67] History, in these texts, consists of a dialectical conflict between opposing forces, protagonists and antagonists. In the late-1960s, the left-wing counterculture came into conflict with the right-wing establishment culture over the war in Vietnam, among other issues, creating a dialectical struggle. Dispatches, *Armies*, and *Campaign Trail* create rhetorical strategies for encompassing the political struggles of this period in American history. Didion's texts comment on more recent historical struggles between dominant and emergent cultures in Miami and El Salvador. These New Journalists continually remind us that they are inscribing their own personal narratives into the collective narrative that constitutes history.

If the New Journalists' view of history is dialectical, it is also dramatic. For Kenneth Burke, the terms dialectic and dramatic are closely related, for history, he explains, "is a 'dramatic'

---

[66] Anderson, 41 "Dramatism."
[67] Lentricchia, 33.

process, involving dialectical oppositions."[68] Competing historical forces, protagonist and antagonist, emergent and dominant culture, are engaged in a dramatic conflict. The dominant class struggles to maintain its hegemony, the process by which, according to Richard Hebdige,

> a provisional alliance of certain social groups can exert 'total social authority' over other subordinate groups, not simply by coercion or by the imposition of ruling ideas, but by 'winning and shaping consent so that the power of the dominant classes appears both legitimate and natural' (Hall, 1977), so that subordinate groups are, if not controlled; then at least contained within an ideological space which does not seem at all 'ideological' [....][69]

Burke argues that, "human affairs being dramatic, the discussion of human affairs becomes dramatic criticism."[70] The New Journalists in this study participate in inherently dramatic events like the war in Vietnam or political struggle in El Salvador; they comment on the drama as it unfolds; and, through their individual literary styles, they dramatize their participation in the events they describe. At the same time, as advocacy journalists, they construct their dramatic presentations of events in ways that privilege one group in the social or political conflict. Thus, Herr and Mailer identify with the anti-Vietnam war left, Thompson openly sides with

---

[68] Burke, *Philosophy*, 107, 109; The following works explore the idea of reality as a performance or dramatic text: Elizabeth Burns, *Theatricality: A study of convention in the theatre and in social life* (London: Longman Group Ltd., 1972); Clifford Geertz, *The Interpretation of Cultures* (New York: Basic Books, Inc., 1973); Erving Goffman, *The Presentation of Self in Everyday Life* (Garden City, N.J.: Doubleday, 1959) and *Frame Analysis: An Essay on the Organization of Experience* (Cambridge: Harvard UP, 1974).

[69] Hebdige, 15-16.

[70] Burke, *Philosophy*, 116.

McGovern in the 1972 presidential campaign, and Didion exposes Anglo Miami's efforts to marginalize Cuban-Americans and condemns Washington's support for El Salvadoran death squads. The element of advocacy or protest in these texts is strong, though never dogmatic or doctrinaire. Anderson argues that much literary nonfiction "recreates the experience of an event rather than logically demonstrating a thesis," exactly what New Journalistic texts do.[71] Mailer, for example, has stated in an interview that "I am never intentionally didactic.... What I try to do is create a state of consciousness that is a fair one, and my hope is that other people will read it and it will change their minds. But I don't have this idea that I want to change everybody's mind in one direction."[72] Orwell's example provides another paradigm here. As a volunteer in the Spanish Civil War, the subject of *Homage to Catalonia*, Orwell was sympathetic to the anti-fascist cause but became seriously disillusioned with the way the Spanish Communist party betrayed the workers' revolution. Like Orwell, then, these writers, while acknowledging their left-wing ideological biases, are also literary artists, and their responses to the political scene are therefore too varied and complex to adhere to the doctrine of any particular political party.

Returning to Burke's Pentad and the consideration of purpose, if we combine these New Journalists' direct participation with a heightened political awareness and overtly political subject matter, we can see even more clearly what differentiates them from other New Journalists of the same era. The subject of *In Cold Blood*, the senseless murders of four people on a Kansas farm, is not "political" in any overt sense, and Capote certainly excludes any interpretive scheme that is explicitly political. Of course, as

---

[71] Anderson, *Style*, 34.
[72] Schroder, 100.

Orwell observed, "no book is genuinely free from political bias. The opinion that art should have nothing to do with politics is itself a political attitude."[73] Nevertheless, we can discern degrees of political awareness and engagement among texts; some writers are simply more politically committed than others. Wolfe's double-edged irony in *Acid Test* ostensibly cuts him loose from any allegiance to the left- or right-wing in the cultural struggle between Kesey's anti-establishment hippies and the un-hip establishment, but as Lehman's reading of Wolfe reveals, the ironic distance Wolfe places between himself and the Pranksters reveals his implicit and perhaps unconscious purpose in *Acid Test*: "to evoke and then arrest the social and political breakout represented by his deep challenge to the journalistic conventions of the 1960s...moving toward a literary realism that more and more has become synonymous with social and political conservatism."[74] Thompson, Mailer, Didion and Herr distinguish themselves from Wolfe and Capote by creating a kind of overtly politicized New Journalism, the purpose of which seems to be consistent with what Orwell cited as the primary motive for his own literary work, "to make political writing into an art."[75] By means of emotionally weighted and self-consciously aesthetic language, they invite readers to share their personal reactions to contemporary political events like the war in Vietnam or the 1972 presidential campaign. Through their texts, these writers engage in a form of political protest, but they are neither dogmatists nor polemicists, and they rarely advocate a specific course of action or political agenda. Again, the experience of George Orwell, a committed leftist but never a member of a political party, provides more useful context here. When Orwell was commissioned by a socialist group to write

---

[73] Orwell, "Why I Write," 312.
[74] Lehman, 77.
[75] Orwell, "Why I Write," 314.

The Road to Wigan Pier, dealing with the conditions under which England's working poor were forced to live, his account was not altogether enthusiastically received by leftists who expected a more doctrinaire analysis. In "Politics and the English Language," Orwell claims that political orthodoxy almost inevitably leads to bad writing, arguing that

> Where it is not true, it will generally be found that the writer is some kind of rebel, expressing his private opinions and not a 'party line.' Orthodoxy, of whatever color, seems to demand a lifeless, imitative style. The political dialects to be found in pamphlets, leading articles, manifestos, White Papers and the speeches of under-secretaries do…vary from party to party, but they are all alike in that one almost never finds in them a fresh, vivid, home-made turn of speech.[76]

Like Orwell, these New Journalists are often suspicious of organized political activity, aware that certain factions, on both the left and right of the political spectrum, use discourse in order to promote their own interests. Michael Herr found that his unique view of the war in Vietnam was met with hostility by both sides in the political conflict: "people of the left," he said, "think that I'm some kind of bloody-minded, militaristic monster, and people of the right think that I'm the worst kind of bleeding-heart sob sister."[77] These New Journalists are also distrustful of the veracity of the mass media which they consider a tool for corporate and government power. Covering the 1972 presidential campaign in *Fear and Loathing: on the Campaign Trail*, for example, Hunter S. Thompson claims that "Even reading and watching all the news,

---

[76] Orwell, "Politics," 165-166.
[77] Schroeder, 26.

there is no way to know the truth—except to be there."[78] For Thompson, as for the other New Journalists in this study, direct participation becomes an moral ethical imperative.

My contention that New Journalists attempt to persuade us to accept their moral and political values conflicts with Mas'ud Zavarzadeh's claim, in *The Mythopoeic Reality*, that these writers concern themselves with "the world-as-it-is," an absurd world, without meaning or purpose.[79] Zavarzadeh argues unpersuasively that New Journalists create "a neutral transcription of experiential situations [...] free from any imposed scheme of meaning or extracted patterns of significance."[80] W. Ross Winterowd disagrees, claiming that "Thematic texts are by definition interpretations: that is the whole purpose of, for instance, the personal essay. However, narratives are equally interpretive, for making a narrative is creating an interpretation."[81] I tend to side with Winterowd, and with V.N. Voloshinov, whose comments about the relationship between language and values have informed my own thinking:

> Any word used in actual speech possesses not only theme and meaning in the referential, or content, sense of these words, but also value judgment: i.e., all referential contents produced in living speech are said or written in conjunction with a specific evaluative accent.... No utterance can be put together without value judgment. Every utterance is above all an evaluative orientation. Therefore, each

---

[78] Thompson, *Campaign Trail*, 199.
[79] Zavarzadeh, 3.
[80] Zavarzadeh, 3.
[81] Winterowd, 41, "Other."

element in living utterance not only has a meaning
but also has a value.[82]

Speech always contains a value judgment because it is generated in a social context where neutrality and objectivity are impossible to achieve. While the values these New Journalists accept are often those shared by the left-wing counterculture of the late 1960s, their direct participation in events means that their own personal values, prejudices, and attitudes will shape their narratives in unique ways. Anderson reads New Journalistic texts as an "effort to convey in words the inexplicable energies, intensities, and contradictions of American experience,"[83] but Anderson overemphasizes the "inexplicable" nature of these changes and underestimates the power of language to recreate experience symbolically and engage the reader in a shared reality. I will argue that these writers' primary concern lies not with the ineffable and extraverbal, as Anderson says, but with direct, immediate experience and how that experience fits into communal patterns of experience. New Journalistic texts do occasionally point to experiences that are extraverbal, as Wolfe does in *Acid Test* when he symbolically recreates an hallucinogenic experience, but more often they concentrate on experiences that are explicitly verbal. As we shall see, these participatory New Journalists are also rhetorical critics, incorporating the discourse of others into their texts in order to test it against their own experience and to subject that discourse to rhetorical scrutiny. My stylistic analyses will demonstrate the ways in which these writers deconstruct the texts of the dominant culture while they symbolically recreate their own experiences of contemporary historical events.

---

[82] Volosinov, 103-105.
[83] Bakhtin, 284.

31

Unlike Zavarzadeh, Anderson does believe that New Journalists attempt to impose an evaluative scheme on their experience. He argues that "the dramatic presentations of contemporary prose argue for values and attempt to persuade us to accept those values," but the "values" he talks about are primarily aesthetic.[84] He neglects to give adequate consideration to the social, political, and moral values that these texts implicitly or explicitly ask us to share. According to Anderson, New Journalism "avoids [...] open deliberation on moral issues," and yet, as I will demonstrate, these texts do sometimes deliberate on questions of social and political reality.[85] In *The Armies of the Night*, for example, Norman Mailer includes a chapter titled "Why Are We In Vietnam?" that features a deliberative argument classical in its construction. The main problem with *Style As Argument* is that Anderson fails to identify the real theme of New Journalism which he proposes is "its own rhetorical dilemma."[86] One may argue that all literary and journalistic texts are, on some level, about the construction of the texts themselves, but Anderson is concerned with the metalinguistic properties of these New Journalistic texts at the expense of the dramatized social interaction between characters and their environment, in which, as V.N. Voloshinov says, "The immediate social situation and the broader social milieu wholly determine—and determine from within, so to speak—the structure of an utterance."[87] A text can never be solely "about" its own language without reference to the social environment that shapes the writer's discourse. As Bakhtin says, "The internal politics of style (how its elements are put together) is determined by its external politics (its relationship to alien discourse)."[88] These New

---

[84] Anderson, *Style*, 2.
[85] Anderson, *Style*, 3.
[86] Anderson, *Style*, 4.
[87] Voloshinov, 86.
[88] Bakthin, 284.

Journalists, as we shall see, demonstrate a keen awareness of the relationship between politics and literary discourse. The dominant theme of the New Journalistic texts under discussion here is the ideological struggle between right-wing and left-wing forces played out on the historical stage. By insisting that New Journalistic texts are autonomous verbal structures, or meta-texts, Anderson overlooks, like John Hellmann, the social context of New Journalism. It must be admitted, however, that Hellmann's thematic interpretations are informed by his understanding of the relationship between the writer and his environment in a way that Anderson's and Zavarzadeh's are not. Hellmann identifies traditional themes in the work of these writers. His discussion of Thompson's *Fear and Loathing in Las Vegas*, for example, focuses on the writer's search for the American Dream.[89] Hellmann's analysis contains much that is valuable, as do his analyses of Mailer, Wolfe and Herr, but my discussion will concern themes and ideas in these works like protest, propaganda, and political struggle that have been largely overlooked by other critics.

Genre: Fiction and Nonfiction

The major shortcoming of *Fables of Fact* lies in Hellmann's insistence that New Journalism is a fictional genre. The generic misnomer originates perhaps with Truman Capote's claim that *In Cold Blood* was a "nonfiction novel."[90] Obviously, New Journalism represents the application of fictional techniques to journalistic material, and such devices as interior monologue, extensive dialogue, and scene by scene construction are common to New Journalism. Nevertheless, I take issue with critics, like Hellmann, who point to the use of these narrative techniques as the

---

[89] Hellmann, 73-85.
[90] Capote.

basis for a discussion of works of New Journalism as novels. Hellmann cites Robert Scholes' observation that "fact" and "fiction" share etymological roots, both meaning "to make," and concludes that to use language to create any sort of narrative is essentially to fictionalize, i.e., to "make up" a story[91] To the extent that New Journalistic works symbolically recreate experience by describing it in their works, one may claim that their texts are "fictions." As semanticists like S.I. Hayakawa long ago discovered, the map (text) is not the territory (reality).[92] However, by the logic of Hellmann's definition, the term "fiction" applies to so many forms of discourse, from Science Fiction and Fantasy to everyday conversation, that it serves little use as a term with which we can make meaningful distinctions between or among the various forms. David Eason accepts the premise that New Journalistic texts may be discussed as fiction by claiming that they can be divided according to the conventional categories of realism and modernism: Wolfe and Capote, he says, are realists, while Mailer, Thompson, and Didion are modernists.[93] It was Wolfe who first suggested that the New Journalists had, in effect, revived literary realism, the convention by which society's manners and morals were given artistic representation, which he believed so many contemporary novelists in the 1960s and 1970s like Roth, Barth, and Pynchon seemed to have abandoned for forms of meta-fiction and fabulism[94] John Hellmann rejects the notion that New Journalists employ conventional realistic techniques but does acknowledge their modernity. He claims that "The basic assumption of nineteenth-century fiction, like that of twentieth-century journalism, lay in the existence of an objective reality

---

[91] Hellmann, 17-18.
[92] Hayakawa, 19-21.
[93] Eason, "Image-World," 192.
[94] Wolfe, 39-41.

simply recorded";[95] however, by the 1960s, "change and fragmentation had come to substitute for the stable body of 'manners and morals'," so that "The realm of the believable had become an extremely doubtful concept."[96] Neither fiction nor journalism could any longer describe the "typical" experience captured by realistic fiction from an earlier era, that of Dreiser or Howells, for example, because the "typical" no longer existed. Given the inapplicability of nineteenth-century techniques to twentieth century phenomena, Hellmann maintains that New Journalists were forced to appropriate the techniques of modernism, such as fragmentation and stream of consciousness narration. Hellman and Eason share an either/or assumption about narrative genres, either realist or modernist, but these categories are too broad to describe the unique qualities of individual texts. Reading Wolfe is as unlike reading Mailer as reading Mailer is unlike reading Didion. Mailer even chose different styles for different journalistic projects. For *The Executioner's Song*, Mailer chose a stripped-down, colloquial style that is completely unlike the complex style he employs in *The Armies of the Night*. Considering the stylistic variety of Mailer's texts, Morris Dickstein writes that "Mailer has been our most protean writer, remarkably consistent in his themes yet always surprising in the ways he finds to pursue them, beginning with his own inimitable style ... no two of Mailer's books would ever be quite alike.... Strategies that worked well would never be exactly repeated."[97] I would further argue that the minimalist style Didion employs in her early journalism, the essays in *The White Album* and *Slouching Toward Bethlehem*, is different than the syntactically more complex style she employs in her later reporting in *Salvador* and *Miami*. Didion

---

[95] Hellmann, 9.
[96] Hellmann, 9.
[97] Dickstein, 118.

herself has said in an interview that "the sentences in my nonfiction are far more complicated than the sentences in my fiction. More clauses. More semi-colons. I don't seem to hear that many clauses when I'm writing a novel."[98] As suggested by Didion's remarks, categories like realism and modernism simply fail to account for the rich stylistic variety of contemporary American literary journalism.

Ronald Weber raises the most common sense objection to the application of the term "fiction" to works of New Journalism:

> The books are not fictions because the writers do not choose to go beyond the facts or invent 'facts' to fit their purposes [...] The difference between fact writing and fiction writing in contemporary writing is not located in the use of factual material or in the employment of novelistic techniques ...What matters is the fact writer's decision to stay within the confines of the evidence as it can be known—and within those confines, if he chooses to write literary nonfiction, to do many of the things fiction writers do.[99]

Daniel Lehman adds that "The subject [of New Journalism] cannot be contained within the imagination of the author; thus the author confronts a living subject as one character to another."[100] As George Dillon argues, "language in [nonfiction narratives] is harnessed to the world; it is accountable to facts not of its own inventing; its descriptions and assertions can be assessed [...] for accuracy, truthfulness, and sincerity."[101] Contrary to Scholes' and

---

[98] Keuhl, 410.
[99] Weber, 47.
[100] Lehman, 50.
[101] Dillon, 197-98.

36

Hellman's claims, New Journalists do not "make" or "invent" characters and events in narratives in the same way fiction writers do. The imaginary world that fiction writers create, which often bears a striking resemblance to the world that most readers know, is nevertheless different from the reality nonfiction writers represent because the nonfictional world is the readers' world as well. Writing of Herr's *Dispatches*, Don Ringnalda observes that "One of the most profound problems in studies of the Vietnam War is the stubborn Euclidean assurance that fact and fiction are easily recognized opposites from two different worlds."[102] He problematizes generic labels by suggesting that "When it comes to *Dispatches* the lines separating fact, fiction, journalism, memoir, history, and autobiography become extremely blurred."[103] Indeed, narratives exist on a continuum with pure fiction and pure nonfiction at each extreme. The term "realistic fiction," which could be considered an oxymoron, dramatizes representative characters in representative situations, but it also contains a plethora of details that are historically factual or autobiographical. Or, to cite a modernist example, how much of Joyce's *Ulysses*, based as it is on Joyce's encyclopedic knowledge of Dublin, is history, how much autobiography, and how much pure fiction?

To substantiate his claim that New Journalism belongs to that category of prose we call fiction, Hellmann relies on Northrop Frye's distinction, set forth in *Anatomy of Criticism*, between imaginative and non-imaginative writing. According to Frye, imaginative writing is self-referential; it creates an autonomous verbal structure that invites aesthetic contemplation; non-imaginative writing, referring primarily to the outside world, is used to carry out the business of everyday communication and

---

[102] Ringalda, 75.
[103] Ringalda, 75.

directs readers' attention to the information, not to the text itself. Hellmann puts the matter this way:

> If we accept Frye's definition of fiction as literary prose, then our division is properly between the fictional and the assertive. This reformulation of the issues eliminates the unfortunate *illusory* separation of fictional and factual writing—illusory because it seems to separate aesthetic form and purpose from a certain subject matter: fact.[104]

I certainly agree with Hellmann's assertion that factual material may be treated with "aesthetic form and purpose," but I see no reason to equate "aesthetic" with "fictional."

New Journalistic Styles

Frye's distinction between the "fictional" and the "assertive" reinforces a traditional, conservative view of language that runs counter to the radical values embodied by these New Journalistic texts. In *Marxism and Literature*, Raymond Williams explains that the view of language Frye and Hellmann have adopted is ultimately reductive:

> The range of actual writing ... surpasses any reduction of 'creative imagination' to the 'subjective,' with its dependent propositions: 'literature' as 'internal' or 'inner' truth; other forms of writing as 'external' truth. These depend, ultimately, on the characteristic bourgeois separation of 'individual' and 'society' and on the older idealist separations of 'mind' and 'world'. The

---

[104] Hellmann, 21.

range of writing, in most forms, crosses these
artificial categories again and again [....][105]

As I will explain later, the "idealist separations of 'mind' and 'world'" to which Williams refers are those promulgated by Plato and later by the Royal Society. They are the same barriers between observers and observed that these New Journalists, through direct participation in their narratives, seek to break down. Following Frye's lead, Hellmann claims that a text must be either entirely literary/fictional or entirely nonliterary/nonfictional; maintains that the language in a text either calls attention to itself or that it does not. As Hugh Kenner argues, however, "the language of fiction cannot be told from that of fact. Their grammar, syntax, and semantics are identical."[106] In *Analyzing Prose*, Richard Lanham traces the origin of this literature/nonliterature or fiction/nonfiction distinction to Aristotelian rhetoric. Lanham claims that Aristotelian thinking about verbal self-consciousness has resulted in the creation of "a method for stylistic judgment that reduces what is obviously a complex gradient of response to a simplistic on/off switch [...]"[107] As Lanham demonstrates, this kind of thinking about language locks us into false alternatives. Fiction/nonfiction and poetry/prose only appear to be polar opposites. As readers, Lanham says, we can locate both pairs of apparent opposites on one stylistic spectrum. Hellmann contends that the literary or fictional properties of New Journalism are determined by "the construction of a text, whatever its subject, as a work of artistic design and intention so that it finally, or ultimately, refers to itself"[108]; but, unlike the seemingly transparent style of most journalists, which pretends merely to reflect the world it reports,

---

[105] Williams, 148.
[106] Kenner, 189.
[107] Lanham, 217.
[108] Hellmann, 23.

pointing only outward, New Journalistic style is at once transparent and opaque, pointing both to its subject and to itself. Zavarzadeh concurs, insisting that New Journalism is not "mono-referential," i.e., it doesn't refer exclusively to itself as text or to the outside world; rather, it is "bi-referential," referring both to itself as text and to the outside world.[109] The final direction of a text, whether in our out, depends, to a degree, on the reader. W. Ross Winterowd emphasizes the crucial role of the reader in determining whether texts are factual or fictional:

> Literariness, fictionality, and poeticality are not functions of the text itself but result from the way in which the reader takes the text, using the appropriateness conditions that constitute the genre. If the reader takes the nonfiction novel to be nonfiction, the essential conditions for assertions would apply: the work would be taken as representing an actual state of affairs. Under this condition, the obviously fictional elements in a text—such as invented dialogue—are taken as authorial interpretations, legitimate hypotheses about reality, not as fictions [....][110]

Lanham similarly speaks of the fictional/nonfictional distinction as "a complex transaction between reader and writer which allows both of them to delineate degrees of self-consciousness in the kind of reality indicated [...]"[111] New Journalistic writing assumes its greatest degree of opacity when the writer's participation in events becomes most emotionally intense. Of course, one reader's transparency may be another's opacity, and

---

[109] Zavarzadeh, 55-56.
[110] Winterowd, 32.
[111] Lanham, 217.

40

any given text is subject to what Phyllis Frus calls a "self-reflexive" reading.[112] Lanham's stylistic spectrum clearly demonstrates that we can locate styles on a spectrum based on the degree of transparency or opacity they display. On Lanham's spectrum, we can see that, for example, there are demonstrable quantitative differences between the concise style and formulaic structure prescribed for journalists by the Associated Press manual and the loose, lyrical style Michael Herr, who received no formal training as a journalist, employs in *Dispatches*.

Anderson maintains that literary journalism is "finally more a way of looking at a text, a way of reading ... than an inherent property of a text," yet his collection of articles on literary journalism contains essays that, by his own admission, "imply that the 'literary' or 'aesthetic' is in some sense a quality inherent in a work."[113] Even given the reader's role in the negotiation of genre and 'literariness', a rich rhetorical and critical tradition has repeatedly shown that we can identify demonstrably different styles. Ancient Greek and Roman rhetoricians devised an elaborate classificatory system of tropes and schemes, all of which can be found in Richard Lanham's *Handlist of Rhetorical Terms*, the primary source for the definitions of terms I will use in my own textual analyses. Lanham's *Analyzing Prose* and Edward P.J. Corbett's *Classical Rhetoric for the Modern Student* offer models for the application of these rhetorical terms to a wide variety of discourses. Dennis Rygiel points out the numerous methods we can adopt from Stylistics to provide an objective description of syntactic, semantic, lexical, and phonological features of texts with an eye toward which features are likely to produce which rhetorical or aesthetic effects. Taking into account a "whole range of

---

[112] Frus, 5.
[113] Anderson, *Literary*, xxii.

41

categories," which could include generic designations like autobiography and journalism, Rygiel outlines how critics can adopt a practical, "holistic" approach to style that sets in motion a "continual dialectic between intuition and analysis."[114] Beginning with the assumption that New Journalism is a genre of fiction, Hellmann analyzes selected New Journalistic texts in traditional novelistic terms like plot, characterization, and symbol. If New Journalism is not fiction, however, it seems inappropriate to discuss it in the way we discuss novels and short stories. Traditional terms like plot divert our attention from questions of style and persuasive purpose, and such terms misrepresent the unique epistemological status of literary nonfiction. Rhetorical analysis allows us to avoid the pitfalls of Hellmann's terminology, and opens the way for a consideration of style and persona. New Journalism (like all nonfiction prose) requires a detailed description of stylistic features and an analysis of how style models motive and behavior.

As Anderson claims in *Style As Argument*, his book does indeed "concentrate on subtleties and details of style,"[115] but his study lacks what every other study of New Journalism omits as well: a genuinely close stylistic/rhetorical analysis of individual passages. I have chosen to appropriate Richard Lanham's "lemon squeezer" method to analyze New Journalistic texts, selecting an extended passage and employing terms from classical rhetoric to name verbal patterns that model the writer's motives and behavior.[116] The stylistically persuasive properties of New Journalistic works make the use of rhetorical terms a particularly appropriate analytical method, as Burke explains:

---

[114] Rygiel, 34-39.
[115] Anderson, *Style*, 3.
[116] Lanham, 140-166.

the notion of persuasion to *attitude* would permit the application of rhetorical terms to purely *poetic* structures; the study of lyrical devices might be classed under the head of rhetoric, when these devices are considered for their power to induce or communicate states of mind in readers, even though the kinds of assent evoked have no overt, practical outcome.[117]

By writing in a self-consciously aesthetic style, employing figurative language, syntactic rhythms, consonance and assonance, etc., New Journalists create what Lanham calls "tacit persuasion patterns."[118] At its most opaque, their prose approaches the condition of verse. As Anderson argues, "though rhetoric and poetry have different aims—one to persuade and move to action, the other to create objects for contemplation and intrinsic pleasure—they can have similar modes or ways of achieving their ends."[119] When the prose reaches these stylistically opaque high points, it achieves, in Burke's term, "pure persuasion."[120] The purely persuasive properties of these texts create the necessary set of preconditions for New Journalists to establish what Burke calls a sense of "identification" between writer and reader.[121] Identification requires collaboration, the active participation of the reader in the creation of meaning. Burke argues that an audience who feels it is collaborating in the development of an assertion is more likely to identify with the speaker and his or her message. After "inducing the auditor [or reader] to participate in the form, as a 'universal' locus of appeal," Burke says, the writer may then

---

[117] Burke, *Rhetoric*, 25.
[118] Lanham, 122.
[119] Anderson, *Style*, xxii.
[120] Burke, *Rhetoric*, 267.
[121] Burke, *Rhetoric*, 55-59.

"include a partisan statement within this same pale of assent."[122] Thus, Michael Herr condemns American involvement in Vietnam by inviting the reader to collaborate in the construction of formal patterns and, at the same time, by stating implicitly or explicitly his own impressions of the scene. The degree of "identification" or "pure persuasion" in New Journalistic texts becomes highest when the writers' reactions to their immediate situation become most intense. As Burke says, "the more urgent the oratory [or text], the greater the profusion and vitality of the formal devices."[123] In these instances, according to Winterowd, literary nonfiction texts achieve the kinds of stylistic intensity that he calls "presence," which he defines as "the means whereby style gives arguments status, vividness, and extralogical power [...] that object or concept to which one directs attention assumes thereby more presence than other objects or concepts ... the act of attention endows presence."[124] I have chosen passages from each text that display this high degree of emotional involvement and stylistic opacity. Each chapter in this study will culminate in a discussion of how the individual writer uses style in order to create a rhetorical persona, comment on other discourse, and dramatize his or her immediate situation. Although I have chosen to appropriate terms from classical rhetoric to name some of the stylistic features of New Journalistic texts, I do not mean to imply that the New Journalists themselves are familiar with these terms, nor that they consciously employ these rhetorical devices. Rhetorical schemes such as chiasmus, anaphora, and parataxis (defined below) are simply part of our collective syntactical repertoire, of both *langue* and *parole*, in Saussure's terms.[125] Conditioned by a lifetime of

---

[122] Burke, *Rhetoric*, 59.
[123] Burke, *Rhetoric*, 57.
[124] Winterowd, "Dramatism," 585.
[125] Ferdinand de Saussure, *Course in General Linguistics* (London: Philosophical Library, 1978).

44

reading, especially of literature, readers and writers internalize these visual and aural patterns whether they know their rhetorical names or not.

Genre: New Journalism and Conventional Journalism

Having examined New Journalism in relation to fiction—the genre it assimilates—we need to turn our attention to journalism itself. The politics of New Journalism, particularly of the type examined here, is best understood in contrast to conventional journalism, which established the rules New Journalists set out to break. Like their counterparts in electronic journalism, conventional print journalists play an important part in the construction of social reality. In *Manufacturing Consent*, Edward S. Herman and Noam Chomsky explain the function of the mass media (television, film, radio, print journalism) in an industrial society: "the mass media serve as a system for communicating messages and symbols to the general populace. It is their function to amuse, entertain, and inform, and to inculcate individuals with the values, beliefs, and codes of behavior that will integrate them into the institutional structures of the larger society."[126] Journalists have considered themselves ethically bound to adopt a dispassionate, detached, and unbiased attitude toward their subject, a necessary stance to substantiate their claim to objectivity. During the 1960s, however, the notion of objectivity had come under attack. John Hartsock explains that conventional journalism during the 1960s found itself in the throes of an "epistemological crisis" regarding the notion of objectivity.[127] Theodore Roszak conceives of the epistemological crisis to which Hartsock refers as a conflict between what he calls "In-Here" versus "Out-There," i.e., between the subjective and the

---

[126] Herman and Chomsky, 1.
[127] Harstock, 15.

objective.[128] Roszak locates this belief at the center of Western metaphysics, arguing that, during the post-WII era, American technocrats assumed that only the "Out-There," the physical universe, that which was empirically verifiable and quantifiable, was ultimately knowable. Hartsock asserts that the New Journalists, rejecting the Aristotelian, "scientific" view, attempted to "narrow the gulf between subjectivity and the phenomenal world in reaction against mainstream objectifying journalisms that were attempting to widen the gulf."[129] More was at stake, however, than a philosophical dispute, as journalists and critics began to understand that objectivity, impartiality, and independence were not only rarely, if ever, attained, but that the media's primary function was not the objective transmission of information but propaganda and social control. Noam Chomsky and Edward Hermann argue that

> the democratic postulate is that the media are independent and committed to discovering and reporting the truth, and that they do not merely reflect the world as powerful groups wish it to be perceived. Leaders of the media claim that their news choices rest on unbiased professional and objective criteria, and they have support for this contention in the intellectual community. If, however, the powerful are able to fix the premises of discourse, to decide what the general populace is allowed to see, hear, and think about, and to 'manage' public opinion by regular propaganda

---

[128] Roszal, 220.
[129] Harstock, 15.

campaigns, the standard view of how the system works is at serious odds with reality.[130]

The bulk of Herman and Chomsky's book is devoted to the ways in which the media did indeed "fix the premises of discourse" on such issues as American involvement in Vietnam and El Salvador. By concealing its own interests and biases, the mass media can more effectively manage public opinion. These New Journalists, on the other hand, openly admit their interests and biases and lay no particular claim to objectivity. In one sense, then, the clash between styles of reporting becomes, in Hellman's words, "a conflict of a disguised perspective vs. an admitted one, and a corporate fiction vs. a personal one."[131] The mass media is an institution that confers authority on its reporters, and its authority rests on its claim to complete independence and impartiality, but as Jack Newfield has observed, even journalists who strive to attain complete objectivity are hampered by values they implicitly, and perhaps unconsciously, share: "Among these unspoken, but organic, values are belief in welfare capitalism, God, the West, Puritanism, the Law, family, property, the two-party system, and perhaps most crucially, in the notion that violence is only defensible when employed by the State."[132] One of the New Journalists' most common tactics is to pull the mask off conventional journalistic accounts in order to reveal their hidden motives and biases. Hartsock suggests that literary journalism "fundamentally has been a reaction in this century against the alienating gulf created by the objectification of news in the American mainstream press."[133] By "objectification" Hartsock means the tendency of mainstream reporters to separate themselves

---

[130] Herman and Chomsky, xi.
[131] Hellmann, 4.
[132] Newfield, 56.
[133] Harstock, 202.

entirely from their subjects, disregarding the role they play in the construction of meaning. Beginning with the premise that the ideal of disinterested objectivity is a sham, a cover for the corporate interests that own and therefore control the media, many New Journalists rejected the standard journalistic assumptions. These participatory New Journalists incorporate conventional news stories into their texts and counter those stories with their own first-hand accounts in order to expose the disingenuousness and limitations of traditional news reporting. The writers whose work I will discuss often see themselves as engaged in a direct conflict with the authority, the corporate establishment, and its propagandists in the mass media. Hollowell observes that:

> In terms of the reporter's attitudes and values, the new journalism reflects a decreased deference toward public officials indicative of the decline in authority throughout society. The conventional reporter typically holds a deferential attitude toward the public officials and must dutifully report their statements. The usual news article often reflects, unwittingly, the official attitudes of those with vested interests in how the news gets reported. The New Journalist, in contrast, strives to reveal the story hidden beneath the surface facts.[134]

In the process, these writers often dramatized the contradictions between officially-filtered propaganda and reality. Texts such as Michael Herr's *Dispatches*, on the war in Vietnam, and Joan Didion's *Salvador*, on U.S. involvement in that Central American country, are two examples.

---

[134] Hollowell, 124.

Having examined the traditional journalist's role in the construction of social reality and the new journalist's effort to reconstruct that reality, we need to turn our attention to the specific methods both types of journalists use to achieve their goals. David Eason summarizes the routine journalists' "doctrine of objectivity" as follows:

> As practically defined, objectivity means customary linguistic usage, structuring information in a rigid pattern sometimes referred to as the 'inverted pyramid,' supplying brief clear answers to the questions Who? What? Where? When? and Why?, using quotations as evidence, and presenting conflicting points of view.[135]

This approach carries certain inherent limitations, however. In "The Working Press, The Literary Culture and The New Journalism," Morris Dickstein maintains that conventional journalism fails to interpret facts, ignoring underlying causes while omitting information that powerful interests wish to suppress.[136] By the mid-1960s, reporting "just the facts" was no longer sufficient. Rather than restricting their accounts to discrete bits of data, the New Journalists sought, in Hollowell's words, to "*reconstruct* the experience as it might have unfolded."[137] As Tom Wolfe explains in his preface to *The New Journalism*, "the basic reporting unit is no longer the datum, the piece of information, but the scene."[138] When Wolfe talks about "the scene" he means essentially the same thing that the 1960s counterculture meant when they used the term: the "scene" is the Gestalt of a given event, a physical,

---

[135] Eason, NJ, "Metaphor," 146.
[136] Dickstein, 875.
[137] Hollowell, 25.
[138] Wolfe, 50.

psychological, symbolic totality, the meaning of which cannot be derived from its individual parts, i.e., the facts. In "New Journalism, Metaphor and Culture," David L. Eason corroborates Wolfe's findings: "Whereas routine journalism focuses on the object of perception, 'the fact,' New Journalism describes the 'world view' which constitutes the facts."[139] New Journalists realized that the conventional 5 Ws approach tended to reduce complex events to their lowest common denominator and thus to distort their reality. They went beyond a mere recording of facts to a discussion of the socioeconomic and psychological factors involved in a given event. By focusing on the "scene" to which Wolfe refers, New Journalism widened the scope of its camera lens; it searched beneath surface events to reveal deeper layers of meaning than those reached by routine journalism. Writing more for magazine and book publication than for daily newspapers, New Journalists were able to write more extended, open-ended narratives that allowed them to treat subjects in profuse detail and with a greater depth of analysis. In a sort of mock-interview with Mailer, novelist William Kennedy succinctly summarizes the writer's attitude toward the constraints placed on conventional journalists: "Think of the poor reporter, who does not have the leisure of the novelist or the poet to discover what he thinks. The unconscious gives up, buries itself, leaves the writer to his cliché, and [he] saves the truth ... for his colleagues and friends."[140] As I will argue later in this chapter, and throughout this book, the kind of autobiographical journalistic approach these writers have adopted allows them heuristically to discover the meaning of their experience in the act of writing about it, drawing on memory, reflection, and reconsideration to a degree most journalists cannot afford. The necessity for these New Journalists to develop their

---

[139] Eason, 146.
[140] Kennedy, 20.

subjects more fully was underscored by news reports on television, the sound-bite medium that, as Neal Postman argues, has encouraged us all to "amuse ourselves to death" by interspersing news of the war in Vietnam and social unrest with commercials for hair spray and dog food, gradually rendering us incapable of distinguishing between the deadly serious and the deadeningly trivial.[141] Herr maintains that the mainstream media's coverage of the war in Vietnam actually prolonged the conflict because "the coverage turned the war into something that was happening in the media wonderland that we are all increasingly living in [...] that horribly homogenized, not real and not unreal, twilight world of television."[142]

In conventional journalism, then, form, the inverted pyramid and the 5Ws, shapes content. The result, predictably, is that the perceptions of traditional journalists are shaped by their medium. They see what their training as journalists conditions them to see. As Gaye Tuchman explains in "Making News by Doing Work," routine journalists "construct and reconstruct social reality by establishing the context in which social phenomena are perceived and defined."[143] Consequently, readers of conventional journalism perceive events in the same context, that of the standard journalistic formula. The form of the conventional news story attempts to assure the reader that the writer has carefully weighed each discrete bit of information and determined its importance prior to composition. This style encourages a passive reading and does not invite the reader to actively engage with the text, to interrogate its meaning. The closed, formulaic style and structure of a routine news story imply a static, authoritarian view of history. Alternatively, because New Journalists view history dialectically,

---

[141] Postman, *Amusing.*
[142] Schroeder, 38.
[143] Tuchman, 129.

their texts therefore remain open. As Hartsock has observed, New Journalistic texts expose the fact that the mainstream media's claim to objectivity and correspondingly transparent style are like "the emperor's invisible clothes, a pose or conceit that makes a claim to critical closure. Subjectivity alone undoes the lie, and in undoing it literary journalists resist coming to critical closure."[144] Unlike the short, simple sentences conventional journalists employ, many New Journalists utilize a paratactic or "running" style in which facts and observations are not ranked in order of importance. Parataxis suggests that historical interpretation is always relative and incomplete. Again, in the texts I will discuss here, the reader often gets the feeling that the writer has recorded thoughts and impressions spontaneously, creating reality in the process of describing it. Of course, like all good writers, New Journalists must revise their prose to achieve a desired effect. Rhetorically, however, what matters is the appearance of spontaneity, the impression that the writer is seeking the meaning of an experience in the act of composition. The appearance of spontaneity contributes to the sense of dramatic urgency and immediacy these texts create. A heuristic approach allows these writers to dramatize not only the events themselves as they rapidly unfold but their own participation in those events. In *Fear and Loathing: on the Campaign Trail*, for example, Hunter S. Thompson uses his frenzied, fragmented, improvisational Gonzo style to dramatize his constant deadline pressure: "Ah yes," he says, "I can hear the Mojo wire humming frantically across the room [...] the pressure is building up. The copy no longer makes sense."[145] At the same time, much New Journalistic writing is, in the Wordsworthian phrase, emotion or experience recollected in tranquility. Accordingly, at the other end of the stylistic spectrum,

---

[144] Harstock, 203.
[145] Thompson, *Campaign Trail*, 169.

these writers, Didion especially, sometimes employ the opposite of parataxis, hyptotaxis, in which subordinate clauses and phrases build to a rounded period, delaying the most important fact or idea to form a climax at the end of the sentence. Hypotactic syntax in these texts allows writers to represent a depth and complexity of understanding that is missing from that of most conventional journalists. The writer's symbolic reenactment of events and their reactions to events invoke readers' participation and engagement.

In the 1960s and 70s, the 5Ws and inverted pyramid journalistic conventions suggested that the world journalists described was stable, rational, and comprehensible, but as John Hollowell explains, the world in the 1960s was unlike any world we had seen before:

> The dominant mood of America in the 1960s was apocalypse. Perpetual crisis seemed in many ways the rule. Throughout the decade the events reported daily by newspapers and magazines documented the sweeping changes in every sector of our national life and often strained our imaginations to the point of disbelief. Increasingly, everyday 'reality' became more fantastic than the fictional versions of even our best novelists.[146]

Hartsock believes that "mainstream journalism, objectifying in nature, failed to adequately account for and make meaning out of the transformations and crises" of the era.[147] Events such as the Kennedy assassinations, the first moon landing, and the countercultural explosion required new modes of perception and understanding. During the turmoil and social upheaval of the 1906s, the New Journalists began to realize (independently of one

---

[146] Hollowell, 1.
[147] Harstock, 195.

53

another) that the standard inverted pyramid/5 Ws approach was no longer useful to describe the rapidly changing world they reported. As Hellmann says, "reporters such as Wolfe, Thompson and Herr found themselves saddled with rules and formulas that made it impossible for them to deal adequately with their subjects."[148] New Journalists saw the need for a new kind of reporting to convey a new kind of reality. In contrast to routine journalism, New Journalists offered their readers alternative perspectives embodied in radically new forms. The texts of the New Journalists follow no standard format; indeed, their stylistic approaches differ widely from one another. By adopting the techniques of fiction—the construction of scenes, the extensive use of dialogue, and the use of stream of consciousness narrative technique—and employing their own unique styles, the New Journalists created literary structures that are highly individual and experimental in form. They refused to shape their perceptions according to the standard journalistic formula, and they attempted to come to their subjects with as few preconceptions as possible. As they did so, they allowed their subjects to determine the way they wrote about them; therefore, their texts are loosely-structured, episodic. In *The Dialogic Imagination*, Mikhail Bakhtin says that "the novelization of other genres, like journalism, results in an indeterminacy, a certain semantic open-endedness, a living contact with unfinished, still evolving contemporary reality (the open-ended present) [...]"[149] Like the contemporary reality that constitutes its subject, New Journalism is a genre in the process of becoming, calling the rules and fundamental assumptions of conventional journalism into question. It no longer claims that reality is fixed or static, and it thus undermines the authoritative versions of reality created by conventional journalism.

---

[148] Hellmann, 2.
[149] Bakhtin, 6-7.

The matter of form leads us back into questions of style, the agency through which these New Journalists create their narrative personae and voice their opposition to dominant cultures. Again, their highly individualized narrative structures and styles are what Kenneth Burke calls stylistic "strategies" for coping with situations: emotional, intellectual, and even physiological responses to stimuli.[150] In contrast to the highly literary styles these writers adopt, mainstream journalists attempt to write prose that will transparently reveal its subject, a prose that does not call attention to itself as language. As Burke argues, however, "Men seek for vocabularies that will be faithful *reflections* of reality. To this end, they must develop vocabularies that are *selections* of reality. And any selection of reality must, in certain circumstances, function as a *deflection* of reality. Insofar as the vocabulary meets the needs of reflection, we can say that it has the necessary scope. In its selectivity, it is a reduction."[151] In *Analyzing Prose*, Lanham locates the origin of the transparent view of language in classical rhetoric. Plato and Aristotle, he says, believed in the self-standing idea, a world that exists independently of our perceptions of it. According to this view, writers were required to call attention to the world they described, not to themselves or to their texts. Stylistic features which called attention to themselves were considered vices. Therefore, Plato and Aristotle sought to eliminate verbal self-consciousness, and conventional journalism has inherited the Platonic view of language. Because conventional journalists claim to offer their readers a completely objective version of events, they need a prose style that transparently reveals, or implicitly claims to reveal, the world it describes, without calling attention to the language itself. However, much recent thinking about prose refutes the belief that language can achieve

---

[150] Burke, *Philosophy*, 1.
[151] Burke, *Grammar*, 59.

absolute transparency. Following an analysis of Michael Herr's style in *Dispatches*, Lanham says that

> The uselessness here of the Aristotelian scheme brings up several important general problems. Perhaps the most obvious are the prose/poetry and fiction/nonfiction distinctions. For Aristotle, these must be absolute distinctions ...When you have a prose which is too poetic for prose, like Herr's frequently, you make up a special name for it— *kunstprosa* or *art prose*—and then forget the problem. When you have a prose that is halfway between fictional and nonfictional prose, again like Herr's New Journalism, you make up a special name for that too—'faction' (fact + fiction) seems to be the preferred new noun—and again forget about the theoretical problem.[152]

Rejecting the kind of epistemology implied by the Platonic/Aristotelian view of language, Lanham argues that "Prose can never be purely transparent because there is no self-subsisting model out there to be transparent to."[153] Following the lead of the Sophists, Lanham proposes that we evaluate prose according to "a spectrum of self-consciousness for verbal styles which measures the whole range from transparent to opaque" without making judgments about virtues and vices.[154] New Journalistic discourse can be located at many points along the spectrum, but unlike the language of conventional journalism, it generally tends toward the opaque rather than the transparent. The language of New

---

[152] Lanham, 216.
[153] Lanham, 3.
[154] Lanham, 204.

Journalism calls attention to itself in a self-consciously persuasive fashion.

This contrast between the intentional transparency of mainstream journalism and the equally intentional opacity of New Journalistic discourse carries significant political implications. David Eason locates the implicit political struggles in the dominant tropes of these respective discourses. According to Eason, the primary difference between the language of conventional journalism and the language of New Journalism is that of metonymy (based on contiguity) versus metaphor (based on similarity). Routine journalism, Eason says, employs the metonymical sign, implying "an intrinsic prior relationship between it and its referent," while New Journalism tends to rely on metaphorical symbols wherein no such "intrinsic prior relationship" exists.[155] Eason argues that a metonymical form of consciousness reflects the perception of a natural connection between past and present realities and a faith that traditional ways of making sense of those realities are still appropriate. In contrast, the emergence of a metaphorical form of consciousness signals the perception of discontinuity between convention and reality and a need to naturalize reality by uniting it with appropriate symbols.[156] Despite Eason's keen insight into these differing styles, the problem with his distinction lies in his use of the word "naturalize" to describe the effects of these New Journalists' stylistic strategies. As we have seen, ideology is the means through which the dominant culture "naturalizes" social reality and thus imposes its hegemony, its cultural and political authority. I would argue that "the perception of discontinuity between convention and reality" Eason finds in the figurative language New Journalists employ

---

[155] Eason, NJ, "Metaphor," 144.
[156] Eason, "Metaphor," 144.

actually denaturalizes the world, or, in Formalist terms, it defamiliarizes the familiar.

Again, conventional journalism presupposes a stable, autonomous reality, a world "out there" that can be accurately and objectively recorded. Through their seemingly objective, transparent style, standard journalists refuse to acknowledge the role they play in shaping the reality they describe. Platonic rhetoric, which makes verbal self-consciousness a sin, commands us to disregard our own participation in the creation of external reality. This way of thinking about the relationship between reality and the language used to describe it became especially dominant during what Lanham calls the "Newtonion Interlude," beginning in the late seventeenth century and continuing, in some ways, into the twentieth.[157] Thomas Sprat and the other members of the Royal Society adopted a supposedly transparent prose model that would allow them to record objective scientific observations. This model is perfectly suited to conventional journalism. As we have seen, the conventional journalists' pretense of "objectivity" allows reporters and their editors to manipulate public opinion more effectively. As Hugh Kenner observes, a "plain" style that seeks not to call attention to itself is still contrived, artificial, a rhetorical appeal to accept its assertions as fact.[158] Indeed, its apparent simplicity and transparency make it all the more effective as a vehicle of deception: "A man who doesn't make his language ornate cannot be deceiving us: so runs the hidden premise," Kenner says.[159] As Eason observes, cultural forms like journalism are

institutionalized and habitualized by societal members, providing a means for the transformation

---

[157] Lanham, 7.
[158] Kenner, 157.
[159] Kenner, 187.

> of knowledge vital to existence into routine.
> Because their function is to 'naturalize' reality, they
> do not raise questions about their own
> appropriateness for revealing 'truth.' Like words
> which through convention come to be considered
> inseparable from their referents, cultural forms
> appear neutral and transparent, natural ways to
> know the world.[160]

Through the institutionalization of the mass media, dominant power structures discourage us from believing that we can play any significant role in the creation of our world. They ask us to accept their versions of the world around us, and they dissuade us from creating alternative versions. By discouraging our participation in the creation of social reality, the mass media promotes not democracy but totalitarianism.

In contrast to conventional journalists, New Journalists freely admit that they are creating their own version of events. Because New Journalism is self-consciously opaque, it encourages active participation, or reader-response, and forces the reader into an awareness of the complex, creative interaction between self, text, and the world at large. Lanham maintains that "To admit self-consciousness into verbal style is to imply that the self is a social being, created by human society and existing only in it [...]"[161] New Journalism often invites readers to look *at*, not *through*, the verbal surface of the text. The reader's awareness of the writer's verbal self-consciousness leads the reader to conclude that the world in the text is, in part, the writer's creation, as well as his or her own. As Lanham says, "when we become self-conscious about words, they come to symbolize our participating creation of the external

---

[160] Eason, 143.
[161] Lanham, 218.

59

reality."[162] By concentrating on an open text which requires them to complete its meaning, readers also become aware of the degree to which they participate in this creative process. Again, passive acceptance is totalitarian, participation democratic.

What are the further political implications of these stylistic differences? In one sense, the conflict between mainstream journalism and New Journalism becomes, in Bakhtin's terms, a clash between "authoritative" and "internally persuasive" discourse.[163] According to Bakhtin, "authoritative discourse permits no play [...] one must either totally affirm it, or totally reject it. It is indissolubly fused with its authority—with political power, an institution, a person—and it stands or falls with that authority."[164] New Journalistic style is, by contrast, "internally persuasive":

> Internally persuasive discourse...awakens new and independent words ... It organizes masses of our words from within, and does not remain in an isolated and static condition. It is not so much interpreted by us as it is further, that is, freely developed, applied to new material, new conditions; it enters into interanimating relationships with new contexts. More than that, it enters into an intense interaction, a *struggle* with other internally persuasive discourses. Our ideological development is just such an intense struggle within us for hegemony among various available verbal and ideological points of view, approaches, directions and values. The semantic structure of an internally

---

[162] Lanham, 217.
[163] Bakhtin, 342.
[164] Bakhtin, 343.

persuasive discourse is not finite; it is *open*; in each
of the new contexts that dialogize it, this discourse
is able to reveal even newer *ways to mean*.[165]

Unlike conventional journalists, who remain detached from the
people and events they describe, New Journalists become
personally involved with their subjects. In this way, they assert
their preference for what Kenneth Burke, in *The Philosophy of
Literary Form*, calls the "poetic" ideal; conventional journalists, by
contrast, hold to the "semantic" ideal.[166] Seeking to attain the
"semantic" ideal, the writer, in Burke's words, stands "aside from
the battle, stressing the role of the observer, whose observations it
is hoped will define situations with sufficient realistic accuracy to
prepare an adequate chart for action."[167] The authority of
conventional journalism derives from its separation between
observer and observed. Burke points out the fallacy that underlies
the semantic approach:

> it fosters, sometime explicitly, sometimes by
> implication, the notion that one may
> comprehensively discuss human and social events
> in a nonmoral vocabulary, and that perception itself
> is a nonmoral act. It is the moral impulse that
> motivates perception, giving it both intensity and
> direction, suggesting what to look for and what to
> look out for.[168]

The writers I will discuss reject the "semantic" ideal in favor of the
"poetic" ideal. They

---

[165] Bakhtin, 345-46.
[166] Burke, *Philosophy*, 138.
[167] Burke, *Philosophy*, 149.
[168] Burke, *Philosophy*, 164.

would contend, by implication, that true knowledge can only be attained *through* the battle, stressing the role of the participant, who in the course of his participation, it is hoped, will define situations with sufficient realistic accuracy to prepare an image for action.[169]

Through their direct participation in events, New Journalists eliminate the distance between observer and observed. They place themselves in the middle of their stories and create personae who speak from within the world being reported. By becoming directly involved with their subjects, the New Journalists' texts embody an emotional quality that is generally excluded from conventional reporting. Holding to the "semantic" ideal, conventional journalists would try, in Burke's words again, "to *cut away*, to *abstract*, all emotional factors that complicate the objective clarity of meaning."[170] In contrast, New Journalists, believing in the "poetic" ideal, would, according to Burke, "try to derive [their] vision from the *heaping up* of all these emotional factors, playing them off against one another, inviting them to reinforce and contradict one another, and seeking to make this active participation itself a major ingredient of the vision."[171] As stated earlier, the poetic qualities of New Journalistic texts become most visible when the narrator's emotional involvement with his or her subject becomes most intense. The following chapters will explore some of those stylistic high points in the context of these New Journalists' dramatized interaction with the people and events in their narratives.

---

[169] Burke, *Philosophy*, 149.
[170] Burke, *Philosophy*, 148.
[171] Burke, *Philosophy*, 148.

Chapter Two:

Michael Herr's *Dispatches*: Journalist as Hipster and Postmodern Hero

History as Drama

Michael Herr's *Dispatches*, an account of the writer's experience during the Vietnam War, dramatizes the ideological conflict between the dominant establishment culture and the left-wing counterculture during the late 1960s. In Herr's text, the establishment assumes the form of the U.S. military, represented by the commanding officers who served in Vietnam and by the corporate media. The anti-establishment forces, with whom Herr symbolically aligns himself, are the lower ranking soldiers or "grunts"—as Herr calls them and as they call themselves--and countercultural reporters like Herr who openly acknowledge their left-wing allegiances. As Thomas Meyers writes, "Attuned to the message that the war is an energized, increasingly uncontrolled performance within redefined mythic space, [Herr] chooses to demonstrate how art and history continually merge in Vietnam [....]."[1] Vietnam, Herr says, was a place "where no drama had to be

---

[1] Meyers, 165.

invented, ever,"[2] indicating that his experience was inherently dramatic. Nevertheless, Herr's text provides a running commentary on the dramatic narrative of the Vietnam War while it also creates, through style and narrative persona, a drama of its own, that of a countercultural reporter tuning in, turning on and freaking out over America's first postmodern war.

Herr contends that the soldiers and correspondents in Vietnam experienced the war as dramatic to a large extent because they had been conditioned to see it that way. He exposes the degree to which ideology, in the form of popular media, informs soldiers' and journalists' perceptions. John Hellman has observed that Herr "sees a deeper gulf between the consciousness of Americans and the actuality of the war that from the beginning produced an artificial, fictive 'reality' conditioning the nature and course of the experience."[3] Herr says it was almost impossible for the reporters in Vietnam to see the war in its own terms, rather than in terms of other wars they had either witnessed, or read about, or seen represented on television or in films. "We'd all seen too many movies," Herr says, "years of media glut had made certain connections difficult" (223). The journalists tended to superimpose one war over another: "There were those whose madness it was not to know which war they were actually in," Herr says, "fantasizing privately about other, older wars, Wars I and II" (200). In some cases, the journalists' perceptions of the drama of war, and of their role in the drama, affect the way they write about it: "Over there," Herr observes, "all styles grew in their way out of the same haunted, haunting romance, Those Crazy Guys Who Cover the War" (200). Herr prefaces Section II of the "Colleagues" section of *Dispatches* with a paragraph-length parody of the conventionally

---

[2] Herr, 262. All subsequent references to *Dispatches* are taken from this edition.

[3] Hellmann, 146.

cynical, war-weary correspondent's voice (199). Later, he demonstrates that some correspondents had adopted this hard-boiled voice in their own prose: "So many stories had run the phrase 'grim reminders of a rainless monsoon,'" he says, "that it became a standard, always good for a laugh" (204). Despite its highly original qualities, however, Herr's own prose occasionally exhibits the same romanticizing tendency, as in the following passage: "Maybe you had to be pathological to find glamour in Saigon, maybe you just had to settle for very little, but Saigon had it for me, and danger activated it" (42). The quixotic yet hard-boiled tone of the sentence above suggests the war correspondence of Edward R. Murrow or Ernest Hemingway, two writers whose combat journalism clearly influenced Herr's own.[4] Walking through the aftermath of battle for the first time, Herr alludes to Hemingway's story, "A Way You'll Never Be," thus demonstrating the degree to which he interpreted his Vietnam experience as a dramatic text informed by other texts (22). Meyers suggests that Herr "redefines journalistic honesty not by retreating from the mythic aspects of war but by emphasizing them, by illustrating that no pure exchange between referent and romantic sensibility is possible."[5] Despite Meyers' overemphasis on Herr's "romantic sensibility," to the point where the correspondent appears almost solipsistic, his interpretation of the narrative point of view in *Dispatches* comes closer to the truth than that of Hellmann, who argues that Herr empathizes "so completely with any and all of the situations and characters that he could gain understanding relatively undistorted by personal attitudes and

---

[4] For an extended discussion of Herr's prose in comparison with Hemingway's, see Richard Locke, "Field Reports: Alaska and Vietnam," rev. of *Dispatches*, by Michael Herr, *New York Times Book Review* 18 Dec. 1977: 3, 26-27.

[5] Meyers, 166.

preconceptions."[6] I would argue that, unlike the mainstream journalists who claim to present an unbiased, objective account of the war, Herr openly asserts his own ideological mindset and subjectivity. While he acknowledges his own influences, however, Herr realizes that Vietnam was unlike other wars, and he ultimately crafts a stylistic approach that captures the war's unique rhythms, voices and nuances of feeling. He appropriates a familiar 1960s metaphor, life as film, in which everybody becomes his own director and star, to describe the tendency of the correspondents and soldiers to interpret their experience in dramatic terms. "We have all been compelled to make our own movies," he says, "as many movies as there are correspondents, and this is mine" (200). Of course, Herr's "movie" shares more in common with *Apocalypse Now*, arguably an anti-war film, for which Herr wrote the voice-over narration, than with a jingoistic, pro-military film like *The Green Berets*. By observing that all war reporters made their own movies, Herr makes the point that they saw and reported the war from a multiplicity of perspectives. He thus undermines the notion that any journalistic account could be entirely objective, much less authoritative.

In contrast to the correspondents' tendency to see life in terms of art, a marine sergeant tells Herr early on, "This ain't the fucking movies over here, you know" (21). Herr acknowledges his naiveté at this point by saying, "I laughed [...] and said that I knew, but he knew that I didn't" (22). The first time Herr puts on a pair of fatigues he describes himself posing in front of a mirror, making heroic moves he says he'd never make again; following that passage, he describes his horror at walking through a corpse-strewn battlefield as a transistor radio plays Sam the Sham and the Pharoahs' "Li'l Red Riding Hood," a metaphor for Herr's

---

[6] Hellmann, 133.

innocence and rite of passage into the war (37). As Hellman has discussed at some length, the sometimes shocking transformation from innocence to experience is one of the major motifs in Herr's text.[7] Of course, war narratives, even ostensibly ironic, anti-war narratives, such as Stephen Crane's *The Red Badge of Courage*, almost inevitably dramatize the rite of passage of young men testing themselves on the field of battle and emerging as older, wiser, and more-self-confident. Perhaps for this reason, Susan Jeffords finds in Vietnam War narratives such as Herr's "the remasculinization of American culture, the large-scale renegotiation and regeneration of the interests, values, and projects of patriarchy [...] taking place in U.S. social relations."[8] At the same time, Herr's narrator is an anti-hero, a terrified, middle-class American young man who emerged from the conflict, as did many Vietnam veterans, badly damaged by the experience. He seems, indeed, to be keenly aware of the destructive nature of war as a test of masculinity. Herr describes his own struggle with pre-formulated notions of war this way:

> The first few times that I got fired at or saw combat deaths, nothing really happened, all the responses got locked in my head. It was the same familiar violence, only moved over to another medium; some kind of jungle play with giant helicopters and fantastic special effects, actors lying out there in canvas body bags waiting for the scene to end before they could get up again and walk it off. But that was some scene (you found out), there was no cutting it. (223)

---

[7] Hellman, 126-38.
[8] Jeffords, xi.

Only in time, through direct experience, does Herr begin to realize the true horror of the war. Returning from combat and relating the experience, he would say, "'Oh man I was scared,' and 'Oh God I thought it was all over'"; it took a long time, he says later, "before I knew how scared I was really supposed to be, or [...] how beyond my control 'all over' could become" (20). Herr gradually begins to think about "what happens to you when you pursue a fantasy until it becomes an experience, and then afterward you can't handle the experience" (72). He reflects afterward, "Talk about impersonating an identity, about locking into a role, about irony: I went to cover the war and the war covered me" (20). The war so permeates Herr's consciousness that he becomes a part of the war, with all of its horror and contradictions, and his prose allegorizes the degree to which he breaks down the barriers between observer and observed.

Before we discuss Herr's unique treatment of his material, we need to examine his relationship to both the grunts and to the members of the Mission, Command Headquarters, key players in Herr's dramatic recreation of the war. Differences between Mission personnel and grunts were based partly on class: the members of Mission who gave out orders were mostly college-educated white men, middle- or upper-middle-class, who had achieved a position of authority within the military hierarchy. The grunts who received the orders, by contrast, were relatively uneducated, many of them black, middle- or working-class young men. The two cultures had two different perspectives on the war: the Command's perspective was often abstract, based on strategies and statistics, but the grunts carried out orders given by the Mission, so their perspective was more concrete. The Mission knew about military strategies; the grunts knew about fighting and trying to survive in a war in which they could not believe and which, apparently, they could not win. In this context it is worth

68

citing Richard Lanham's definition of "grunt," quoted here from his discussion of *Dispatches* in *Analyzing Prose*: "'Grunt,' in the war became an anti-heroic heroic term, the perfect embodiment of dogged bravery built on incredible mistakes and hopeless wrong."[9] In a series of symbolically suggestive vignettes, Herr elicits the reader's sympathy for the grunts' predicament.

Like the correspondents, the grunts had their war fantasies, often of the John Wayne variety. Still, their stories were much closer to the truth of the battle than the prefabricated versions provided by the Mission, Command Headquarters. Sensing that the real story in Vietnam was to be found not at military briefings but out in the field where the fighting took place, Herr and some of the other countercultural reporters, Sean Flynn and Tim Page, for example, established a special relationship with some of the grunts. Herr says, "Between all of the grunts turning on or tripping out on the war and the substantial number of correspondents doing the same thing, it was an authentic sub-culture" (252). In Herr's text, this subculture presents an alternative to the dominant culture, the Mission culture. Despite the reporters' willingness to identify with them, the grunts initially display a deep distrust of the reporters, whom they have good reason to suspect are merely mouthpieces for the military establishment. This suspicion causes them to view the reporters as outsiders, curiosities or even threats: "As far as any of them knew," Herr says, "we were crazy, maybe even dangerous. It made sense: They *had* to be here [....] We did *not* have to be here" (202). Therefore, Herr and the other reporters find it difficult to gain acceptance by the grunt subculture. No matter how high the degree of identification between the grunts and reporters becomes, their status is different. Herr describes the peculiar effect a group of reporters has on an outfit when they arrive unexpectedly on the

---

[9] Lanham, 214.

eve of an operation; their presence inspires fear and suspicion in the grunts, who are certain that a major battle is about to occur. This situation affords the reporters a certain "power" which Herr describes in anthropological terms:

> Then, it didn't matter that we were dressed exactly as they were and would be going exactly where they were going; we were as exotic and fearsome as black magic, coming on with cameras and questions, and if we promised to take the anonymity off of what was about to happen, we were also there to watchdog the day. (203)

Initiation into grunt subculture is carried out through the exchange of language. As Herr and some other reporters enter a particular camp, he observes that "none of them was talking to us yet, they were sort of talking for us, trying to make us out [....] It was like a ritual, all the preliminary forms had to be observed" (202). Once the grunts begin talking *to* Herr and his colleagues, they have to some degree assimilated the reporters into their own subculture. Despite the difference in status between soldiers and reporters, and the fact that Herr and his colleagues were generally better educated and therefore more articulate than the grunts (the word "grunt" suggests a rudimentary level of verbal competence), they all shared a common language, that of the late-1960s counterculture. Language is the bridge which allows Herr and his colleagues to cross the divide and establish a sense of identification with the enlisted men.

One factor that breaks down barriers between the grunts and the reporters is their adoption of the late-1960s styles. The grunt subculture partly takes its style from the dress and behavior of the anti-war counterculture. The grunts wore peace symbols on their helmets, listened to rock 'n' roll, and took consciousness-altering drugs. Herr lists various status details, objects appropriated by the grunts to symbolize their participation in the war, relics, Herr says, "picked off an enemy they'd killed, a little transfer of power," or objects of an iconic, ritualistic or religious nature: "Bibles and St. Christophers, locks of hair, photographs of family members or counterculture heroes like John Lennon or Che Guevara" (50). He pays close attention to the semiotic style of the grunt subculture, emphasizing its eclecticism, which was part of late-1960s, postmodern style. In the following passage, Herr describes a collage created by one of the grunts:

> It included glimpses of burning monks, stacked Viet Cong dead, wounded Marines screaming and weeping, Cardinal Spellman waving from a chopper, Ronald Reagan, his face halved and separated by a stalk of cannabis; pictures of John Lennon peering through wire-rimmed glasses, Mick Jagger, Jimi Hendrix, Dylan, Eldridge Cleaver, Rap Brown; coffins draped with American flags whose stars were replaced by swastikas and dollar signs; odd parts clipped from *Playboy* pictures, newspaper headlines (FARMERS BUTCHER HOGS TO PROTEST PORK PRICE DIP), photo captions (*President Jokes with Newsmen*), beautiful girls holding flowers, showers of peace symbols; Ky standing at attention and saluting, a small mushroom cloud forming where his genitalia should have been; a map of the western United States with the shape of Vietnam reversed and fitted over California, and one large, long figure that began at the bottom with shiny leather boots and rouged knees and ascended in a microskirt, bare breasts, graceful shoulders and a long neck, topped by the

71

burned, blackened face of a dead Vietnamese woman. (186-187)

Don Ringnalda reinforces the notion that the war in Vietnam was inherently dramatic by observing that the collage confronts readers with "the disorienting truth that in America's trillion-dollar Vietnam movie, we were all actors, not audience" (89).[10] Thomas Meyers maintains that the "organic form" of *Dispatches* results from the journalist's "sympathetic union with his data,"[11] and the passage above is a good example of how Herr achieves this "sympathetic union" with the grunts. Stylistically, Herr dramatizes the juxtaposed images with a rounded period, which builds to a shocking climax with the head of the dead Vietnamese woman. The visual eclecticism of the collage, with its bizarre, disorienting juxtapositions and black sense of humor, is representative of the countercultural style, and it demonstrates Herr's sense of verbal identification with his subject. Like an anthropologist attempting a "thick description" of an alien culture, Herr records as many concrete details of the grunt subculture as possible.[12]

Herr chronicles the way the grunts, in the face of incalculable suffering and mechanized means of destruction, resort to primitive superstition to protect themselves. In a further anthropological observation on superstition which, according to Herr, ran high in Vietnam, he says that some soldiers were felt to be charmed, or impervious to harm. Herr finds himself staying close to these men in combat, and he doubts "whether anything could be as parasitic as that," or, he adds, "as intimate" (242). Herr indicates that the parasitical relationship was reciprocal: "We covered each other" (70). The analogy between journalism and

---

[10] Ringalda, 89.
[11] Meyers, 156.
[12] Geertz, 3-33.

firepower, coverage and cover, runs throughout *Dispatches*. Herr plays with two meanings of the verb, to cover, which from his point of view denotes both gunfire and reporting. During the battle at Hue, Herr asks a marine to cover him and another correspondent; then, as they run up the street, the question Herr has just asked strikes him as humorously ironic: "'Oh man,' he asks the other correspondent, 'do you realize that I just asked that guy back there to *cover us*?'"(225). Herr explains that this "exchange of services" between reporters and grunts worked until one night he found himself "at the wrong end of the story [...] with a .30-caliber automatic in my hands, firing cover [...]" (70-71). With the appropriation of a weapon to cover, or to fire cover, Herr adopts, literally and symbolically, the role of combatant. Then, he says, "I wasn't a reporter, I was a shooter" (71). Herr then feels qualified to say, "I was in many ways brother to these poor, tired grunts, I knew what they knew now, I'd done it" (220). The degree of identification here between writer and subject is very high. Meyers suggests, "The reporters' willingness to accept the same risks as those threatening the grunts—the immediate dangers of personal immersion—is often the key to finding at least a temporary solidarity."[13] Unlike the conventional journalist, who remains detached from his subject, Herr in this passage eliminates the distance between observer and observed. Ringnalda maintains, "The story that [Herr] got was that Vietnam was a story. The term 'nonfiction' lost its currency in a hurry. Being 'covered' by the war does not mean simply that Herr was overwhelmed by the war; it means he was written by it. The time-honored Western distinction between subject and object simply disintegrated."[14] In the process,

---

[13] Meyers, 167.
[14] Ringnalda, 77.

Herr takes Wolfe's concept of "saturation reporting," i.e., complete immersion in one's subject, to its extreme.[15]

In order to show just how closely aligned his interests were with those of the grunts, Herr frequently turns to metaphor. As we have seen, he sometimes conceptualizes the relationship between the grunts and the correspondents as parasitic. A quote from the Bob Dylan song, "Visions of Johanna," "Name me someone that's not a parasite/ And I'll go out and say a prayer for him," serves as the epigram for the "Colleagues" section in which Herr focuses on the role of the correspondents in Vietnam and their relationship to the grunts. Sometimes that relationship is ghoulish: "You [the correspondent] took your living from their deaths" (221). If the correspondents were parasites, the fighting in Vietnam and its resulting casualties served as host. Herr says, "If you photographed a dead marine with a poncho over his face and got something for it, you were *some* kind of parasite" (243). But the situation becomes more complicated than that: "What were you if you pulled the poncho back first to make a better shot," he asks, "what were you if you stood there watching it, making a note to remember it later in case you might want to use it?" (243-44); the answer, "Some other kind of parasite, I suppose" (244). As is evident from the moral indignation and self-reproach in the passage quoted above, Herr is clearly uncomfortable with the idea that he was in Vietnam to feed on and to profit from death and human suffering. His attitude sets him apart from some of the other correspondents to whom the dead were statistics, merely anonymous grunts. When another correspondent asks Herr what he finds to talk to the grunts about, he is surprised to find that Herr does not find the grunts as uninteresting as he does (232).

---

[15] Wolfe.

Contrasting himself to the journalists who most often ignored the grunts and relied instead on official, second-hand, and therefore pre-packaged accounts of the war, Herr seeks his information first-hand; he goes directly to the most reliable source, the grunts who actually fought and died in the war. Herr spent so much time talking to and listening to the grunts, getting to know them personally, that he found it impossible to remain objective. All their stories, he observes, shared one common rhetorical purpose: They all said, "'Put yourself in my place'" (31). Herr's adoption of the grunt point of view indicates that he is interested in reporting more than the mere "facts" relating to troop movements and kill ratios. He is determined to allow the grunts to tell their own stories, stories American viewers did not see on the six o'clock news or read in the evening newspapers. In formalistic terms, he foregrounds emergent, subcultural voices which the dominant culture's mass media had suppressed. Like the other New Journalistic texts under examination here, *Dispatches* is, in Bakhtinian terms, heteroglossic. Grunt voices engage Mission voices in a dialectical interplay. It is as if all the voices of the war were recorded on one reel of tape, then mixed by the corporate media so that only one voice, the unified voice of Mission leaders, could be heard; Herr remixes the tape, amplifying voices which had not been audible before. The grunt stories often disclose information that Mission leaders would have preferred undisclosed. One soldier reveals that U.S. troops shot South Vietnamese peasants who were holding on to a U.S. helicopter as it attempted to lift off from a combat site: "'They could sure as shit believe Charlie was shooting them,' he says of the shocked South Vietnamese, 'but they couldn't believe that we was doing it too [...].'" (30). Another soldier exposes Mission's practice of falsifying combat statistics: "'I went out and killed one VC and liberated a prisoner,' he says, 'Next day the major called me in and

75

told me that I'd killed fourteen VC and liberated six prisoners'" (182). To report the grunts' experience as faithfully as possible became a moral imperative for Herr. He repeatedly makes the point that the grunts felt their side of the story wasn't being told by the dominant media. Through his appropriation of grunt voices, and his close identification with the grunts, the reporter privileges one source of information over another and, in the process, undermines the authority of official sources, i.e., Mission, Command Headquarters.

While his sympathies are with the grunts, not Mission personnel, Herr occasionally expresses disgust at the brutal methods the grunts sometimes used, throwing people out of helicopters, for example, or setting dogs on them. "I stood as close to them as I could without actually being one of them," he says, "and then I stood as far back as I could without leaving the planet" (70). As a middle-class, college-educated, professional journalist, Herr feels detached from many of the grunts, who share neither his class privileges nor his educational background. He cannot wholly assimilate himself into the grunt subculture, and his alienation places him, like the other New Journalists in this study, in a marginalized position, caught between the emergent counterculture and the dominant culture.

Herr as Rhetorical Critic

At this point we need to further examine Herr's specific opposition to the primary antagonist in *Dispatches*, the Mission, Command Headquarters. If Herr occasionally finds himself alienated by the grunts, his criticism of the Mission, the military officials who represent the dominant establishment culture in Vietnam, is completely unambiguous. He devotes much of *Dispatches* to an attack on the narrative account of the war inscribed by Mission. He refers to its language as "uni-prose," an

76

Orwellian-sounding phrase suggesting the military establishment's effort to present a single, authoritative version of the war and to exclude alternative versions (226). Through the assimilation of grunt voices into his text, Herr accumulates as many readings of the war, including his own, as possible. By incorporating examples of Mission discourse into his text, he points out the glaring contrast between the official version of events and the reality of events as he perceived them.

In their attempt to win support for the war, military officials employ bureaucratese, a language devoid of individual expression that pretends to point to some transparent, objectively verifiable truth. Hellmann acknowledges that *Dispatches* is "permeated by examples of the gulf between official language and actuality," but maintains that discrepancies between events and Mission's version of events serve to "call special attention to Herr's own language."[16] Hellmann reads the official language in much the same way that military spokesmen wanted it to be read. He looks *at* Herr's prose but *through* the official version, accepting its discourse as a transparent medium. Herr foregrounds his own prose, certainly, but he foregrounds military language at the same time. He asks that the reader's At/Through switch, to borrow Lanham's term, be turned to 'At' at all times. Through his close rhetorical scrutiny of the Mission's "uni-prose," Herr calls attention to the role the official version plays in creating the reality it describes. The Mission ran a public relations campaign in order to paint an optimistic picture of the war, glossing over unpleasant facts altogether, or phrasing them euphemistically in a deliberate attempt to conceal, distort or cosmetically alter reality. Herr refers to the Mission's daily press briefing as "standard diurnal informational freak-o-rama, Five O'Clock Follies, Jive at Five"

---

[16] Hellmann, 129-130.

(37). He says that the news media, for the most part, were "ultimately reverential toward the institutions involved" in the war, including "the Office of the President, the Military, America at war and, most of all, the empty technology that characterized Vietnam" (228). Whenever news media executives visited the front, the Mission manipulated what they saw; then, Herr says, "a real story would develop" (228). He appropriates the passive construction, "story would develop," which bureaucrats typically used to conceal a story's origin; then, he attaches a mock headline, "Snow In The Tropics," to the Mission's story in order to parody the use of public relations techniques to distort reality and paint a positive, optimistic picture of the war for the folks back home. To emphasize the degree to which the Mission distorted facts, Herr described the daily briefings as a "psychotic vaudeville," and notes that a term such as "pacification" was nothing more than "a swollen computerized tit being forced upon an already violated population, a costly valueless program that worked only in press conferences [...]." (229). Herr's shocking, far-fetched metaphors, "psychotic vaudeville," and "swollen computerized tit," convey a sense of the bizarre unreality of the military's fabrications. Unlike its supposedly transparent discourse, Herr's self-consciously opaque language emphasizes the writer's role in the creation of meaning. Before analyzing Herr's discourse in detail, however, we need to take a closer look at the ways in which he establishes a contrast between the Mission's language and his own.

Herr describes the briefings as "an Orwellian grope through the day's events as seen by the Mission" (105). As Orwell did throughout his career, Herr exposes the intention on behalf of official spokespersons, in this case the U.S. Armed Forces, to misrepresent reality. During the failed attempt by U.S. forces to secure Khe Sanh, Herr claims that Mission "caused heavy causalities to be described as light, routs and ambushes to be

78

described as temporary tactical ploys, and filthy weather to be described as good and even excellent" (152). He incorporates numerous examples of Mission distortions, which he labels "language fix," into his own text: like "'discrete burst' (one of those tore an old grandfather and two children to bits [...]), 'friendly casualties' (not warm, not fun), 'meeting engagement' (ambush), concluding usually with 17 or 117 or 317 enemy dead and American losses described as 'light'" (237). By interspersing his own comments between the Mission's phrases, Herr reveals the face of horror behind the mask. The Mission's language, he says, created a sense of "mindless optimism, the kind that rejected facts and killed grunts wholesale" (154). He says that its "cheer-crazed" language "seemed to be the only kind of talk that any of them was capable of," and he incorporates examples in an ironic context: "'Excellent,' 'real fine,' 'outstanding,' 'first rate' [...]" (154). In one instance, Herr foregrounds the official, bureaucratic jargon by juxtaposing an off-the-record remark with the version recorded by the press:

> Most would say that they either had it wrapped up or wound down: 'He's all pissed out, Charlie's all pissed out, booger's shot his whole wad,' one of them promised me, while in Saigon it would be restructured for briefings, 'He no longer maintains in our view capability to mount, execute or sustain a serious offensive action' [....]. (49)

The Mission strives, in Burkean terms, for the "semantic" ideal, a language that attempts to present a detached, objective reconstruction of events.[17] By contrasting the bureaucratic version of events with the colloquial version supplied by the grunts, Herr demonstrates how Mission's language strips any given event of its

---

[17] Burke, *Philosophy*, 147-50.

emotional content at the same time that he brings that content to the foreground. Herr thus asserts his preference for the "poetic" ideal.[18] As a correspondent, Herr makes it clear that the information provided by Mission, even when it was accurate, could not convey the emotional quality of an event: "There were all kinds of people who could give you the background," he says, "the facts [...] but only a correspondent could give you the exact mood that attended each of the major epochs [...]." (241). Mood is an emotional factor, generally omitted from the official, bureaucratic accounts supplied by Mission. Meyers argues that one of Herr's most significant achievements in *Dispatches* is "the careful juxtaposition of intuitive response and imaginative extension with the most glaring omissions of the official narrative."[19] As we shall see in the stylistic analysis below, Herr's prose dramatizes emotions, attempting symbolically to reproduce not only the facts of war, but the way it felt to the participants, and primarily to him.

Stylistic Analysis

The language of *Dispatches* presents an alternative, if not an outright challenge, to Mission's language. Unlike the flat, emotionless, seemingly transparent plain style that asks not to be noticed, Herr's style is highly expressive and opaque, calling attention to itself as language. The opacity of Herr's prose emphasizes the degree to which the writer and reader must participate in the process of creating meaning. To demonstrate his opposition to the Mission's language and the view of the war that language implies, Herr relies partly on what Burke calls "pure" persuasion, or formal "identification," in which the speaker creates a highly self-conscious, literary style that gains the reader's assent

---

[18] Ibid.
[19] Meyers, 161.

to his argument.[20] At its most dramatically self-conscious, Herr's prose demonstrates the carefully wrought structures and lyricism associated with verse. Hellmann regards Herr's style as a synthesis of journalism and "fictional techniques."[21] By "fictional techniques" Hellmann means such devices as stream-of-consciousness narration and characterization, qualities which *Dispatches* certainly contains, but the "fictional techniques" he detects in Herr's prose are really features that apply to larger units of discourse than the individual sentence. The closest Hellmann comes to a detailed stylistic analysis of Herr's prose is to note its "clipped words; violent images of ascent and descent, expansion and contraction" and its "rhythmic embodiment of total abandonment and complete control,"[22] without providing much in the way of specific examples. Ringnalda writes of Herr's style that it is "a freewheeling collage of straightforward remembering, hallucination, irony, acid sarcasm, jump cuts, freeze frames, stream of consciousness, incongruous juxtaposition, realism, surrealism, Dadaism, and metafiction."[23] Ringnalda's description is a jumble of cinematic metaphors, genres, and -isms that describe larger units of discourse than the individual sentence or passage. Jim Nielson objects to stylistic criticism of *Dispatches* by pointing out, "Reviewers frequently cited long passages with little or no discussion, as if the connection between Herr's prose and the war were self-evident."[24] Indeed, both Hellmann's and Ringnalda's discussions of style lack specificity and an accurately descriptive terminology for the discussion of language. Lanham's stylistic analysis of Herr's "metachopper" passage is the most detailed available. Lanham chooses to focus on Herr's description of a

---

[20] Burke, *Rhetoric*, 55-59.
[21] Hellmann, 127.
[22] Hellmann, 131.
[23] Ringnalda, 81.
[24] Nielson, 137.

specific object rather his direct experience of ground contact,[25] but I have chosen to analyze a passage from *Dispatches* which is more representative of Herr's primary thematic concern—the horror of war. Like Lanham, though, I will appropriate terms from classical rhetoric to name stylistic features, demonstrating how Herr's prose dramatizes his experience of the Vietnam War. When his emotional involvement with his subject is at its peak, Herr's prose becomes most purely persuasive and opaque. These moments tend to occur when Herr vents his outrage at Mission's bureaucratic falsehoods, or when he recalls his numerous encounters with extreme violence, as in the following extended passage:

> Sometimes you'd step from the bunker, all sense of time passing having left you, and find it dark out. The far side of the hills around the bowl of the base glimmering, but you could never see the source of the light, and it had the look of a city at night approached from a great distance. Flares were dropping everywhere around the fringes of the perimeter, laying a dead white light on the high ground rising from the piedmont. There would be dozens of them at once sometimes, trailing an intense smoke, dropping white-hot sparks, and it seemed as though anything caught in their range would be made still, like figures in a game of living statues. There would be the muted rush of illumination rounds, fired from 60-mm. mortars inside the wire, dropping magnesium-brilliant above the NVA trenches for a few seconds, outlining the gaunt, flat spread of the mahogany trees, giving the landscape a ghastly clarity and dying out. You

---

[25] Lanham, 210-16.

could watch mortar bursts, orange and gray-smoking, over the tops of trees three and four kilometers away, and the heavier shelling from support bases farther east along the DMZ, from Camp Carrol and the Rockpile, directed against suspected troop movements or NVA rocket and mortar positions. Once in a while—I guess I saw it happen three or four times in all—there would be a secondary explosion, a direct hit on a supply of NVA ammunition. And at night it was beautiful. Even the incoming was beautiful at night, beautiful and deeply dreadful.

I remembered the way a Phantom pilot had talked about how beautiful the surface-to-air missiles looked as they drifted up toward his plane to kill him, and remembered myself how lovely .50-caliber tracers could be, coming at you as you flew at night in a helicopter, how slow and graceful, arching up easily, a dream, so remote from anything that could harm you. It could make you feel a total serenity, an elevation that put you above death, but that never lasted very long. One hit anywhere in the chopper would bring you back, bitten lips, white knuckles and all, and then you knew where you were. It was different with the incoming at Khe Sanh. You didn't get to watch the shells very often. You knew if you heard one, the first one, that you were safe, or at least saved. If you were still standing up and looking after that, you deserved anything that happened to you.

Nights were when the air and artillery strikes were heaviest, because that was when we knew the NVA was above ground and moving. At night you could lie out on some sandbags and watch the C-47's mounted with Vulcans doing their work. The C-47 was a standard prop flareship, but many of them carried .20- and .762-mm guns on their doors, Mike-Mikes that could fire 300 rounds per second, Gatling style, "a round in every square inch of a football field in less than a minute," as the handouts said. They used to call it Puff the Magic Dragon, but the Marines knew better: they named it Spooky. Every fifth round fired was a tracer, and when Spooky was working, everything stopped while that solid stream of violet red poured down out of the black sky. If you watched from a great distance, the stream would seem to dry up between bursts, vanishing slowly from air to ground like a comet tail, the sound of the guns disappearing too, a few seconds later. If you watched at close range, you couldn't believe that anyone had the courage to deal with that night after night, week after week, and you cultivated a respect for the Vietcong and the NVA who had crouched under it every night now for months. It was awesome, worse than anything the Lord had ever put down on Egypt, and at night, you'd hear the Marines talking, watching it, yelling, "Get some!" until they grew quiet and someone would say, "Spooky understands." The nights were very beautiful. Night was really when you had the least to fear and feared the most. You could go though some very bad numbers at night.

84

Because, really, what a choice there was; what a prodigy of things to be afraid of! The moment that you understood this, really understood it, you lost your anxiety instantly. Anxiety was a luxury, a joke you had no room for once you knew the variety of deaths and mutilations the war offered. Some feared head wounds, some dreaded chest wounds or stomach wounds, everyone feared the wound of wounds, the Wound. Guys would pray and pray—Just you and me, God. Right?—offer anything, if only they could be spared that: Take my legs, take my hands, take my eyes, take my fucking *life*, You Bastard, but please, please, please don't take *those*. Whenever a shell landed in a group, everyone forgot about the next rounds and skipped back to rip their pants away, to check, laughing hysterically with relief even though their legs might be shattered, their kneecaps torn away, kept upright by their relief and shock, gratitude and adrenaline.

There were choices everywhere, but they were never choices that you could hope to make. There was even some small chance for personal style in your recognition of the one thing you feared more than any other. You could die in a sudden blood-burning crunch as your chopper hit the ground like dead weight, you could fly apart so that your pieces would never be gathered, you could take one neat round in the lung and out hearing only the bubble of the last few breaths, you could die in the last stage of malaria with that faint tapping in your ears, and that could happen to you after months of firefights and rockets and machine guns.

Enough, too many, were saved for that, and you always hoped that no irony would attend your passing. You could end in a pit somewhere with a spike through you, everything stopped forever except for the one or two motions, purely involuntary, as though you could kick it all away and come back. You could fall down dead so that the medics would have to spend half an hour looking for the hole that killed you, getting more and more spooked as the search went on. You could be shot, mined, grenaded, rocketed, mortared, sniped at, blown up and away so that your leavings had to be dropped into a sagging poncho and carried to Graves Registration, that's all she wrote. It was almost marvelous.

And at night, all of it seemed possible. At night in Khe Sanh, waiting there thinking about all of them (40,000 some said), thinking that they might really try it, could keep you up. If they did, when they did, it might not matter that you were in the best bunker in the DMZ, wouldn't matter that you were young and had plans, that you were loved, that you were a noncombatant, an observer. Because if it came, it would be in a bloodswarm of killing, and credentials would not be examined. (The only Vietnamese many of us knew was the words "Bao Chi! Bao Chi!"—Journalist! Journalist! or even "Bao Chi Fap!"—French Journalist!, which was the same as saying Don't shoot! Don't shoot!) You came to love your life, to love and respect the mere fact of it, but often you became heedless of it in the way somnambulists are heedless. Being

86

"good" meant staying alive, and sometimes that was only a matter of caring enough at any given moment. No wonder everyone became a luck freak, no wonder you could wake at four in the morning some mornings and *know* that tomorrow it would finally happen, you could stop worrying about it now and just lie there, sweating in the dampest chill you ever felt.

But once it was actually going on, things were different. You were just like everyone else, you could no more blink than spit. It came back the same way every time, dreaded and welcome, balls and bowels turning over together, your senses working like strobes, free-falling all the way down to the essences and then flying out again in a rush to focus, like the first strong twinge of tripping after an infusion of psilocybin, reaching in at the point of calm and springing all the joy and all the dread ever known, *ever* known by *everyone* who *ever* lived, unutterable in its speeding brilliance, touching all the edges and then passing, as though it had all been controlled from outside, by a god or by the moon, And every time, you were so weary afterwards, so empty of everything but being alive that you couldn't recall any of it except to know that it was like something else you had felt once before. It remained obscure for a long time, but after enough times the memory took shape and substance and finally revealed itself one afternoon after the breaking off of a firefight. It was the feeling you'd had when you were much, much younger and undressing a girl for the first time. (139-144)

87

Dispatches is written in a colloquial, informal style. Herr speaks with the voice of a young, college-educated American of the late 1960s. His prose is filled with countercultural slang as well as literary and pop cultural allusions, which lend his voice a familiar ethos. Many critics have noted that, in *Dispatches*, style equals content. Lanham, for example, demonstrates that Herr's style "allegorizes" his subject matter:

> The prose models the war: self-conscious, mannered, media-aware to within an inch of its life, yet suddenly switching to impossibly real and bloody and pointless. Vietnam *was* unlike other wars. Herr is trying to tell us how and why this was so. It was not a war fought on one level of self-consciousness. It was not a war whose emotional and moral and psychological orientation we could all agree on, as say, World War II was. It was fought in extreme self-consciousness. This, the prose both says and embodies.[26]

Nielson objects to arguments, like Lanham's, that "Herr was believed to have constructed a book whose nonlinear structure and kinetic prose [...] seemed to mirror the war itself" (136),[27] contending that "any assertion that there is a natural and direct connection between Herr's aesthetic and the war, that there exists a correspondence between narrative strategy and historical period is itself shaped by historical and cultural imperatives."[28] However, Nielson's statement is, in turn, "shaped by historical and cultural imperatives"; further, Nielson begs the question by assuming that critics writing on Herr's style do, in fact, suggest a "natural"

---

[26] Lanham, 216.
[27] Nielson, 136.
[28] Nielson, 138.

connection between Herr's style and the people and events it describes. As a work of literature, *Dispatches* is an example of imitative form, symbolically recreating a real-life event from the perspective of one witness-participant named Michael Herr who writes in a highly stylized reportorial prose that seems designed to call attention to itself as a rhetorical performance; therefore, there's nothing particularly "natural" about it. Hellmann focuses less on the mimetic quality of Herr's prose and more on its meta-linguistic properties: "Herr's book," he says, "is assertively *about* [my italics] its own language and form."[29] While recognizing Herr's verbal self-consciousness, Hellmann underestimates Herr's journalistic and rhetorical purposes, which make *Dispatches* more than an experiment in meta-narrative; *Dispatches* is reportage, and what it reports about is Herr's experience of the war in Vietnam.

The passage quoted above ends with a hypotactic structure, in which clauses or phrases are arranged in a dependent or subordinate relationship. Subordinate clauses create a hierarchy of importance in which the most important unit of discourse appears last. Hypotaxis suggests that the writer has carefully considered his subject matter and come to some definite conclusions about it. There are some instances in which Herr feels certain enough about the meaning of his experience to draw conclusions. In the passage we have just read, Herr uses a hypotactic structure to dramatize a situation: the intense emotional experience of combat, building to a final realization of the link between fear and eroticism, about which I will have more to say later. The opposite of hypotaxis is parataxis, in which clauses or phrases are arranged independently in a coordinate, rather than a subordinate, structure. A loose, rambling, paratactic syntax is more representative of Herr's style than its hypotactic counterpart. Most of the time, the action in

---

[29] Hellmann, 128.

Vietnam occurred so quickly and violently, and created such terror and confusion, that Herr finds it necessary to adopt a style that will enable him to dramatize that terror and confusion; in those instances, the paratactic style best suits his purposes. Because so much of Herr's experience remains incomplete, open to further interpretation, the paratactic style allows him to probe the meaning of his experience as he writes about it. Herr's paratactic style carries political implications as well: its openness models his view of the war as an ongoing historical process that must continually be reassessed. The prose being issued from Command Headquarters, by contrast, implies a static, authoritarian view of history in which meaning becomes fixed in time, becomes Truth. Herr's refusal to draw final conclusions indicates that he views history dialectically, that is, as open and inconclusive.

Herr's paratactic prose is polysyndetic, which is to say it contains lots of connectors and coordinating conjunctions. It is comma-laden, clauses and phrases flowing out from one another, either picking up a narrative line, or stringing out definitions and qualifications. Connectors, of course, make connections between things. In Herr's case, connectors help him make a kind of symbolic order out of the chaos of war. Again, the use of coordinate rather than subordinate conjunctions indicates that Herr has not yet ranked disparate elements of his experience in order of importance, i.e., one element has not become subordinated to another. Coordinators allow him to accumulate data still in the process of becoming meaning; he allows that process of discovery to become part of the very fabric of the text. Herr's paratactic or "running" style models his concern with the present moment. While reading *Dispatches*, the reader enters symbolically into a mind in real-time interaction with its immediate environment; the prose imitates the mind in the act apprehending and coping with events as they rapidly unfold. Herr relies heavily on verb phrases, in this case present participles: "Flares were dropping everywhere [...] laying dead white light on the high round rising from the piedmont [...] trailing an intense smoke, dropping white hot sparks [...]." Within this same paragraph, however, Herr switches to past participles: "I remembered the way a Phantom pilot had talked about how beautiful the surface-to-air missiles looked as they drifted up toward his plane to kill him [...]." The continual shift from present to past and back again emphasizes the importance of immediate experience and of memory; the chronological structure of *Dispatches* corresponds to Herr's highly selective, subjective mindset.

Herr's point of view oscillates not only between present and past but between first and second person, sometimes, as in this passage, within the same paragraph: "You could watch mortar bursts [....] Once in a while—I guess I saw it happen three or four times in all—there would be a secondary explosion [...]." Herr switches to a second-person construction when he wants to describe phenomena or narrate events which were common to most Americans in Vietnam. The use of second person also helps him to create a sense of dramatic immediacy: "Night was really when you had the least to fear and feared the most. You could go through some very bad numbers at night." Just as important, Herr's use of second person invites the reader to participate in the experience, symbolically, of course, in a more direct fashion than the first person does: "Once it was going on, things were different. You were just like everyone else, you could no more blink than spit." The shift back and forth from second person to first also models, in a sense, Herr's shifting role from reporter or observer, remaining detached and receiving special treatment and consideration due to his non-combatant status, to his role as participant, seeking cover from enemy fire and trying simply to survive like the grunts. Herr tends to use "I" most often when discussing his journalistic role

91

and "you" when he experienced the war the same way the soldiers did. Sometimes Herr narrates the war from the interior point of view of a soldier: "Guys would pray—and pray—Just you and me, God. Right?" He occasionally switches to the first person plural, "we," generally indicating either the U.S. military command in Vietnam—"us" as opposed to "them," the North Vietnamese—or referring to himself and whomever he is with at that particular time. The shifting point of view allows Herr to convey a sense of the disorienting effects of the war on its participants; it also allows him to multiply perspectives on the war, a war in which, as we have seen, no single point of view completely encompasses all the others.

Because all interpretations of the war are relative, Herr's prose demonstrates a tendency toward parenthetical qualification, as in the following passage: "Because, really, what a prodigy of things there was to be afraid of! The moment that you understood this, really understood it, you lost your anxiety instantly." The phrase, "really understood it," sets non-participants at a distance from participants; only a participant can "really" understand the horror of war. Sometimes definitions qualify other definitions: "Anxiety was a luxury, a joke you had no room for once you knew the variety of deaths and mutilations the war offered." Herr describes the feeling of witnessing the battle below from a helicopter hovering above as a "dream," as a feeling of "total serenity" and "an elevation that put you above death." Here again, perspective is all important. The appositives and parenthetical qualifiers that permeate Herr's text give the reader a sense of the complex reality of war.

Herr sometimes makes use of chiasmus, a scheme in which two parts of a sentence appear as reverse mirror images of the other, forming an ABBA structure. Here are two examples from the passage we are examining. "And at night [a rocket explosion] was beautiful. Even the incoming was beautiful at night [....]." The word, "beautiful" and the phrase, "at night," appear in reverse order here. The complementary structure of the two sentences allegorizes a point Herr makes fairly frequently: warfare could seem both horrible and paradoxically beautiful. He returns to this idea when he describes, in a passage quoted above, the feeling of serenity he experienced watching the battle from the relatively safe perspective of a helicopter. At the end of that same paragraph, Herr once again creates a chiasmus: "Night was when you really had the least to fear and feared the most." The degree of "fear" changes from "least" to "most," but the chiasmic structure remains intact. Herr presents the reader with another paradox here; the chiasmus allows him to make the point that, in Vietnam, things turned into their opposites, and nothing was necessarily what it seemed.

In many passages Herr uses anaphora, the repetition of a word or words at the beginning of successive clauses or phrases. Here, for example, Herr offers two different perspectives on artillery fire: "If you watched from a great distance [....] If you watched at close range [...]." In this passage, Herr simply develops the idea that the war's reality depended heavily on one's perspective. In the next paragraph, Herr uses anaphora and its opposite, epanaphora (or epiphora), the repetition of a word or words at the end of successive phrases or clauses: "Some feared head wounds, some dreaded chest wounds or stomach wounds, everyone feared the wound of wounds, the Wound." This meditation on "the Wound," obviously a genital wound, shifts into the soldier's interior perspective as he prays to God to spare his testicles, and here the anaphoric structure becomes most opaque: "Take my legs, take my hands, takes my eyes, take my fucking *life*, You Bastard, but please, please, please, don't take *those*." The sentence just quoted also displays an isocolonic structure, in which

93

phases and clauses are arranged in units of equal length, but the italicized *"those"* with which the sentence climaxes indicates that, as far as the soldier is concerned, not all parts of the body are equally valuable. This passage contains other interesting features: for instance, conduplicatio, the repetition of a word or words in successive phrases or clauses: "Some feared head wounds, some dreaded chest wounds or stomach wounds, everyone feared the wound of wounds, the Wound." Here again, the isocolons seem to rank all parts of the body equally, until the sentence ends abruptly with the "the Wound," capital "W," indicating instead a hierarchy of value attached (no pun intended) to the body. Herr also employs epizeuxis here, the repetition of a word with no words in between—"please, please, please"—which emphasizes the urgency of the soldier's plea. Herr uses anaphora most dramatically in the passage describing the seemingly endless variety of deaths Vietnam had to offer: "You could die in a sudden bloodburning crunch […] you could take one neat round in the lung […] you could die in the last stage of malaria [...]." The phrase, "you could," occurs a total of seven times in this passage, building to the following conclusion: "You could be shot, mined, grenaded, rocketed, mortared, sniped at, blown up and away [...]." The omission of conjunctions between words, "shot, mined, grenaded," etc., is called brachylogia, and Herr's use of this scheme suggests that the participants in the war might face any number of these perils simultaneously.

In the next two paragraphs, the conclusion of this passage, Herr uses pronouns to tie disparate elements of his experience together. The key words here are "them," "they" and, especially, "it." The repetition of a word in a different or contrary sense, "it," is called antistasis, or, another possibility, ploce, the repetition of a word with a new signification after the intervention of another word or words. The repetition of a word or words in succeeding clauses, "they," is, again, conduplicatio. At night, Herr says, "all of it seemed possible." The antecedent of the pronoun "it," in this case, is the plethora of potential deaths mentioned above. In Khe Sanh, the G.I.s sat up at night "thinking that they might really try it," "they" being North Vietnamese forces, referred to indirectly to suggest their uncanny and unsettling ability to remain hidden. The pronoun "it" changes its referent here: suddenly, "it" refers to an enemy attack. The clauses which follow, "If they did, when they did," structured isocolonically, convey a sense of the total lack of certainty and control the participants felt when confronting an invisible enemy. "If they did, when they did," Herr says, "it might not matter that you were in the best bunker in the DMZ, wouldn't matter that you were young and had plans, that you were loved, that you were a non-combatant, an observer." The isocolons, "didn't matter [...] wouldn't matter," and "that," dramatize the way combat reduced all other considerations to the same level— zero. Combat, Herr suggests, is the great neutralizer, nullifying ideals of God, country, family, all the ideals for which the American people believed their country was fighting. Herr finally names "it," both metaphorically and literally, "as a bloodswarm of killing"; the neologism, "bloodswarm," connotes savage and senseless slaughter. Herr says that, some mornings, "you could wake at four [...] and *know* that tomorrow it would finally happen, you could stop worrying about it," again conveying a sense of helplessness and lack of control. Paradoxically, within the same paragraph, "it" becomes life: "You came to love your life, to love and respect the mere fact of it, but often you became heedless of it [...]." In the next paragraph, "it" swings from death to life again, preparing the reader for a highly metaphorical, hypotactic passage which builds to an unexpected climax. "But once it was actually going on," Herr reflects, "it came back the same way every time [...]." At first, "it" refers to combat, then "it" becomes the response

95

to combat, an experience Herr dwells on for the remainder of the passage. In a highly descriptive, expansive sentence, the isocolons stretching out until the suspension of meaning threatens to snap, Herr explores the meaning of "it," the experience of combat:

> It came back the same way every time, dreaded and welcome, balls and bowels turning over together, your senses working like strobes, free-falling all the way down to the essences and then flying out again in a rush to focus, like the first strong twinge of tripping after an infusion of psilocybin, reaching in at the point of calm and springing all the joy and all the dread ever known, *ever* known by *everyone* who *ever* lived, unutterable in its speeding brilliance, touching all the edges and then passing, as though it had all been controlled from the outside, by a god or the moon.

Alliteration, "balls and bowels turning over together [...] senses working like strobes," works in this passage to symbolically recreate the feeling of shock and disorientation. Herr constructs a neat parallel, "free-falling all the way down to the essences and then flying out again in a rush to focus," in which participles and prepositional phrases propel the reader into the self and back out again, a different kind of disorientation.

Herr tends to pile layers of metaphorical meaning on top of one another. In this passage, Herr first compares "it" metaphorically to "the first strong twinge of tripping after an infusion of psilocybin," then personifies "it," "reaching in at the point of calm and springing all the joy and all the dread [...]." The mixture of "joy and dread" controls this passage and describes Herr's paradoxical reaction to his experience. The repetition of words from the same root but with different endings, "ever known, *ever* known by *everyone* who *ever* lived," is called polyptoton. The verbs in this passage, initially present participles, "reaching [...] springing [...] touching [...] passing," shift to a passive construction, "as though it had all been controlled from the outside"; the passive construction again dramatizes the lack of control, in this case control given over to "god" or "the moon," two more metaphors arranged in isocolons.

In the sentences that follow, Herr sets the reader up for a hypotactic climax:

> And every time, you were so weary afterward, so empty of everything but being alive that you couldn't recall any of it, except to know that it was like something else you had felt once before. It remained obscure for a long time, but after enough times the memory took shape and substance and finally revealed itself one afternoon during the breaking off of a firefight. It was the feeling you'd had when you were much, much younger and undressing a girl for the first time.

Here, the hypotactic structure builds not on an individual sentence but several sentences. Herr explores a feeling, an "it" that "remained hidden" and then "revealed itself" one final time, metaphorically, as "the feeling you'd had when you were much, much younger and undressing a girl for the first time." The "joy and dread" mentioned earlier becomes a combination of fear and eroticism, just one more paradoxical element of Herr's experience. Herr's repetition of "much" in "much, much younger" is interesting considering that he went to Vietnam in his mid-twenties, the implication being that the experience of combat aged him much more rapidly than life would have otherwise.

There are a few other elements that should be mentioned here. One is the allusiveness that, as we have seen, so permeates Herr's narrative. "It was awesome," Herr says of the sheer amount of firepower directed at the enemy, "worse than anything the Lord had ever put down on Egypt." This Biblical allusion is deliberately hyperbolic; it requires the reader to use his or her imagination in an attempt to grasp phenomena almost beyond imagination. Herr's text also contains a great number of references to military jargon. He talks about "C-47's," for example, or "Mike-Mikes," terms with which a non-participant in the war is unlikely to be familiar. Even readers who know what a C-47 is might be unaware that the grunts referred to this weapon as "Puff the Magic Dragon" or "Spooky." Here again, Herr offers us a glimpse of the war as the grunts saw it. Even though Herr occasionally alludes to major battles in the war's historical development, such Dien Bien Phu and Khe Sanh (to which he devotes an entire chapter), he nevertheless approaches his subject more as a journalist than as an historian. Gordon Taylor calls attention to the limitations of an historical account of the war:

> The closer the historian gets to the heart of combat, the greater the problems. Soldiers expecting a violent end, in the clamour and horror and chaos of battle, do not make reliable eyewitnesses and it is upon eyewitnesses that those who actually seek the truth about combat must usually depend. Investigating and interpreting what happens at the heart of the combat experience involves wrestling with the confused, the contradictory, the irrational, and often the incredible. It involves trying to strip away layers of deception, self-deception ... perhaps

to make the experience comprehensible or credible
[...].[30]

Herr assumes a fair amount of background knowledge on the part of his readers. Many of the "facts" about the war are available to anyone who wants to do the research. Herr's account does not attempt to provide a comprehensive history of the war, only of his direct experience of it. He seems to suggest that no account can be completely comprehensive; in that sense, *Dispatches* supplements other accounts of the war, none of them definitive.

Conclusion

Herr's consciousness is the central consciousness of the book. Because he draws no final, explicitly stated conclusions, not only about his personal experience, but also about the historical significance of the Vietnam War, the structure of his text is open-ended. Herr's loose, rambling syntax and the arrangement of larger units of discourse follow the same internal logic: that of memory and association; he replays experiences again and again, looking for some symbolic meaning. Hellmann says, "Having experience, acquiring new facts, is not in itself the same as acquiring new information"; he stresses that the writer "must also relive that experience through memory and art, shaping the facts into a personally constructed form that will embody a meaning."[31] Herr writes about Vietnam to discover what he thinks and feels about it, what it means, to him at least. Hellmann also notes that the text's fragments "are subsumed within the larger structure of Herr's meditating consciousness as he probes for the essential meaning of his Vietnam experience."[32] Pursuing the logic of his argument one step further, Hellmann contends that Herr wrote *Dispatches* "not as

---

[30] Taylor, 14.
[31] Hellman, 132.
[32] Hellmann, 128.

a direct report on the Vietnam War, but as an exploration of his *memory* of the war."[33] Hellmann centers his discussion of the text on Herr's central consciousness, arguing that Herr "makes the necessity of exploring and ordering the events in Vietnam, not the events themselves, his true subject."[34] Herr refers to this process of exploring and ordering very rarely, however; *Dispatches* is not a meta-text in the same way as *The Armies of the Night*, containing numerous references to the writer brooding over the construction of the text, troubling over whether the text is a novel or a historical account. *Dispatches* is partly about its own language, certainly, but its primary subject is not the writing of the text itself. Its real subject is the war in Vietnam.

As a central consciousness who reckons his position as observer into his observations, Herr demonstrates an interest in the way his consciousness processes information. He is conscious of human factors such as "mind slip and memory play," which account for the reporter's selectivity and subjectivity (272). Hellmann sees Herr's experience as an "emblem of the national consciousness's difficult journey toward self-discovery in Vietnam."[35] There are several indications in the text, however, that the journey is far from over, that the shock waves of the war still reverberate, and that the processing of information never stops. The correspondent calls attention to the now familiar plight of Vietnam veterans still attempting to come to terms with their experience of war. Herr talks about the difficulty of readjusting to so-called "'normal circumstances'" in the U.S. (262): "Back in the World now, and a lot of us aren't making it," he says of the return home (260). It is clear that the war remains with the people who participated in it, whatever the nature of their involvement; it

---

[33] Hellmann, 127-28.
[34] Hellmann, 128.
[35] Hellmann, 136.

continues to be waged in memory and in dreams. Herr describes a dream which, he says, "like a piece of shrapnel [...] takes years to work its way out" (72). And, like the hero in Joseph Campbell's "mono-myth,"[36] who finds it difficult to translate his dark-world experience into light-world terms. In comparing Herr's narrator with Conrad's Marlow in *Heart of Darkness*, Ringnalda suggests that:

> both men realized that what they had witnessed in the heart of darkness was simply beyond any kind of conventional storytelling, and perhaps beyond even unconventional storytelling. Their experiences had been altogether too dark, or, because of what they revealed about Western behavior in Third-World countries, altogether too light. All 'straight history' and straight anything became seriously compromised [....]. The only illumination Marlow and Herr did experience was the illumination of the disintegration of their confidently straight Western consciousnesses.[37]

Nielson objects to Ringnalda's interpretation by stating that he, like other critics of *Dispatches*, seems "completely unaware of the mystification involved in identifying Vietnam as an irrational place beyond the grasp of logic."[38] Unlike Marlow's narrator, perhaps, Herr finds that he is not alone in his inability to communicate his experience: "Everybody knew someone who had been in Vietnam and didn't want to talk about it," Herr says. "Maybe they just didn't know how" (268). Herr describes his own dilemma this way:

---

[36] Campbell, 3-42.
[37] Ringnalda, 72.
[38] Nielson, 143.

And if they just asked, 'What was your scene there?' I wouldn't know what to say either; so I'd say I was trying to write about it and didn't want to dissipate it. But before you could dissipate it you had to locate it, Plant you now, dig you later: information printed on the eye, stored in the brain, coded over skin and transmitted by blood, maybe what they meant by 'blood consciousness.' And transmitted over and over without letup on increasingly powerful frequencies until you either received it or blocked it out one last time, informational Death of a Thousand Cuts. (268)

Taylor argues further that Herr's text:

sought to do what it accepted [...] as impossible and it is no answer simply to dismiss every attempt to depict combat as doomed to failure. The world of war may not be entirely comprehensible but it seems not to be escapable either and in history, literature and film efforts continue to offer insights into the experience of combat and the nature of war. The question is: which forms provide the most effective insights?[39]

Taylor's comment suggests that readers benefit from exposure to multiple perspectives on the Vietnam War, no single one of which need be considered definitive. His question as to which forms produce the "most effective insights," however, seems to contradict his earlier assertion. I would argue that the question is not which forms or genres achieve the greatest degree of insight or verisimilitude, but which texts.

---

[39] Taylor, 15.

Unlike the conventional novelist, who resolves all the dramatic conflicts by the narrative's conclusion, Herr resists imposing a false sense of closure on his own historical narrative. Paul Gray says in his review of *Dispatches* for *Time* magazine that Herr "preaches no sermons, draws no morals, enters no ideological disputes."[40] Nielson argues that comments such as Gray's "reveal the non-ideological ideology (a concern for the transcendent human condition and a focus on textual complexities and sophistication) that has long defined literary culture. This retreat from ideology reveals literary culture's complicity in rewriting the war."[41] Nielson takes literary critics to task because, in his view, they "focus on the aesthetics of postmodernism rather than the political economy behind it,"[42] but aesthetics has always been and will continue to be one of the concerns of literary, as opposed to historical, analysis.

Herr's message is certainly not a didactic one, but permeated as it is with the discourse of rival factions, *Dispatches* is inescapably ideological and dialectical. As such, his text conflicts with revisionist texts written by the dominant culture in an attempt to rewrite the history of the war that will reflect more favorably on the U.S. government's motives and successes in Vietnam. Chomsky writes:

> The popular movement of opposition to the war was doubly threatening to U.S. elites. In the first place, the movement developed out of the control of its 'natural leaders,' thus posing a grave threat to order and stability. What is more, the general passivity and obedience on the part of the population that is a

---

[40] Gray, 119.
[41] Nielson, 146.
[42] Nielson, 152.

basic requirement in a state committed to counterrevolutionary intervention was overcome in significant measure, and dangerous feelings of sympathy towards movements of national liberation in the third world.[43]

Nielson adds, "It is an important task for the intelligentsia in the postwar period to reconstruct the ideological system and to reinstate the patterns of conformism that were shattered by the opposition and resistance to the war in Indochina."[44] He further attacks critics who, he claims, argue that Herr's "slang-filled, self-reflexive style in and of itself can begin to reorganize a popular consensus that has been shaped by the mass media seems more wish-fulfillment than an actual consideration of the power and reach of media institutions and other ideological state apparatuses."[45] Nielson here distorts by oversimplification. No critic really claims that Herr's style "in and of itself" can reshape public opinion about the war, especially about a war that many Americans have long ago concluded should never have been fought. Can any one book bring about such a shift in the national consciousness? Neilson seems to suggest that critics of *Dispatches* are asking Herr to do the impossible. When asked whether the United States has ever recovered from the wound the Vietnam War left in its national psyche, Herr replied in the negative, "because we would have to call things by their real names, shave off all the rhetoric and defuse a lot of emotionally inflated words."[46] One of the reasons the experience is difficult to talk about is that it is still, in a sense, incomplete. "Those who remember the past are condemned to repeat it too" (272).

---

[43] Chomsky, "After the Cataclysm," 17.
[44] Nielson, 140.
[45] Nielson, 149.
[46] Schroeder, 37.

As I mentioned at the outset, *Dispatches* plays out, symbolically, the struggle between the dominant culture, represented by the Mission, Command Headquarters, and the emergent culture, represented by Herr and the grunts, over the war in Vietnam. That conflict was played out not only in Vietnam, but also here in the United States. Herr says, "There'd been nothing happening there," meaning Vietnam, "that hadn't already existed here, coiled up and waiting, back in the world," the "world" being a term used by military personnel to refer to the U.S., to home (268). Herr's metaphor, "coiled up," obviously a reference to a snake, archetypal symbol of evil, conveys the writer's attitude to the forces that initiated the Vietnamese conflict. Herr doesn't name explicitly what was "coiled up and waiting," but it is plausible to conclude, given Herr's left-wing bias, that he means U.S. imperialism, domination and oppression, all in turn motivated by the interests of American capitalism. Back in the "world," Herr says he had trouble distinguishing "the Vietnam veterans from the rock and roll veterans" (276). He explains, "The Sixties had made so many casualties, its war and its music had run power off the same circuit for so long they didn't have to fuse" (276). Herr describes the appearance of a grunt who has just told him a terse, harrowing story of war: "His face was all painted up for night walking now like a bad hallucination, not like the faces I'd seen in San Francisco a few weeks before, the other extreme of the same theater" (5). Herr's pun on "theater" is significant. His literary representation of his experience suggests that the theater of war in Vietnam was theatrical indeed. Ultimately, Herr's text on Vietnam, like his consciousness of the event, remains open. In dialectical fashion, the dramatic conflict between the establishment and the anti-establishment over the subject of Vietnam remains unresolved.

Chapter Three:

Norman Mailer's *The Armies of the Night*: Journalist as Novelist and Intellectual

History as Drama

Like Michael Herr's *Dispatches*, Norman Mailer's *The Armies of the Night* plays out the dramatic historical conflict between the right-wing establishment and left-wing anti-establishment over the war in Vietnam. Mailer recreates his participation in an anti-war march that took place in Washington, D.C. in October 1967, dramatizing his experience by means of a highly self-conscious style, the clash of opposing discourses, and his own rhetorical persona which conflicts with both the establishment and, at times, the anti-establishment. Mailer's text is also similar to Herr's in that the writer places himself in the center of his story, assuming the position of central consciousness as well as protagonist. As we shall see, however, Mailer admits that while he assumes a central role in the text, he was not necessarily a principal player in the events themselves. Mailer conceives his role as that of one participant in an ongoing dramatic performance involving thousands of others. Myriad participants set the scene for the historical drama, the results of which, as Mailer makes clear,

107

are unknown. Mailer's text is again like Herr's in that the narrator draws no conclusions about the larger historical significance of events; in *Armies*, the dramatic conflict remains unresolved.

Although I have chosen the history-as-drama metaphor to discuss Mailer's treatment of his material, I am aware of the inherent danger of pushing this metaphor too far. A number of critics have unsuccessfully attempted to impose a pattern on *Armies*. Barbara Lounsberry, for example, detects in *Armies* an underlying archetypal pattern representing a rite of passage.[1] Certainly, Mailer's experience, symbolically recreated in *Armies*, can be interpreted as a re-enactment of the archetypal journey of the hero Joseph Campbell calls the "mono-myth,"[2] involving the three stages of separation, initiation, and return, but the term "rite of passage" more commonly refers to the formative experiences of a young person, as in a bildungsroman or a kunstlerroman, not to a middle-aged man. Herr's *Dispatches*, relating the experiences of a young reporter encountering the horrors of war, could more properly be called a rite of passage. In "Mailer's March: The Epic Structure of *The Armies of the Night*," Kenneth Seib misrepresents Mailer's text in a different way by enumerating characteristics of the classical epic and demonstrating how Mailer's text displays each one.[3] By pouring the text into an epic mold, however, Seib distorts its shape by oversimplifying it. The present discussion of *Armies* does not maintain that it satisfies any conventional set of generic criteria. To call these narratives dramatic, as I have done, is only to assert that the authors' styles, their rhetorical personae, and their narrative structure contribute a sense of drama to inherently dramatic events such as, in the case of *Armies*, the march on the Pentagon.

---

[1] Lounsberry, 152-168.
[2] Campbell, 3-42.
[3] Seib, 89-94.

One of Mailer's key dramatic techniques is the creation of a persona who becomes the narrative's protagonist locked in struggle with various antagonistic forces. As Schroeder has observed, Mailer's work reflects "the notion that without tension, without dialectical opposition, things don't get better."[4] His fundamental conflict in *Armies*, both as a participant in the event and as a writer, is with the establishment, represented in the text by the Johnson administration, the Pentagon, the police, and middle-class conservatives. These are familiar antagonists for Mailer. Throughout his career, from *The Naked and the Dead* to *Armies* and beyond, one of Mailer's primary themes has been totalitarianism, specifically, the individual in conflict with an oppressive, dehumanizing state. In *Armies*, however, Mailer's protagonist finds himself at odds with virtually everyone with whom he comes into contact. Warner Berthoff speaks of Mailer's "obsession [...] with conflicts of power [...] with pitting himself against rivals,"[5] including, in *Armies*, everyone from President Johnson to friend Robert Lowell. James Breslin claims that "style in Mailer always has an aggressive aspect—as in 'style of attack', a cliché that Mailer really means [...] given the weight of the surrounding deadness, the act of manifesting style becomes an heroic act [...]."[6] Standing apart from organized political factions, thinking and acting largely on his own, Mailer places himself in a marginal position. Robert Erlich finds an early impression of Mailer's unique political persona in his essay, "The White Negro," which deals with the phenomenon of the modern alienated hero, or existential hipster:

> If the hipster is the result of a society that is politically, socially, intellectually and economically

---

[4] Schroeder, 101.
[5] Berthoff, 323.
[6] Breslin, 161.

oppressive, his salvation lies in his consciousness of his condition, in a heightened readiness to maintain the inviolability of the self, both of which can only result from an intense, active engagement with the outside world in a unique and, most often, solitary manner. The possibility for collective political action is limited because of the exhausting psychological demands placed upon the hipster, and the restrictions upon the fullest amount of self-expression that is imposed in the very act of making a serious political commitment. The result is that when the political commitment is made, it is often so rich and confusing as to defy any existing political categories.[7]

As an existentialist, Mailer places a high premium on direct experience and on his own critical acumen and intuitive insight, steadfastly refusing to interpret events through the myopic eyes of left- and right-wing ideologues. By positioning himself as protagonist and narrator, the focus of his own narrative, Mailer makes himself an easy target for charges of egotism. Breslin is particularly critical of Mailer's style and persona, charging that his language is "not the means of communicating the feel of a subject, but the means of enacting his own grandiose self-conception,"[8] but given that Mailer stakes no claim to objectivity, on what basis does Breslin know that what Mailer describes is not the "feel of the subject" to Mailer himself? Breslin assumes that the events had a "feel" independent of an active participant in the events. Mailer's fiercely individualistic stance has come under attack from left-wing critic Robert Merideth, who argues that Mailer's ego-

---

[7] Ehrlich, 11.
[8] Breslin, 167.

assertion and attacks on segments of the left make *Armies* a reactionary, if not counter-revolutionary text.[9] I would argue that one of Mailer's functions as a participant in the event, and one of his purposes as narrator, is to act as a catalytic agent to set the drama in motion. In his real and imagined encounters with the other participants he creates multiple conflicts drive the narrative forward.

Unlike other New Journalists, Mailer refers to himself not in the first person but the third; in *Armies*, he refers to himself as "Mailer." By referring to himself in the third person, Mailer creates a certain distance, sometimes ironic, between himself and his narrator. John Hellmann detects the presence of an ironic, Fieldingesque narrator in *Armies*, observing that Mailer "adopts an ironically superior attitude toward the 'comic hero' ("Mailer," or more precisely Mailer as participant in the event, thus separated by time and role from Mailer as narrator of the event)" (38).[10] Mailer's conception of his role in the drama is more ambiguous, however. Exploring that ambiguity, Mailer asks of his persona: "is he finally comic, a ludicrous figure with mock-heroic associations; or is he not unheroic, and therefore embedded somewhat tragically in the comic? Or is he both at once, and all at once?"[11] Mailer goes on to suggest that there may be no answers to these questions, just as the ambiguity of the event itself may never be resolved: "The march on the Pentagon," he says, "was an ambiguous event whose essential value or absurdity may not be established for ten or twenty years—if indeed ever" (67). Identifying activists Jerry Rubin and David Dellinger as main characters in the drama, Mailer says, "their position in these affairs, precisely because it was central, can resolve nothing of the ambiguity" (67). Marc

---

[9] Merideth, 433-49.
[10] Hellman, 38.
[11] All references to *The Armies of the Night* are taken from this edition.

Weingarten argues that the narrator's use of the third person "liberates Mailer from the 'housing projects of fact and issue' that he felt prevented traditional reportage from examining the often complex matrix of impulses and root causes behind a mammoth act of resistance such as the march on the Pentagon."[12] Laura Adams infers Mailer's belief that "journalists and historians are incapable of handling the ambiguous."[13] Mailer indeed suggests that history is an ambiguous and dynamic process, a sequence of events the meaning of which cannot be ascertained simply by reporting the facts; Mailer's text further suggests that the significance of events must continually be reassessed, and from as many points of view as possible.

Mailer's conception of history and of his own role in the historical drama overlap. Kathy Smith argues that in *Armies* "the self's preemption of the story, the self *as* story, is the only strategy that can precipitate a radical rethinking of how history provides cohesive explanations of ambiguous events."[14] If Mailer conceives of contemporary history as fundamentally ambiguous, even absurd, his role as participant is similarly ambiguous and absurd, in Mailer's view. Hellmann observes that Mailer "casts himself as a protagonist able to bridge self and event through action and metaphor,"[15] and indeed, in one of the text's central metaphors Mailer compares history to a "crazy house" that the reader gains entrance to via Mailer's persona as "bridge" (68). Mailer says that:

> If the event took place in one of the crazy mansions,
> or indeed *the* crazy house of history, it is fitting that
> any ambiguous comic hero of such history should
> be not only off very much to the side of the history,

---

[12] Weingarten, 192.
[13] Adams, 130.
[14] Smith, 187.
[15] Hellman, 37.

112

but that he should be an egotist of the most startling misproportions [...] yet in command of a detachment classic in severity [....] Such egotism being two-headed, thrusting itself forward the better to study itself, finds itself therefore at home in a house of mirrors [....] Once History inhabits a crazy house, egotism may be the last tool left to History. (8)

Mailer's metaphor is appropriate to his method. The "crazy house," typically found in an amusement park, is constructed in this case of events which seem to defy conventional methods for making sense of experience. As in a "house of mirrors," one's senses become disoriented, and nothing is what it seems. The sense of distortion and disorientation is magnified by mass media accounts of the march and by doctrinaire analyses on the left and right. Mailer's "crazy house" metaphor implies that, given the confusion and baffling complexity of events, it would be unethical, if not simply inaccurate, for the writer to omit that element of distortion or disorientation from his text. Mailer's perspective, "very much off to the side," also deemphasizes the centrality of the writer's position in the midst of the event and allows him to make observations relatively free from any dogmatic or polemical limitations and to view events with a sense of distance. To report truthfully on an ambiguous event requires a central consciousness that is not only ambiguous but somewhat detached, lacking a particular agenda: "an eyewitness who is a participant but not a vested partisan is required," Mailer says (67). At the same time, "egotism" implies subjectivity, the necessity to seek the truth of the event within one's own experience; this "truth" can only be discovered within a "house of mirrors," where the writer may examine his experience by seeing his reaction to diverse phenomena reflected back.

113

Mailer's subjectivity and personal involvement in the demonstration allow him a closer perspective than an historical account, based on secondary research (newspaper reports, interviews, etc.), can achieve. Mailer's extended "Novel Metaphor," which introduces Book Two, makes the point:

If you would see the horizon from a forest, you must build a tower. If the horizon will reveal what is significant, an hour of examination will yet do the job—it is the tower which takes months to build. So the Novelist working in secret collaboration with the Historian has perhaps tried to build with his novel a tower fully equipped with telescopes to study—at the greatest advantage—our own horizon. Of course, the tower is crooked, and the telescopes warped, but the instruments of all sciences—history so much as physics—are always constructed in small or large error; what supports the use of them now is that our intimacy with the master builder of the tower, and the lens grinder of the telescopes (yes, even the machinist of the barrels) has given some advantage for correcting the error of the instruments and the imbalance of his tower. May that be claimed of many histories? In fact, how many novels can be put so quickly to use? (For the novel—we will permit ourselves this parenthesis— is, when it is good, the personification of a vision which will enable one to comprehend the other visions better; a microscope—if one is exploring the pond; a telescope upon a tower if you are scrutinizing the forest). The method is then exposed. The mass media which surrounded the March on the Pentagon created a forest of

114

inaccuracy which would blind the efforts of an historian; our novel has provided us with the possibility, no, even the instrument to view our facts and conceivably study them in that field of light a labor of lens-grinding has produced. (245)

Mailer's extended metaphor contains three parts: the horizon represents the demonstration activities themselves; the forest represents the biased and distorted accounts provided to the American public by the corporate media; the tower, telescope, and microscope initially represent Mailer's own text that allows the reader to view the horizon over the forest. Mailer's insistence that one must "build" the tower emphasizes that the text is something shaped or made by the writer's own personality. Michael L. Johnson points out that "Mailer's esthetic ... involves a bringing into play of the full power of the reporter's imagination and sensibility as essential to anything like an honest and relevant, if necessarily imperfect, journalism."[16] Mailer's journalism is "imperfect," according to Johnson, because it is created out of the subjective perceptions of one individual. The tower, telescope, and microscope, then, come to stand not only for Mailer's text, but for the reporter himself. By pointing out that "the tower is crooked, and the telescopes warped," Mailer acknowledges the imperfection or subjectivity of his vision. Mailer's admission that his perceptual apparati are imperfect is an effective rhetorical strategy. As James Breslin notes, "the main use of Mailer's self-irony is to allow him to make criticisms of himself before we can make them, and thus to ward them off."[17] Paradoxically, Mailer protects himself from charges of personal bias by openly admitting his biases. Then, as Stanly T. Gutman says, "the reader can easily become aware of the

---

[16] Johnson, 179.
[17] Breslin, 168.

biases and weaknesses of Mailer's vision and thus compensate for them."[18] The corporate media cannot share Mailer's candor about the role they play in shaping events, for it is in their interest to appear disinterested. The pretense of objectivity, as Edward S. Herman and Noam Chomsky document in *Manufacturing Consent,* allowed the mass media in the U.S. to run an effective propaganda campaign in support of the war.[19] Mailer's claim that the "instruments of all sciences—history so much as physics—are always constructed in small or large error," based on the discovery of modern physics that even scientific observation contains some degree of relativity or subjectivity, further corrects the "error" and "imbalance" of his perceptual instruments by calling attention to them. Once the reader understands that the writer's perspective is determined by his personality and ideological biases (frankly acknowledged, if not foregrounded, throughout the text), the reader may factor those elements into an understanding of both text and event. Mailer's subjectivity also frees him from the obligation, shared by many journalists and historians, to appear objective and disinterested. He can then dramatize the event as he chooses.

Mailer's tower metaphor suggests that the primary distinction between history and fiction exists in the realm of experience: the historian writes his account after the fact, basing it on research, assimilating other accounts, direct or indirect, into his own text; the novelist, by contrast, writes from direct experience. Another difference between history and journalism on the one hand, fiction or new journalism on the other, is that conventional historical or journalistic accounts tend to regard significant events as exterior, residing in the realm of empirically verifiable facts, while fictional or new journalistic texts take interior factors, the

---

[18] Gutman, 162.
[19] Herman and Chomsky, 1

writer's private thoughts or emotions, for example, into consideration. Philip H. Bufithis draws the following distinction between fiction and history in *Armies*: "The book is novelistic because it sensitively describes the effects of the march on a participant-protagonist, Norman Mailer, and historical because it scrupulously describes the *fact* of the march."[20] Mailer says that "the novel must replace history at precisely that point where experience is sufficiently emotional, spiritual, psychical, moral, existential, or supernatural to expose the fact that the historian in pursuing the experience would be obliged to quit the clearly demarcated limits of his historical inquiry" (284).

. History, Mailer says, is "interior" (284), indicating that history is a lived experience, not a compilation of data which bear a purely external relation to the individuals involved. *Armies* contains a multitude of facts about the anti-war demonstration, but Mailer's primary concern is with the feel of the event, the emotional factors that cannot be conveyed by the conventional 5Ws approach—Who, What, When, Where and Why. He cites Dwight McDonald's advice to "look to the feel of the phenomenon. If it feels bad, it *is* bad" (37).

In an article citing and synthesizing Mailer's many pronouncements on the distinctions among narrative forms, Michael Lennon concludes that Mailer sees:

> a fundamental dichotomy between the novel and forms of narrative nonfiction, history and journalism especially. For Mailer the novel is spontaneous, resonant and intended to illumine questions. History and journalism are pre-digested, concrete and intended to provide answers to

---

[20] Bufisthis, 86.

questions they raise. Novels are open, immediate, and overbearing; they intensify consciousness and difficulties of moral choice. History and journalism are lucid and organized; their outcomes are usually predetermined by selected evidence; they deliver buttressed conclusions. In the novel everything is slightly murky, swirling, and when meaning does emerge it does so in a flash of brilliant intuition. Conversely, history and journalism are courts where evidence is presented systematically; at the end of the trial, the accretion of linked facts is overwhelmingly indisputable. Fiction for Mailer is 'the high road,' and its plots are complex and usually open-ended. History and journalism are 'the low road,' and their plots are ordered and predictable. Time in the novel accelerates and then dawdles; it moves at no certain speed. In history and journalism time has been bought and labeled; time has already been consumed.[21]

Lennon's summary faithfully represents Mailer's own observations. The question is whether Mailer's critical principles are consistent with his practice as a writer as well as with the journalistic practices of his contemporaries: Wolfe, Capote, Herr, Thompson, Didion, and so on. A related question: when Mailer references history and journalism, is he referring to what he considers standard historiographic and journalistic practice, or his own? The dichotomy that Lennon brings to light suggests that Mailer conceives of history and journalism as those forms are traditionally understood.

---

[21] Lennon, 97.

When we look closely at *Armies*, however, a work of New Journalism, we can see that the text embodies many of the qualities Mailer associates with fiction. First, as I will demonstrate later in this chapter, Mailer's heuristic style gives to *Armies* a sense of spontaneity and immediacy. Further, Mailer's focus on his own perceptions and impressions does at times intensify the reader's consciousness in sympathetic union with the narrator's, and some of the more deliberative passages, such as the "Why Are We in Vietnam?" chapter, present the reader with the difficult moral choices such as how to end the war in Vietnam without creating even greater instability in southeast Asia. As I will further demonstrate in my discussion of the narrative's conclusion, the form of *Armies* is ultimately open-ended and inconclusive. Finally, as my discussions of Herr, Thompson, and Didion illustrate, their texts make absolute distinctions among the narrative forms of fiction, history, and journalism extremely difficult to establish.

Mailer's distinction between his novelistic method and the methods adopted by historians or the corporate media is similar to the distinction Kenneth Burke makes between the "semantic" and "poetic" ideals.[22] At one end of the spectrum, the historian, striving to achieve the "semantic" ideal, stresses the role of the observer, combining the rigorous documentation of facts with reasoned, objective analysis; at the other end, Mailer, believing in the "poetic" ideal, stresses the role of the participant who shares his subjective observations and feelings about the scene. Mailer's primary concern, which I will demonstrate through a discussion of style, is with preparing a dramatically persuasive image which will invite the audience's symbolic participation in an historical struggle. Through a dramatic, "poetic" presentation of events,

---

[22] Burke, *Philosophy*, 138-164.

Mailer urges his readers to give their assent to his observations and reactions.

One element of the text's dramatic structure results from the fact, often referred to by Mailer, that the march had no "center" (22): no individual or group of individuals was completely in charge; no definite route had been decided upon in advance. Mailer's direct participation in an unpredictable and uncertain event points to an important difference between his account and other, more straightforwardly historical accounts that, he says, "can assume that certain ... dramatic issues were never in doubt" (276). Mailer incorporates his uncertainty, anxiety, and fear into the text heuristically, determining the text's structure in the act of writing. As Stanley T. Gutman remarks, the writing of *Armies* represents "a search for meaning," one that has "no known end but only a guideline for its investigation," to seek the meaning of the experience in the experience itself.[23] Gutman calls the march on the Pentagon "a paradigmatic existential situation because it has no preordained conclusion or significance,"[24] and indeed, the uncertainty of the outcome feeds Mailer's appetite for the existential moment: "we are up, face this, all of you," he tells the crowd assembled at the Ambassador Theater, "against an existential situation—we do not know how it is going to turn out, and what is even more inspiring of dread is that the government doesn't know either" (51). The "dread" produced by existential uncertainty raises a dramatic question Mailer asks repeatedly throughout the text: will the march result in violence? Mailer's fear of a violent response on behalf of the police or military creates some of the text's dramatic tension. The thought of being maced, or even worse, struck on the head with a billy club, inspires a

---

[23] Gutman, 167.
[24] Gutman, 167.

"small horror" in the narrator (70). On the morning of the March, Mailer becomes susceptible to the "mood" of the proceedings, which he compares to "a hint of hurricane calm" (98). Mailer's metaphor foreshadows future brutality on the steps of the Pentagon.

Appropriately, *Armies* also contains numerous martial metaphors which suggest the possibility of violence; the title itself, of course, an allusion to Matthew Arnold's poem "Dover Beach," "where ignorant armies clash by night,"[25] refers to combat, an inherently dramatic event, but the protestors march on the Pentagon, Mailer says, "not to capture it, as in actual combat, where victory depends on the acquisition or reclaiming of territory, but to wound it *symbolically*" (68); nevertheless, Mailer continues, "the forces defending that bastion reacted as if a symbolic wound could prove as mortal as any other combative rent" (68). The Pentagon, Mailer reasons, must consider the symbolic value of an attack on the protestors: "An open white riot in the streets of the Capital after the summer riots in the Negro ghettoes would telegraph a portrait of America to Global Village as an extremely unstable nation, therefore a dangerous nation on whom to count for long-term alliances [...]" (268). Mailer considers himself engaged in an act of "symbolic civil disobedience" (294). He knows how important it is for the protestors to appear, symbolically, to have gained a victory, and he is acutely aware of the importance of media coverage to the success of the anti-war movement: "A protest movement which does not grow loses power every day, since protest movements depend upon the interest they arouse in the mass media. But the mass media are interested only in processes which are expanding dramatically or collapsing" (259). Through its dramatic presentation of events, *The Armies of the*

---

[25] Arnold, 56-57.

Night represents Mailer's attempt to feed the fires of the protest movement. As I have indicated, however, Mailer is reluctant to claim victory, setting the stage for dramatic conflict but leaving the drama unresolved.

Restating his interest in the existential moment, Mailer says that "if the March did more or less succeed ... it would be as a result of episodes one had never anticipated, and the results might lead you into directions altogether unforeseen" (102). A march with no predictable outcome is conducive to Mailer's rejection of well thought-out schemes in favor of spontaneity and inspiration. Mailer's style of revolt, shared by many of the student radicals, causes conflict between the writer and the middle-class left, who prefer, he says, "the unassailable logic of the next step," a program of resistance that follows from careful and deliberate planning (103). The uncertainty of the outcome does not trouble the most radical factions of the march who, like Mailer, prefer "revolution by theater and without a script" (249). Mailer claims that, for the radicals, revolution preceded ideology: "you created the revolution first and learned from it," he says, "learned of what your revolution might consist and where it might go out of the intimate truth of the way it presented itself to your experience" (104). Mailer's notion of revolution first, ideology later actually forms in reaction to the programmatic and therefore uninspiring example of the Old Left, with its endless speeches, pamphlets, and committee meetings, and even that of the New Left, which Mailer feels is compromised by its complicity with the enemy, "technology land." He says that the "mediocre, middle-class, middle-aged masses of the Left were ... the first real champions of technology land: they could not conceive of a revolution without hospitals, lawyers, mass meetings, and leaflets passed out at the polls" (113). Mailer's final allegiance, he says, is with the hippies and yippies on the radical fringe, but that is only to say that he aligns himself with a loosely structured, unorganized faction of the left, essentially anarchistic in spirit, which also prefers "revolution by theater and without a script" (249). The formless theatricality of the hippie, or more specifically (given the key participation of figures like Abbie Hoffman and Jerry Rubin), yippie aesthetic most closely suits Mailer's own politics and dramatically self-conscious, heuristic style. Nevertheless, Philip H. Bufithis points out, "While Mailer admires the demonstrators' pluck and wholeheartedly sympathizes with their moral stand against the state's authority, he makes it clear that both sides possess their share of lies, delusions and dogmas."[26] Mailer may have been hip—in the 1950s he was an early hipster—but he was, of course, neither a hippie nor a yippie. Forty-four years old at the time of the march, veteran of World War II, husband and father, Mailer belonged to a different generation. Ultimately, he views hippies and yippies with the same degree of detachment with which he regards every other group.

Mailer as Rhetorical Critic

Aligning himself more or less with the radical fringe, Mailer's opposition to the war is clear throughout; but, unlike some of the war's opponents, he is neither a professional revolutionary nor an ideologue. Robert Ehrlich asserts that, despite Mailer's political radicalism, the writer "considers himself primarily an artist for whom events attain their ultimate significance when an active engagement with the external world gives rise to the process of writing."[27] Mailer frequently suggests that "one's own literary work was the answer to the war in Vietnam" (19). Movements, political parties, and acronyms are anathema to his aesthetic sense and anarchistic sensibility. Mailer's ideological make-up is eclectic, composed of various influences,

---

[26] Bufisthis, 91.
[27] Ehrlich, 16-17.

none of which assumes priority over the other. Mailer often reflects on his previous involvement with radical causes and left-wing periodicals and concludes that "his private mixture of Marxism, conservatism, nihilism, and large parts of existentialism could no longer produce any polemical gravies for the digestive apparatus of scholarly Socialist minds" (35). Labeling himself a "Left Conservative," Mailer establishes his marginal position (208). As Kathy Smith writes, "It is with this label in mind that Mailer wants us to receive his impressions about why we are in Vietnam. They are presented in such a way as to complicate the apparently polarized positions: you are either for the war or against it."[28] Mailer's chapter, "Why Are We In Vietnam?" illustrates the reductive oversimplifications of For or Against positions, and his final refusal to accept whole-heartedly any position other than his own allows him to remain somewhat detached, a necessary precondition for artistic and intellectual freedom.

At the same time, Mailer attempts to foreground as many conflicting voices into his text as possible. In Bakhtinian terms, *Armies* is a "heteroglossic" text; Bakhtin, we recall, defines heteroglossia as *"another's speech in another's language,* serving to express authorial intentions but in a refracted way."[29] Mailer incorporates the language of others into his own text by playing the various voices off one another dialectically, multiplying perspectives so that no particular ideological viewpoint assumes hegemony over the others. As Chris Anderson points out, Mailer assumes the role of "rhetorical critic."[30] Indeed, much of *Armies* consists of a critique of pro-and anti-war rhetoric. For example, Mailer condemns what he calls "totalitarianese," quoting a reply by a Pentagon official who responds to charges of excessive brutality

---

[28] Smith, 187.
[29] Bakhtin, 324.
[30] Anderson, 98.

against the protestors: "We feel our action is consistent with objectives of security and control faced with varying levels of dissent" (315). Mailer repeats the spokesman's words in italics to indicate his indignation and utter disbelief: *"Consistent with objectives of security and control! levels of dissent!"* (315). He then explains that the spokesman was speaking "totalitarianese, which is to say, technologese, which is to say any language which succeeds in stripping itself of any moral content" (315). "Technologese" exemplifies what Bakhtin calls "authoritative discourse," language that is "indissolubly fused with its authority" and "permits no play."[31] As we shall see, Mailer answers the establishment's "authoritative discourse" with his own "internally persuasive discourse."[32] Loosely structured, figurative, and self-consciously aesthetic, Mailer's style presents a challenge to the authority of the Establishment's discourses, further developing the fundamental dramatic conflict in the text. Before I discuss the specific ways in which Mailer's "internally persuasive" discourse works, we need to examine his rhetorical critique of the discourse of others in more detail.

Mailer's criticism of language is not limited to establishment discourse. Robert Ehrlich observes that "Mailer continually indicates his dissatisfaction with the 'jargon-mired' children of the Counter-Culture, whose few curt expressions, 'entropies of vocabulary,' are used to describe experiences which require much more elaboration."[33] Of a young protestor speaking on the occasion of turning in his draft card, Mailer says, "one did not look forward to a revolution which would substitute 'thing' for better words" (91). Abstractions like "'thing,'" Mailer implies, lack the quality of concreteness necessary for effective political

---

[31] Bakhtin, 342-43.
[32] Bakhtin, 345-46.
[33] Ehrlich, 13.

125

rhetoric (250), and he expresses boredom at the interminable round of speeches delivered on the steps of the Department of Justice (84-96). He says, "Rhetoric hand in hand with reason put no spirit of war in revolutionary boys" (294). Anderson says, "As Mailer listens to speech after speech before and during the March on the Pentagon, he becomes increasingly convinced that such step-by-step, careful programmatic expression is not only stylistically uninteresting but finally useless."[34] Mailer demonstrates the uselessness of such programmatic rhetoric when he is arrested and put in jail for breaking a police line. While inside, he meets a young revolutionary named Walter Teague, a Leninist; Teague's line is the party line. Mailer recreates Teague's speech to the other prisoners, but he does so in the third person to emphasize the impersonal tone of much political rhetoric:

> One worked for the revolution twenty-four hours a day ... one explained, one instructed ... one took the collective experience of the revolutionary activity [in this case, the assault on the Pentagon] and one analyzed the experience, one extracted the revolutionary content from the less-than-revolutionary chaos of mixed intents, compromised programs and sell-outs. (201-202)

Mailer's use of anaphora here, phrases or clauses beginning with the same word or group of words, "One ... one ... one," creates the impression of stylistic uniformity and tireless repetition, thus demonstrating the tendency of the ideologue to analyze events reductively. No originality of expression means no originality of thought. Mailer states that truth is arrived at in. the process of creating meaning: "a good half of writing," he says, "consists in being sufficiently sensitive to the moment" (40). Teague's

---

[34] Anderson, 100.

discourse is dogmatic, closed; Mailer's is heuristic, open. Mailer doesn't object to the content of Teague's speech but to the form: "Everything Teague said was probably true," the narrator explains, "and yet the indictment was too easy—it had all the hard firm impact of the sound-as-brickwork-logic-of-the-next-step" (202). Robert Ehrlich makes the point that individuals on the right or left who think, speak, and act according to the "sound-as-brickwork-logic-of-the-next-step," assuming a stable set of conditions that can be logically and methodically changed, "are ultimately trapped by rigid ideological applications which do not acknowledge the complexity of experience, especially the subtle workings of the irrational in our daily lives."[35] Mailer's own view of history and human motives is far more complex than Teague's, whose Leninist rhetoric, he claims, "was built to analyze a world in which all of the structures are made of steel" (202); in 1967, however, "the sinews of society were founded on transistors so small Dragon Lady could hide them beneath her nail" (202). Mailer disdains practical suggestions while he thrives on inspiration and dialectical confrontation. He clearly admires activist Jerry Rubin who, when he is told that the police could easily stop protestors from crossing the various bridges leading from Washington, D.C. to northern Virginia, site of the Pentagon, advocates simply turning around and marching to the Capitol instead. "A true visionary," Mailer says of Rubin, "may [...] always defeat a practical suggestion, for he absorbs any necessary kernel of the detailed from the aura of the other debater" (252). Rubin's dialectical strategy, which allows him to work with given conditions and to improvise, is consistent with Mailer's own. In the end, Mailer asserts his preference for mystery, or the unknown, over logical certainty: "belief was reserved for the revelatory mystery of the happening where you did not know what was going to happen next; that was what was good

---

[35] Ehrlich, 125.

about it" (103). Mystery, the sense of the unknown, supports the text's dramatic structure. Mailer quotes here from a speech by writer/social activist Paul Goodman to the members of the Pentagon:

> 'You are the military industrial [sic] of the United States, the most dangerous body of men at the present in the world, for you not only implement our disastrous policies but are an overwhelmingly [sic] lobby for them, and you expand and rigidify the wrong use of brains, resources, and labor, so that change becomes difficult.' (115)

Again, Mailer reacts here to the form of Goodman's speech, not the content: "everything he said was right, so naturally it had to be said in a style which read like LBJ's exercises in Upper Rhetoric, examples of which are "'at the present in the world' [...] 'implement' [...] 'disastrous policies' [...] 'expand and rigidify'" (115). By comparing Goodman's rhetoric to President Johnson's, Mailer blurs the distinction between left and right, both of whom express themselves in technologese, both of which follow the "sound-as-brickwork-logic-of-the-next-step." As rhetorical critic, Mailer reads Goodman's text in a way that makes it appear compromised by, if not complicit with, the deception practiced by the U.S. government.

In addition to speeches by various participants, *Armies* incorporates numerous journalistic accounts of the march on the Pentagon. Mailer lodges bitter complaints against the conventional media's distortion of reported speech: "The papers [...] wrenched and garbled and twisted and broke one's words and sentences until a good author always sounded like an incoherent overcharged idiot in newsprint [...] It really did not matter what was said— dependably one was elliptic, incomprehensible, asinine" (80).

128

Mailer quotes these sources for several reasons. First, he wishes to highlight their limitations and distortions, thus to subvert their authority. The problem with conventional journalism, from Mailer's point of view, is that it must necessarily atomize phenomena in order to satisfy space requirements; the conventional media condenses the participants' words and quotes them out of context, creating an impression of events which is ultimately simplistic and therefore distorted. Mailer's account of the scene at the Ambassador Theater, juxtaposed to *Time* magazine's account, exemplifies this reductive tendency on behalf of the conventional media (40-66). At the beginning of his own text, Mailer cites *Time* magazine's brief, biased, elliptical account of the speeches at the Ambassador Theater, in which Mailer is described as an obscene, incoherent, belligerent drunk (13-14). Following the account, and closing Book I, Section 1, the narrator says, "Now we may leave *Time* in order to find out what happened" (14). In a sense, the first several sections of *Armies* supplement and refute the *Time* account. Mailer bashes both the corporate and underground press for their glaring inaccuracies and distortions: "the journalistic information available from both sides," he says, "is so incoherent, inaccurate, contradictory, malicious, even based on error that no accurate history is conceivable" (284). He says, "Psychedelic underground papers consider themselves removed from any fetish with factology" (286). Mailer multiplies perspectives on a given event, "The Battle of the Wedge," for example (289-292), in order to demonstrate that no particular point of view can be definitive or authoritative.

As we have seen, Mailer blasts members of the corporate media for their lies and misrepresentations, but he also criticizes them for "creating a psychology ... in the average American which made wars like Vietnam possible [...]" (95). Mailer is not explicit about his use of the term "psychology" in this context, but it is clear that he holds the mass media responsible for helping, directly or indirectly, to promote the war. Ehrlich makes the following distinction between the mindset of conventional journalists, who often lent implicit support for the war, and of Mailer as hipster:

> Unlike the hipster who has forged a vision out of the processes of his experience, the conventional journalist cannot distinguish between his real feelings and the emotional encrustations of society. The endless process of socialization tends to turn the journalist's nervous system into a reflex of the most powerful men in America.[36]

Herman and Chomsky document the way conventional journalists marginalized the dissenting, anti-Vietnam war position and suppressed information which would damage the government's credibility.[37] Robert J. Begiebing says that the *Time* magazine story cited above "clearly illustrates the biases of *Time* in favor of the Establishment cause."[38] As Mailer's remarks regarding media coverage of the war make clear, the corporate press attempted to manipulate public reaction to the march on the Pentagon in a way that ultimately privileged the (316). He quotes a James Reston account in the New York *Times* in which condemnation of the protestors is clear (317). Mailer also notes that he found no specific mention, in any of the corporate press accounts, of "The Battle of the Wedge" (316-317). The corporate media conveniently omits "The Battle of the Wedge" from its accounts in order to promote the interests of the military-industrial complex. Viewing the corporate media as an agent of the enemy, Mailer dramatizes "The Battle of the Wedge" to counter the Pentagon's attack (298-316).

---

[36] Ehrlich, 115.
[37] Herman and Chomsky, 169-296.
[38] Begibing, 42.

Stylistic Analysis

A number of critics have pointed out that Mailer presents his own style as an alternative to mass media and establishment discourse. Bufithis observes that:

> The continual modulations of mood, the convoluted and energetically reflective prose, that fills this book constitute Mailer's counterthrust against the mass media which, he believes, seduce the mind and make American society...impatient with ideas, with situations of complexity, with the habit of reflection, the discerning of distinctions, the weight of nuance.[39]

One of the ways Mailer poses an alternative to establishment discourse is through the inclusion of multiple voices. In Voloshinovian terms, Mailer's "multiaccentual" style provides numerous alternatives to the "uniaccentual" discourse of the mass media and political factions.[40] The voice of the establishment attempts to drown out the voices of the opposition and to speak in only one voice, its own; Mailer's rhetorical purpose, on the other hand, is to make those voices heard. In addition to the voices of left-wing protestors, those the establishment attempts to silence, Mailer speaks in numerous voices of his own: there is Mailer the reporter, reporting facts, conveying information; Mailer the social critic, attacking complacency on the left and totalitarianism on the right; and Mailer the prophet, dimly foretelling, as we shall see in the conclusion, the future of America. Through his use of various styles, Mailer wages ideological war on left- and right-wing discourse. In a self-interview published in *Cannibals and*

---

[39] Bufisthis, 91.
[40] Voloshinov, 23.

Christians, Mailer says that the form or style of literary work is "the record of a war" between the writer and his environment.[41] In the case of *Armies,* the war becomes, on one level, a dialectical struggle among competing discourses. In reference to Mailer's discussion of liberal protest organizations, for example, Richard Poirier says that the protagonist finds himself "in dialectical opposition to the prevailing mood" and uses his language to counter the stale, cliché-ridden quality of political rhetoric.[42] Michael L. Johnson asserts that Mailer "clearly wants to avoid freezing his exploratory attitude into any kind of dogmatism; he wants to keep his ideas free, changing, his mind open to the forces of the moment,"[43] so his style, correspondingly, becomes ever-changing, open, and free. The consequence of Mailer's open-style rhetorical subversion is the liberation of his reader's consciousness, which has been imprisoned by institutionalized language and thought.

Mailer's style is highly self-conscious and opaque, calling attention to itself as language. When his style is at its most opaque, or self-consciously rhetorical, it approaches the rhythms and sound patterns associated with poetry. Mailer's prose occasionally displays the qualities of play and delight in language for its own sake that Kenneth Burke calls "pure persuasion."[44] At the same time, Mailer does wish to persuade his readers to share his attitudes, beliefs, and prejudices. To this end, his prose establishes what Burke, again, calls "identification."[45] The formal identification in Mailer's prose becomes closest when the writer's emotional pitch is at its highest, or when his philosophical musings

---

[41] Mailer, *Cannibals,* 370.
[42] Poirier, 91.
[43] Johnson, 181.
[44] Burke, *Rhetoric,* 267-94.
[45] Burke, *Rhetoric,* 55-9.

lead him astray from the narrative. Conversely, the more detached Mailer is, the less self-consciously persuasive is his style. James Berlin states that "distance from the specific continually results in flabbiness in Mailer's own prose [....] Metaphors [...] are often stilted, forced attempts to lift banalities into elevated prose [...]."[46] The opening chapters of Book Two, for example, in which Mailer relates events occurring prior to his direct participation in the march, are the least stylistically interesting in the text, low points so to speak. Before discussing Book Two in detail, however, I would like to look more closely at one of the stylistic high points in Book One. Once again, I will appropriate Lanham's method—the use of terms from classical rhetoric to describe stylistic features and how they function—set forth in *Analyzing Prose*. There are numerous rhetorical high points in *Armies* that lend themselves to close stylistic analysis; I have chosen to examine one passage in which Mailer confronts the enemy, totalitarianism, in the form of its most prominent symbol in this text—the Pentagon. In the following excerpt from Book One, Part III, Chapter 5, Mailer reflects on his first sighting of the Pentagon building:

> Since the parking lot was huge as five football fields, and just about empty, for they were the first arrivals, the terminus of the March was without drama. Nor was the Pentagon even altogether visible from the parking lot. Perhaps for that reason, a recollection returned to Mailer (alive as an open nerve) when they had seen it first, walking through the field, just after the March had left the road on the Virginia side of the Potomac; there, topping a rise, it appeared, huge in the near distance, not attractive. Somehow, Mailer had been anticipating it would look more impressive

---

[46] Breslin, 165.

than its pictures, he was always expecting corporation land to surprise him with a bit of wit, a hint of unexpected grace—it never did. The Pentagon rose like an anomaly of the sea from the soft Virginia fields (they were crossing a park) its pale yellow walls reminiscent of some plastic plug coming out the hole made in flesh by an unmentionable operation. There, it sat, geometrical aura complete, isolated from anything in nature surrounding it. Eras ago had corporation land begun by putting billboards on the old post roads?—now they worked to clean them up—just as the populace had succeeded in depositing comfortable amounts of libido on highway signs, gasoline exhausts, and oil-stained Jersey macadam—now corporation land, here named Government, took over state preserves, straightened crooked narrow roads, put up government buildings, removed unwelcome signs till the young Pop eye of Art wept for unwelcome signs—where are our old friends?—and corporation land would succeed, if it hadn't yet, in making nature look like an outdoor hospital, and the streets of U.S. cities, grace of Urban Renewal, would be difficult to distinguish when drunk from pyramids of packaged foods in the aisles of a supermarket.

For years he had been writing about the nature of totalitarianism, its need to render populations apathetic, its instrument—the destruction of mood. Mood was forever being sliced, cut, stamped, ground, excised, or obliterated; mood was a scent which rose from the acts and calms of nature, and totalitarianism was a deodorant to nature. Yes, and

134

by the logic of this metaphor, the Pentagon looked like the five-sided tip on the spout of a spray can to be used under the arm, yes, the Pentagon was spraying the deodorant of its presence all over the fields of Virginia. (135-136)

This passage progresses from narration (Mailer's reactions to events become narrative events, as in a "recollection returned [...]") to description to analysis. Throughout *Armies*, Mailer steps off the narrative path, asks us to look closely at something, and then discusses its significance; he frequently digresses for several pages before returning to the story of the march. The use of an observation or fact as a point of departure for a further, related observation is called paradiegesis, a characteristic feature of much of Mailer's prose.

Another feature of this passage is Mailer's mixture of hypotactic and paratactic structures. Hypotactic sentence elements are arranged in a subordinate relationship; they build to a dramatic climax, as in the last two sentences in this passage. In a paratactic sentence, the grammatical elements are ranked equally in a coordinate relationship, as in "There, it sat, geometrical aura complete, isolated from everything in nature surrounding it." Parataxis allows Mailer to string together fragments of experience which may have seemed, up to the moment of writing, unrelated; in this sense, parataxis functions heuristically. Anderson accurately describes Mailer's composing process as follows: "Rather than start from the standpoint of what he has learned after all is said and done, he begins at the beginning, recording his first impression and then the second, then the third and fourth, as well as the principle of movement that emerges as he changes."[47] The use of interjections, "yes," for example, occurs frequently in Mailer's

---

[47] Anderson, 90.

prose, and offers evidence of its heuristic qualities; the interjections suggest a mind in the process of creating meaning, discovering what it wants to saying the act of saying it. The final metaphor in this passage, in which Mailer interjects "yes" on two occasions, also suggests this heuristic quality. Hellmann argues persuasively that Mailer's use of metaphor is a "natural expression of his epistemology, since it openly displays meaning as an individual consciousness's active participation of its ordering and interpretive activities upon the world around it."[48] Anderson adds, "Metaphors in Mailer's text are meant as points of departure rather than fixed images. Tenors change and evolve as Mailer discovers the unfolding implications of the vehicle."[49] Mailer credits Dwight McDonald with giving him "the hint that the clue to discovery was not in the substance of one's idea, but in what was learned from the style of one's attack" (37). He claims that "a good half of writing consists of being sufficiently sensitive to the moment to reach for the next promise which is usually hidden in some word or phrase just a shift to the side of one's conscious intent" (40). Mailer likens this process to "speaking-in-public" which, as opposed to "public speaking [...] an exercise from prepared texts," allows the speaker to improvise (40).

A heuristic approach most appropriately suits Mailer's subject matter. Mailer says he wrote his account quickly, "as if the accelerating history of the country forbade deliberation" (241). This process of creating meaning occasionally produces a highly unusual, even eccentric, syntax. A. Alvarez observes that Mailer "has abandoned formal rules in order to arrive at a medium which will follow precisely the certainties and hesitations of his sensibility in action. This is the technical, stylistic parallel of the

---

[48] Hellman, 42.
[49] Anderson, *Style*, 95.

larger drift of the book [...]."[50] Sentences such as the one beginning, "Eras ago," with its convoluted syntax—question marks followed by dashes, shifts in mood—provide examples of anacoluthon, the ending of a sentence with a different structure than that with which it began. Mailer's use of anacoluthon suggests not only that he wrote his sentences too quickly to revise as he did so but that he made a conscious decision not to revise, allowing the structure of the sentence to allegorize, as it were, its complex meaning. Richard Poirier argues, "If [Mailer] is to effect a revolution in our consciousness, it will not be by making merely the usual kind of sense. It will be by virtue of a style subversive of the ways such problems are customarily handled."[51] Occasionally, caught up in the rhythms and sounds of his prose as his mind wanders freely from phrase to phrase, Mailer seems to lose sight of his direction, as in the last sentence in the first paragraph. The phrase "difficult to distinguish when drunk" needs a modifier (Who is drunk? The narrator or "the streets of U.S. cities"?); the confused syntax, however, actually conveys the confusion and the sensory disorientation Mailer experiences in "corporation land."

Despite Mailer's assertion that "the terminus of the March was without drama," he nevertheless dramatizes his first glimpse of the Pentagon. Mailer's bringing of that moment to memory is called commemoratio: "a recollection returned to Mailer of that moment (alive as open nerve) when they had seen it first ... there, topping a rise, it appeared ..." The three short elements following in quick succession, "there, topping a rise, it appeared," convey the impression of a sudden sighting. However, the sentence is finally anti-climactic: "huge in the near distance, not attractive." The use of "not attractive" instead of "unattractive" not only makes a

---

[50] Alarez, 352.
[51] Poirier, 10.

137

judgment but expresses Mailer's disappointment. Another passage, "There, it appeared, geometrical aura complete, isolated from anything in nature surrounding it," recalls the one just mentioned. The descriptive observations in both passages are examples of paradiegesis, mentioned above, prompting Mailer's further observations about "corporation land." Following the short, staccato, "there, topping a rise, it appeared," Mailer stretches out a few isocolons, phrases of approximately equal length and corresponding structure: "Mailer had been anticipating ... he was always expecting." The rhythm slows down as Mailer's anticipation fades into disappointment. The abrupt, "it never did," speeds things up again, and prepares us for the striking metaphor which follows and which I will discuss at greater length below. Tricolon patterns isocolons in threes: "highway signs, gasoline exhausts, and oil-stained Jersey macadam...." Isocolons commonly appear in groups of three, and establish here the kind of formal expectation Burke associates with identification.[52] More isocolons follow, this time in a group of four, all constructed verb-adjective-noun: "took over state preserves, straightened crooked narrow roads, put up government buildings, removed unwelcome signs ..." The isocolons in these last two passages allow Mailer to create a litany of specific indictments against the enemy—"corporation land."

In the first paragraph, Mailer uses parenthesis, a word, phrase or sentence inserted as an aside in a sentence complete in itself: "(alive as an open nerve) ..." Mailer's prose is heavily parenthetical, allegorizing a complex view of the world and functioning as a direct rebuke both to the dogmatic, stilted language of political parties and the reductive, stripped-down style of the mass media. Additional parenthetical elements like "Where

---

[52] Burke, *Rhetoric*, 55-9.

are our old friends?" provide examples of subjectio, commonly known as a rhetorical question, in which the person asking the question suggests his own answer. In these instances, the answers are merely implied. The two clauses, "Eras ago had corporation land begun by putting billboards on the old post roads?" and "Now they worked to clean them up" omit an implied "yes." The effect, once again, is heuristic; Mailers asks himself questions in the process of writing in order to discover the answers.

The effectiveness of Mailer's rhetoric depends in large degree on his ability to discuss the abstract in concrete terms. For example, he personifies "corporation land" in this passage in order to make it more tangible: "he was always expecting corporation land to surprise him with a bit of wit, a hint of unexpected grace [....]" Mailer also employs metonymy, and here I take my definition from Kenneth Burke's *A Grammar of Motives*: metonymy, Burke says, is the reduction of an incorporeal or intangible state in terms of the corporeal or tangible,[53] as in "grace of Urban Renewal" in the form of "the streets of U.S. cities." Faced with the bewildering complexity and rapid change of events in the late-1960s, and the myriad (often unseen) threats totalitarianism presents to the individual, Mailer's use of personification and metonymy connect disparate phenomena. He forces the reader—whose perceptions have become habitually dulled by the local newspaper and the evening news—to see the world in new ways; in Formalist terms, Mailer defamiliarizes the familiar.

Another device that allows the writer to make connections between things is, of course, figurative language. Let us now return to some figures in the first paragraph quoted above: "The Pentagon rose like an anomaly of the sea from the soft Virginia fields [...] its

---

[53] Burke, *Grammar*, 506.

pale yellow walls reminiscent of some plastic plug coming out of the hole made in flesh by an unmentionable operation." Following the initial simile, "like an anomaly," the metaphor is extravagant, unexpected, bizarre; it is the type of metaphor classical rhetoricians would have labeled catechresis, the rhetorical purpose of which is to shock or threaten the reader into awareness. A quick look at some of Mailer's other similes, "huge as five football fields," and "making nature look like an outdoor hospital," shows just how striking the metaphors are in comparison. Mailer asks that we see the Pentagon in a different way, as a malign presence, and indeed, throughout his career as a writer he has described totalitarianism as a disease. In *Cannibals and Christians*, to cite just one example, Mailer writes, "The country was in disease. It had been in disease a long time. There was nothing in our growth which was organic."[54] The metaphor which closes our passage returns to the same idea:

> Mood was a scent which rose from the acts and calms of nature, and totalitarianism was a deodorant to nature. Yes, and by the logic of this metaphor, the Pentagon looked like the five-sided tip of a spray can to be used under the arm, yes, the Pentagon was spraying the deodorant of its presence all over the fields of Virginia.

Both metaphors are examples of accumulatio, the heaping up of praise or, in this case, accusation, to emphasize or summarize points which have already been made. More specifically, the metaphors exemplify cohortatio, which Lanham defines, somewhat coincidentally in this context, as follows: "Amplification that moves the hearer's indignation, as when the horrors of an enemy's barbarities are dwelt upon to promote patriotism."[55] Mailer's

---

[54] Mailer, *Cannibals*, 42.
[55] Lanham, *Handlist*, 24-5.

metaphor becomes syllogistic in its progression: roughly paraphrased, the major premise asserts that totalitarianism deodorizes nature; the minor premise claims that the Pentagon resembles a deodorant can; Mailer concludes that the Pentagon is, therefore, totalitarian. In the first simile, Mailer describes the Pentagon as an "anomaly of the sea," again suggesting something distinctly unnatural in the building's presence. To drive home the point, Mailer places the Pentagon's "aura" at a distance, "isolated from anything in nature surrounding it," thus resonating with Wallace Stevens' line "like nothing else in Tennessee" from the poem "Anecdote of the Jar,"[56] and criticizing the institution from a Romantic perspective. Breslin observes that to Mailer the Pentagon represents "the absence (in fact, the suppression) of style [...] to look at a building so thoroughly purged of any hint of the human is to feel nothing—nothingness, the void—or, more accurately, to confront the terrifying 'totalitarian' effort to destroy feeling and impose an alien and (dead) abstract form of order on the individual."[57] The Pentagon is either devoid of spirit, because cut off from nature, or, as the Exorcism of the Pentagon conducted by poets Ed Sanders, Allen Ginsberg, and Tuli Kupferburg suggests, possessed by evil spirits and in need of a spiritual cleansing (139-143). Mailer's observation that "the populace had finally succeeded in depositing comfortable amounts of libido on highway signs" etc. makes the further point that Americans have sublimated (following Mailer's Freudian metaphor) their natural instincts into the construction of "corporation land."

There are other elements of verbal play or "pure persuasion" in these metaphors that should be pointed out. First, in both we find an ironic pun, perhaps subconscious, almost certainly

---

[56] Stevens, 76.
[57] Breslin, 160.

unintentional, on "rose." "The Pentagon rose," and "mood was a scent which rose [...]" A totalitarian rose, Mailer implies, by any other name would smell as foul. The classical term for a pun, incidentally, is paronomasia. (We may detect another pun, based on a reference to a cartoon character Popeye the Sailor in "the young Pop eye of Art.") Both the figures we have been examining rely partly on sound patterns for their effect. In the first, "sea" and "soft," and "plastic plug" are alliterative or consonant; "unmentionable operation," with its repetition of "-tion" sounds, falls somewhere between consonance and assonance. In the second, "tip on the spout of a spray can" is an example of parechesis, the repetition of the same sound in close or successive words: "tip on the spout of a spray can" is also onomatopoeic. Other examples of alliteration in this passage are "five football fields," "difficult to distinguish when drunk," and "pyramids of packaged foods." The second metaphor also displays polyptoton, the repetition of the same word with a different ending, "spray" and "spraying"; in this case the progression from "spray" to "spraying" takes what may at first seem only a potential threat and activates it. All of the sound devices and puns in this purely persuasive passage allow Mailer to gain his readers' assent, at least during the moment of reading.

The last paragraph also displays anadiplosis, the repetition of the last word of one sentence or clause to begin the next: "mood. Mood" Conduplicatio, the repetition of a word or words in succeeding clauses, also functions here: "mood. Mood [...] mood [....]" (The repetition of "unwelcome" in the first paragraph is another example of conduplicatio.) In the second paragraph, Mailer uses anadiplosis and conduplicatio to create links in his chain of thought; repetition allows disparate phenomena to cohere on the page. We detect in Mailer's use of "mood" and "Pentagon" in this passage additional instances of paradiegesis, the use of each word leading to further observations on its significance. Mailer's use of "mood" and "Pentagon" also establishes a pattern called anaphora, the repetition of the same word or words at the beginning of successive clauses: "Mood was [...] mood was [...]" and "The Pentagon looked [...] the Pentagon was [...]" In Mailer's world view, as we have seen from the discussion of metaphor above, "mood" and the Pentagon are dialectically opposed; in the last paragraph, Mailer's use of anaphora balances the two terms while placing them in an antithetical relationship Significantly, Mailer switches to a passive construction, "mood was forever being sliced," to indicate that the Pentagon is the oppressor, mood its innocent victim. The clause, "Mood was forever being sliced, cut, stamped, ground, excised, or obliterated," is an example of brachylogia, the omission of conjunctions between words, suggesting here a sense of mechanized violence.

The "pure persuasiveness" and "formal identification" of Mailer's prose, as exemplified in the passage above, stand dialectically opposed to the type of logical reasoning and tedious argumentation represented by the "sound-as-brickwork-logic-of-the-step." Nevertheless, as Anderson observes, "Mailer is not hesitant about marshaling evidence and advancing premises himself, particularly in his long and calculated argument against the Vietnam War."[58] The argument to which Anderson refers can be found in the chapter, "Why Are We In Vietnam?" Anderson identifies syllogisms (abbreviated or otherwise), reiteration, and magnification as some of the argumentative tools Mailer uses in this chapter (108). In this rhetorical set piece, Mailer presents a logical argument, which could have been based, directly or indirectly, on Aristotle's criteria for an effective speech. In Book III of the *Rhetoric*, Aristotle states that a good speech must be

---

[58] Anderson, 108.

composed of four parts: the introduction or proem: an outline or narration of the subject, or statement of the case; the proofs for and against the case, or the argument: and the summary, or epilogue.[59] Mailer introduces his subject in this way: "He knew the arguments for the war, and against the war—finally they bored him. The arguments in support of the war were founded on basic assumptions which had not been examined and were endlessly repeated—the arguments to withdraw never pursued the consequences" (204). He then provides the reader with a brief historical narrative of events since World War II which culminated in the Cold War, the Domino Theory, and finally the war in Vietnam (204-205). In the next part of this chapter Mailer reviews the position of both Hawks and Doves, marshalling arguments for and against the case put forth by both (205-208). Mailer chooses to discuss the Hawks first so that he may use certain arguments of the Doves to refute those of their opponents, thus privileging the Dove's position, but only slightly; finally, Mailer accepts neither position. "The Hawks were smug and self-righteous," he says, "the Doves were evasive of the real question" (208). Mailer then begins to advance his own position that the U.S. should "pull out of Vietnam completely" (209). He admits that the consequences of a complete withdrawal are unknown: perhaps the Communists would assume power, as the Hawks feared and the Doves found inexpedient to discuss (209). Mailer reasons, however, that "the more Communism expanded, the more monumental would become its problems [....] In the expansion of Communism was its own containment" (211). The form and content of Mailer's argument seem to contradict one another. He appropriates the skeletal form from classical rhetoric, and in that sense the form would seem closed. However, the form serves a heuristic function, providing Mailer a mold into which he may pour the content of his ideas. In

---

[59] Aristotle, 200.

144

the epilogue, he speculates that America might have become "schizophrenic," suffering a split between mind and soul, between the love of Christ, representing mystery, and the love of the corporation, a force antithetical to mystery (211-212). The opposition between the love of mystery and the love of no mystery is one of the key dramatic conflicts in the text. Mailer's final argument, that the U.S. should open the doors of Southeast Asia and let history run its unpredictable course, once again asserts his preference for freedom over domination, for open over closed systems, and for an ongoing historical drama without clear-cut resolutions.

Both the "Why Are We in Vietnam?" chapter and the passage I discussed at length above appear in Book One, which most critics writing on *Armies* have found more interesting than Book Two. Alan Trachtenburg asserts, "Taken by itself, Book Two is not nearly so persuasive or compelling a piece of writing as the earlier part, from which it takes its aesthetic justification as counterpart. It seems too much a muted coda, adding information but not really extending insight and feeling beyond Book One."[60] Bufithis also maintains that there is a stylistic difference between Books One and Two:

> When Mailer departs from his novelistic rendering of material, the book loses its thrust. The narrative-descriptive style, in which explicit details triumphantly cohere with implicit moral movements, gives way to the oracular-ruminative style which dotes on abstractions and cultural *cum* philosophical questions.[61]

---

[60] Bufisthis, 94.
[61] Trachtenburg, 701.

As I am attempting to show, however, the entire text dramatizes the march on the Pentagon, and Book Two is not devoid of drama. Both books contain their share of poetry *and* philosophy. Kathy Smith astutely observes that the "as" in Mailer's subtitles, "History as a Novel" and "the Novel as History," "denotes a metaphorical relationship between history and fiction, implying not only that history is *like* fiction, and vice versa, but that one always contains the other.... Mailer uses 'as' to complicate the terms, allowing them to merge into one another."[62] The key difference between the two books is in the degree to which Mailer actually participates in the events described. In Book One, Mailer personally witnesses everything he writes about. His direct participation accounts for the higher degree of emotional involvement; therefore, his language is more poetic, more emotionally charged. Book Two is based much more, though not exclusively, on secondary research; the higher degree of detachment causes a corresponding decrease in stylistically energized prose. In Book Two, Chapters 2-5 deal with the months of planning leading up to the march, including negotiations and compromises between various leftist factions and between the protestors and the U.S. government. There is little drama here. Mailer's concern is less with his own responses and impressions than with facts external to himself and gathered by way of research, precisely the method he himself associates with historiography. Mailer's lack of participation in the events related in Book Two affects his style; it becomes plain, unself-conscious, prosaic. No longer emotionally involved, Mailer's narrative voice loses its passion, its sense of conviction and engagement. There is less indictment of right- and left-wing positions, more conjecture regarding strategies of negotiation. The narrator continues to analyze events, but the analysis becomes less philosophical, less metaphorical.

---

[62] Smith, 191.

146

However, if the opening chapters of Book Two are less self-consciously dramatic than Book One, both in terms of the nature of the events described and the narrator's reaction to those events, Book Two, Chapter 6 quickens the dramatic pace. All of the events related up to this point lead to the principal confrontation between demonstrators and U.S. troops in front of the Pentagon. Mailer begins Book Two, Chapter 6 with the following assertion: "It is on this particular occasion that the conceit one is writing a history must be abandoned" (283). He explains that if "the first book is a history in the guise or dress or manifest of a novel...the second is a real or true novel ... presented in the style of a history," thus blurring the distinction between the two forms of writing (284). Indeed, *Armies* becomes more novelistic from this point on. The narrative drive shifts into a higher gear, and Mailer's imagination goes to work. The narrator is able to dramatize certain details of the action not because he personally witnessed them (by this point he had been arrested), but because his participation in the march up to the arrest was sufficient to enable him to recreate the mood of the proceedings.

Book Two also introduces a new dramatic conflict. As I have stated, throughout most of *Armies* the main conflict is between the establishment and anti-establishment. In Book Two, Chapter 6, the conflict between troops and demonstrators becomes, in part, a conflict between working class and urban middle class youth. This conflict comes as a surprise, as Mailer notes: "It would take the rebirth of Marx for Marxism to explain definitively this middle class condemnation of an imperialist war in the last Capitalist nation, this working class affirmation" (287). The narrator muses on this apparent contradiction. The urban middle class, he reasons, owns neither property nor the means of production and so are cut off from the real source of power; feeling themselves the most alienated, they are therefore the most critical

147

of their government's policies. The working class, by contrast, "is loyal to friends, not ideas," so alienation is less likely (287). "No wonder the Army bothered them not a bit," Mailer says (287). The working class has the authority and the guns but the urban middle class feels it has the moral advantage. Mailer imaginatively recreates the message the urban middle class youth brings to the troops: "I am morally right and you are wrong and the balance of existence is such that the meat of your life is now attached to my spirit. I am stealing your balls" (288). Later, however, in a dramatic reversal, the antagonistic forces of the U.S. Military reassert their dominance. After dark, when many of the protestors have left the grounds of the Pentagon, the Military rotates its forces; the troops form a wedge and begin moving through the crowd to separate it, kicking and clubbing at the demonstrators. The narrator quotes several accounts of "The Battle of the Wedge" which describe the violence and brutality in graphic detail (302-307). Mailer points out that much of the violence was directed at women, in what he interprets as a symbolic attempt on the part of the military to emasculate the male demonstrators. The working class youth "had plucked all stolen balls back," he says (308). Various demonstrators point out that the military had no legal right to attack protestors acting under the protection of a permit. Mailer states that "The Army had been guilty of illegal activity and knew it," appealing to the moral indignation of his readers (309).

Book Two, Chapter 10 concerns the repercussions of the march and follows up on continued protest activities. Many of the activists served extended prison sentences and were brutally mistreated for non-cooperation with their incarcerators. In the following passage, Mailer dramatizes their experience:

> Several men at the D.C. jail would not wear prison
> clothing. Stripped of their own, naked, they were

thrown in the Hole. There they lived in cells so
small that not all could lie down at once to sleep.
For a day they lay naked on the floor, for many days
naked with blankets and mattress on the floor. For
many days they did not eat nor drink water.
Dehydration brought them near to madness. (318)

Mailer uses ellipsis, the omission of a word easily understood,
"Stripped of their own [clothing]," to suggest the protestors'
degradation and humiliation by the authorities. By stating that the
protestors were "Stripped of their own," he implies that they were
deprived of more than clothing, that their fundamental rights and
dignity were also taken from them. The repetition of the phrase
"for many days" emphasizes the terrible relentlessness of their
punishment, and creates through its rhythmic pattern a Biblical
tone, leading Mailer finally to ask about protestors, "Who was to
say they were not saints?" (319). He closes this chapter by
imaginatively recreating the protestors' prayer that their suffering
be accepted by God as penance for the sins of their country in
Vietnam.

Conclusion

The final chapter of *Armies* consists of a pair of extended
metaphors which capture the ominous uncertainty, the mixture of
hope and dread Mailer feels in the wake of the march. These final,
emotionally charged metaphors are crucial to an understanding of
the text's dramatic structure:

Whole crisis of Christianity in America that the
military heroes were on one side, and the unnamed
saints on the other! Let the bugle blow. The death of
America rides in on the smog. America—the land
where a new kind of man was born from the idea
that God was present in every man not only as

149

compassion but as power, and so the country belonged to the people; for the will of the people—if the locks of their life could be given the art to turn—was then the will of God. Great and dangerous idea! If the locks did not turn, then the will of the people was the will of the Devil. Who by now could know where was what? Liars controlled the locks.

Brood on that country who expresses our will. She is America, once a beauty of magnificence unparalleled, now a beauty of leprous skin. She is heavy with child—no one knows if legitimate—and languishes in a dungeon whose walls are never seen. Now the first contractions of her fearsome labor begin—it will go on: no doctor exists to tell the hour. It is only known that false labor is not likely on her now, no, she will probably give birth, and to what?—the most fearsome totalitarianism the world has never known? or can she, poor giant, tormented lovely girl, deliver a babe of a new world brave and tender, artful and wild?

Rush to the locks. God writhes in his bonds. Rush to the locks. Deliver us from our curse. For we must end on the road to that mystery where courage, death and the drama of love give promise of sleep. (320)

Hollowell interprets this final chapter as the dramatic conflict between Manichean opposites: "All of the opposed forces—totalitarianism and democracy, age and youth, technology and humanism, the Devil's curse and God's grace—come together on a

150

weekend in October 1967."[63] Mailer suggests these "opposed forces" through the use of balance and antithesis, the controlling stylistic principle of the final chapter. He says that "the military heroes were on one side, the unnamed saints on the other," and that America was "once a beauty of magnificence unparalleled," but is "now a beauty of leprous skin." Inverting the word order, he states, "the will of the people—if the locks of their life could be given the will to turn—was then the will of God [...] If the locks did not turn, then the will of the people was the will of the Devil." Finally, he asks whether America will give birth to "the most fearsome totalitarianism the world has ever known," or "a new world brave and tender, artful and wild." Mailer also personifies America as "She," a woman about to give birth, in order to phrase a highly complex question in concrete, humanly compelling terms. To dramatize the uncertainty of the outcome, Mailer asks a series of rhetorical questions. The first question, "Who by now could know where was what?" is followed by an answer: "Liars controlled the locks." In this instance, Mailer employs a rhetorical device called sermocinatio in which he answers his own question in order to express his doubt and frustration. Mailer then asks of America, "she will probably give birth [...] and to what?" This question is followed not by an answer but by more questions, compounding the dramatic tension. We see in this passage further evidence of Mailer's heuristic method, the interjection "no" suggesting a mind attempting to come to terms with the uncertainty of the moment. Closing with a series of short, quick sentences in the imperative mood, "Brood on that country that expresses our will [...] Let the bugle blow [...] Rush to the locks [...] Deliver us from our curse," Mailer emphasizes the urgent need for direct action.

---

[63] Hollowell, 100.

Critics have often failed to interpret the conclusion satisfactorily. Mailer's text concludes, according to Hollowell, with the hope that good will ultimately triumph over evil.[64] Hollowell's interpretation disregards the political implications of Mailer's conclusion; instead, he sees Mailer involved in a moral struggle somewhat disengaged from historical reality. What Hollowell discusses in theological or moral terms, Stanley T. Gutman interprets dialectically:

> Though [Mailer] had always believed that struggle between opposing forces is the condition of existence, he had also affirmed a need for synthesis between opposing forces to resolve, if only temporarily, the struggle at the core of all existence. What he is claiming here [in this passage quoted above] is that in contemporary America there seems little possibility of synthesis, and that the dynamics of dialectical process have deteriorated into unresolvable antithesis. Opposites may not longer be reconciled; what appears to lie ahead is the effort of each half of a divided society to destroy the other.[65]

Gutman's speculation is grim, and not altogether warranted. Mailer's metaphorical "babe of a new world brave and tender" suggests not the imminence of mutual destruction but the possibility of social and political regeneration. At the same time, when asked whether the child has been born, Mailer has replied in the negative and suggested that "it gives every promise of being a monster," and yet, in the same interview, he expressed optimism

---

[64] Hollowell, 101.
[65] Gutman, 171.

about the country's future.[66] In any case, as the text concludes, the dialectical opposites are still firmly locked in struggle. Mailer has said, "When you're writing about a period that has not finished itself, you don't know the end, and this keeps you open."[67] Warner Berthoff suggests that the "metaphors of parturition and ambiguous new birth with which the book ends [...] have the heart-sinking beauty of an entire fitness to this fearful, intimately American occasion [...] it is hard not to feel that they from a climax ..."[68] Mailer's metaphors form a climax, perhaps, but not a resolution to the dramatic conflict. The birth Mailer prophesies has yet to occur. Mailer's text and his assessment of the significance of the march remain open. *Armies* does conclude on a note of hope, as Mailer urges his readers to "Rush to the locks," i.e., to take control of America's future. Mailer's exhortation reminds us that the curtain is not closed, and that we all have our roles to play in the historical drama; this final chapter is perhaps our cue.

---

[66] Schroeder, 105.
[67] Schroeder, 104.
[68] Berthoff, 327.

Chapter Four:

Hunter S. Thompson's *Fear and Loathing: On the Campaign Trail*

'72: Journalist as Prankster and Prophet

History as Drama

In *Fear and Loathing: On the Campaign Trail '72*, Hunter S. Thompson dramatizes the conflict between the dominant establishment culture, represented chiefly in this text by right-wing politicians like Richard Nixon, and the emergent anti-establishment counterculture, represented by left-wingers like George McGovern and by Thompson himself. Thompson's persona comments on the 1972 presidential campaign—an event with a built-in narrative structure, consisting of the primaries, the conventions, and the general election—while he creates a narrative of this own, that of a radical left-wing journalist attempting to see the truth through the veil of political rhetoric and implicitly conservative media bias. Declaring his open subjectivity, the writer violates journalistic norms by means of a digressive, stream-of-consciousness style, thus engaging the establishment discourse in a dialectical relationship and undermining its authority. He also uses his highly self-conscious literary style to dramatize his own

155

participation as a campaign journalist and to develop his drugged and deranged outlaw, "Gonzo" persona: part prankster, part prophet. When the campaign culminates in Nixon's landslide re-election, questions remain as to the final meaning of events, questions the narrator cannot answer. His participation in events comes to an end, but the historical narrative continues; *Campaign Trail* resists narrative closure.

By pitting left wing against right wing, protagonist against antagonist, Thompson regards the campaign as an inherently dramatic event. Given the campaign's dramatic structure, commentary on the campaign becomes dramatic criticism, an evaluation of the event's form and significance. Thompson recognizes that presidential elections are not only matters of necessity in a democratic society; they have become social rituals which political myths have been invented to explain. In *Campaign Trail*, he detects patterns of mythic significance beneath the surface narrative of the campaign. Specifically, he sees in the presidential campaign a reenactment of the myth of the dying king. "We've come to the point," he says, "where every four years this national fever rises up—this hunger for the Savior, the White Knight, the Man on Horseback [...]."[1] The American people, according to Thompson, collectively believe that presidents, like kings, become feeble or corrupt, and must abdicate, and a new king step to the throne. Facing political pressure from the left over the subject of the Vietnam War, for example, Lyndon Johnson decides not to seek reelection, an event which Thompson compares to "driving an evil king off the throne" (140). In 1972, Nixon reigns as the evil king, and the nation is sick, chaotic. Poverty, racism, and the Vietnam War threaten to tear the country apart. Thompson

---

[1] Thompson, *Fear and Loathing on the Campaign Trail.* All subsequent references are to this edition.

compares Nixon to "the monstrous Mr. Hyde," implying that Nixon's opponent, George McGovern, represents the kindly, rational, civilized Dr. Jekyll (417). Indeed, the metaphor "monstrous" further develops a theme that recurs constantly in Thompson's text, the transformation of man into beast as a symbol of social breakdown. Nixon, Thompson says later, in an image that he could have borrowed from the Book of Revelations, "speaks for the Werewolf in us; the bully, the predatory shyster who turns into something unspeakable, full of claws and bleeding string-warts, on nights when the moon comes to close [...]" (417). The rhetorical name for an extravagant, far-fetched metaphor of the type we find above is catechresis, a deliberate exaggeration intended to shock, a typical feature of Thompson's hyperbolic style.

In his condemnation of Nixon, Thompson speaks for many in the counterculture who were dissatisfied with the old order and struggled to bring in the new, post-capitalist order. Thompson sets out in quest of a challenger to defeat Nixon, and finds George McGovern. The democratic nominee poses a threat not only to Nixon's presidency, but to the middle-class conservative values Nixon shares with many democrats, most notably, in Thompson's text, George Wallace, Ed Muskie, and Hubert Humphrey. In a world of ambiguity and uncertainty, where appearances often deceive, Thompson regards Nixon and McGovern as polar opposites:

> There is almost a Yin/Yang clarity in the difference between the two men, a contrast so stark that it would be hard to find any two better models in the national politics arena for the legendary duality— the congenital Split Personality and polarized instincts—that almost everybody except America

157

has long since taken for granted as the key to our
National Character. (416)

The word "congenital," with its connotation of disease, and the
notion that the nation's personality is "Split," its instincts
"polarized" between good and evil, further develops the sickness
motif that runs throughout the text. Thompson experiences this
sickness—social, political, spiritual, even physical—and considers
his own ills similar to those of the entire nation. He sees America
as a wasteland, a country in need of collective rebirth. Thompson's
"Yin/Yang" comparison suggests analysis on a deeper poetic or
symbolic level than most journalists reach and establishes a clear
dramatic conflict in the narrative. In his quest for a hero,
Thompson discovers that the American people share his sickness
yet collectively deny their condition; therefore, they resist the
attempts by left-wingers like Thompson and McGovern to remind
them of it. The voices of dissent are voices they wish to silence;
Nixon, in denial himself, wishes to persuade the American people
he can silence the voices. The key dramatic question in Campaign
Trail asks whether any dramatic challenger, including and
especially McGovern, can mount an attack on the collective
consciousness. Only a few even come close. Covering George
Wallace's campaign "performance" in Wisconsin, Thompson is
reminded of Robert Kennedy, a former challenger to the throne:
"Kennedy," Thompson says, "like Wallace, was able to connect
with people on some kind of visceral instinctive level that is
probably both above and below 'rational politics'" (127). If
"above" suggests transcendence, "below" penetrates to the depths
of the collective unconscious, where demons lurk, but the
possibility of redemption also lies. Finally, Thompson reflects:

No presidential candidate who even faintly
reminded the 'typical voters' of the fear and anxiety

158

they'd felt during the constant 'social upheaval' of the 1960's had any chance at all of beating Nixon.... All they wanted in the White House was a man who would leave them alone and do anything necessary to bring calmness back into their lives— even if it meant turning the whole state of Nevada into a concentration camp for hippies, niggers, dope fiends, do-gooders and anyone else who might threaten the status quo. (466-467)

Thompson frequently uses prison metaphors to embody his own feelings of repression and fears of a totalitarian future. The notion that he and McGovern both represent ideological factions that threaten the status quo places both characters in a marginal relationship to the rest of society. Thompson, of course, is far more marginal than McGovern, and it is Thompson who ultimately emerges as the protagonist in the campaign narrative, asking us to identify with his predicament, that of a political underdog battling insurmountable odds.

Despite his marginalized status, Thompson declares his "out front bias in favor of the McGovern candidacy" (19). As far as Thompson is concerned, most Democrats and all Republicans represent the establishment, along with most of the working press, union leaders, and the majority of the American people. Thompson calls the Democratic Party "a bogus alternative to the politics of Nixon" (125); he later claims that the 1968 Nixon-Humphrey race signaled "the de facto triumph of a One Party System in American politics" (205). Weingarten observes that Thompson "held out little hope for anything the Democratic Party had to offer, and he had no qualms about saying so in his articles. The party itself was in trouble, in Thompson's view, unless it was purged of the hacks and toadies, organized labor money, and the 'peace with honor' prevarications that echoed the Nixon administration's Vietnam policy."[2]

McGovern, of course, is also a Democrat, but with a difference: his positions on domestic issues and the war in Vietnam are, by American standards, radically left-wing. Assessing McGovern, Thompson concedes that he must "sympathize in some guilt-stricken way with whatever demented obsession makes him think he can somehow cause this herd of venal pigs [the establishment] to see the light and make him their leader" (125). The phrase "see the light" resonates with Thompson's allusion to T.S. Eliot's "The Hollow Men": "Between the Idea [sic] and the Reality [...] Falls the Shadow" (81). The reference to Eliot not only reinforces the dying king or wasteland theme, it establishes the idealism which Thompson and McGovern share. For all its cynicism, *Campaign Trail* contains much of the idealism that characterized the counterculture movement of the late-1960s. Presumably, Thompson's narrator is "guilt-stricken" because he feels that McGovern seeks to champion the causes that many Sixties radicals, including Thompson himself, had by that point abandoned, and that he seeks to reclaim. In his role as champion of the left, McGovern rejects what Thompson calls the "Madison Avenue School of campaigning," i.e., a campaign run by a highly paid public relations firm, and chooses to believe that grassroots organization and populist appeal can win the day. If McGovern is naive, Thompson seems willing to share his naiveté. However, when McGovern chooses Tom Eagleton (one of the establishment's own) as his running mate, he compromises his integrity, at least in the eyes of the mainstream media. As the campaign progresses, McGovern begins to look less like a countercultural hero and more like a conventional politician.

---

[2] Weingarten, 256.

Consequently, he begins to treat Thompson more like a conventional journalist, limiting the reporter's access to off-the-record remarks that he is almost certain to print. Thompson observes, "My contempt for the time-honored double standard in political journalism might not be entirely compatible with the increasingly pragmatic style of politics that George was getting into" (19). McGovern himself has noted that Thompson "'hated the hypocrisy of the establishment. Basically, I think he wanted to see this country live up to its ideals.'"[3] Increasingly disillusioned with the candidate, Thompson interprets McGovern's campaign as a final, failed attempt to transform the late Sixties ideal into reality. Instead of new hope, *Campaign Trail* ends on a note of ominous foreboding represented by the prospect of four more years of Richard Nixon.

Thompson as Rhetorical Critic

By openly declaring his support for McGovern, Thompson violates journalistic norms of objectivity. As Norman Mailer explains in the tower metaphor in *The Armies of the Night*, admitting his own bias allows the writer, paradoxically, to achieve a higher kind of objectivity.[4] William McKeen observes, "By offering the reader his prejudices, Thompson ensures that all biases are open and honest."[5] John Hellmann goes further, arguing that Thompson "can flatten and warp his representations of reality without falsifying them, because he has clearly represented them as products of a flattening and warping mind."[6] Wayne C. Booth, among others, has called Thompson to task for his highly subjective approach: Thompson's "reality," he says, "is openly—

---

[3] Weingarten, 268.
[4] Mailer, *Armies*, 245.
[5] McKeen, *Thompson*, 46.
[6] Hellmann, 69.

161

one might say deliberately—biased."[7] Responding to criticism that his political analysis lacks objectivity, Thompson responds, "Well [...] shit, what I can say? Objective journalism is a hard thing to come by these days. We all yearn for it, but who can point the way?" (47). Thompson's question implies what he states more explicitly elsewhere, that no version of events, however seemingly detached, is completely objective. (The irony implicit in "We all yearn for it" suggests that everybody in the journalism game knows the game is fixed.) In a passage closely following the one quoted above, Thompson adds,

> So much for objective journalism. Don't bother to look for it here—not under any byline of mine; or anyone else I can think of. With the possible exception of box scores, race results, and stock market tabulations, there is not such thing as Objective Journalism. The phrase itself is a pompous contraction in terms. (48)

News stories, like any other from of discourse, are shaped or made by individuals, who are always motivated or influenced (perhaps unconsciously) by personal or institutional factors like pressure from editors and advertisers. The notion that language can reflect an objective picture of the world is a "pompous contradiction," in Thompson's words, because it allows journalists to deceive themselves, and the public, that they are unbiased. Thompson is no more biased than many journalists; he is simply more candid about it.

Traditionally, journalists have maintained a deferential attitude toward political leaders. Thompson suggests that this arrangement between journalists and politicians works in the

---

[7] Booth, 7.

interest of both groups: the journalists gain access to the information they need to do their jobs while the politicians receive favorable treatment from the journalists. McKeen makes the case:

> Other journalists, with the somber reporting of what politicians and others in authority say, end up parroting the party line and preserving the myths, institutions, legends, and popular heroes of society. Thompson takes his stance as a destroyer of these and implies that gonzo is the truest form of journalism because it does not have to report what someone in authority says.[8]

Thompson criticizes the "clubby/cocktail personal relationships that inevitably develop between politicians and journalists" and maintains, "When professional antagonists become after-hours drinking buddies, they are not likely to turn each other in [...]" (18). Weingarten observes that Thompson "had contempt for the Washington press corps, who he felt coddled the city's power players at the expense of doing their jobs responsibly. It was unfathomable to him that a reporter with his eyes wide open could live in Washington and not deride it at every turn. The political process was corrupt and noxious, and Thompson was going to call it the way he saw it."[9]

As a reporter for *Rolling Stone*—founded in 1967 and by the early Seventies still considered a left-wing, "underground" publication—and as an outsider in relationship to the Washington establishment, Thompson becomes even more marginalized. "My relations with the White House were extremely negative from the start," he says. "My application for press credentials was rejected out of hand" (101). Thompson's adversarial relationship to both

---

[8] McKeen, *Thompson*, 38.
[9] Weingarten, 254.

politicians and other journalists contributes to his image of himself as an "outlaw" journalist, a rebel. As an outsider, Thompson assumes an adversarial stance toward both the journalistic and political establishments. He begins with the assumption that political discourse is intended either to mislead, to manipulate, or to say nothing at all. Thompson says, "Politics has its own language, which is often so complex that it borders on being a code, and the main trick in political journalism is learning how to translate—to make sense of the partisan bullshit that even your friends will lay on you—without dropping your access to the kind of information that allows you to keep functioning" (17). He often points to discrepancies between "the official public version" of events and what politicians say "off the record" (370). Thompson generally refuses to allow "off the record" remarks to remain a secret. His integrity and high regard for truth are important aspects of his rhetorical persona, the speaker of truth to power.

Of course, the relationship between journalists and politicians can and often does become adversarial, if not confrontational, but most journalists are confined or confine themselves within certain boundaries. Thompson claims, "The double-standard realities of campaign journalism ... make it difficult for even the best of the 'straight/objective' reporters to write what they actually think and feel about a candidate" (209). Thompson's combative persona consistently crosses the line between what is considered acceptable and unacceptable professional practice. In a flagrant violation of journalistic norms, Thompson's narrator engages in a series of savage verbal assaults on McGovern's opponents. "Hubert Humphrey," he says, "is a treacherous, gutless old ward-heeler who should be put in a goddamn bottle and sent out with the Japanese current" (135). Sometimes the narrator breaks off his discourse to address some figure directly in an apostrophe, often to threaten or cajole him:

"Remember me, Hubert?" (188). This type of invective is characteristic of Thompson's style and rhetorical ethos. Most readers are unaccustomed to seeing their elected representatives treated in this derisive, mocking fashion. In his distorted representations of Humphrey, Nixon and other political figures, Thompson defamiliarizes reality in order to make us see it more clearly.

Unlike conventional journalists, who consider themselves ethically bound by a professional obligation to confirm their reports, Thompson frequently engages in speculation, mostly about the outcome of various primaries and their significance. At times, the reader cannot easily determine whether to take Thompson's musings seriously, as, for example, when the journalist entertains a rumor (one he later admitted to having invented) that Edmund Muskie's erratic behavior on the campaign trail might have resulted from his use of an exotic Brazilian drug called Ibogaine (150-54). The Ibogaine story signals one of those moments in Thompson's text when fact and fiction become difficult to distinguish. Hartsock writes that Thompson "occupies an anomalous position in relation to narrative literary journalism. Part of the difficulty is that while his work is often narrative, it also engages in outrageous satire and the boundary between fiction and nonfiction is unclear."[10] In another transgression of the rules of conventional journalism, Thompson entertains actual rumors, including one about an underworld plan to provide Humphrey with secret campaign funds for a last-minute blitz in the California primary (229-235). Thompson admits that this "flat-out Byzantine spook story" is a fiction, but publishes it anyway (232). As a journalist, Thompson places less emphasis on accuracy, that which is verifiably factual, than on what might be true in spirit, if not in

---

[10] Harstock, 200.

actual fact. Given Thompson's profound contempt for and distrust of Humphrey, and his cynical attitude toward American politicians in general, he seems to feel justified in suggesting that while there is no proof that Humphrey received (or even planned to receive) secret funds, the senator was certainly capable of such a moral and ethical transgression. Occasionally, driven to distraction by the tedium of the campaign, or feeling the need to vent his anger at the state of the nation in general, Thompson creates pure fictions, like his story about a convention delegate who is blackmailed to swing votes for a particular candidate (264-66). Wayne C. Booth has complained that, given Thompson's admission of subjectivity, and tendency to fictionalize, it becomes impossible to believe him even when he claims to tell the truth.[11] Even though Thompson does admit that the Humphrey story is speculation, Booth's objection is perfectly logical, yet it is based on an assumption that readers might not choose to make. Readers might ask why Thompson would consciously choose to lie or mislead his them about any given detail, particularly one that has been confirmed or denied by any number of other sources. Further, as far as I am aware, no one has publicly accused Thompson of any serious falsehood, much less verified one. By "serious" falsehood, I mean one that can be shown to have been stated deliberately and that caused harm to individuals involved. In *Campaign Trail*, Thompson often combines the "mixture of the fantastic with the probable" and the "comic intent" which, according to James E. Caron, place "Gonzo" journalism in the tradition of the American tall tale.[12] Caron further observes that "Gonzo" tales generally contain what Mark Twain called a "snapper," which Caron defines as "the moment when the narrative becomes so absurd that if the reader has missed the fact that the story has been a lie all along, he or she cannot now fail to

---

[11] Booth, 7.
[12] Caron, 3.

understand."[13] Does anyone familiar with former NBC newsman John Chancellor seriously believe that he and Thompson once split a dose of LSD? One of the characteristics of gonzo journalism, according to McKeen, "is a lack of clarity about what is truth and what is fiction, and a gonzo reader must not care about the distinction too much."[14] Thompson's readers enter into an implicit contract in which they give him the benefit of the doubt, expressing their willingness to accept his assertions as fact unless their own knowledge or experience give them a reason to doubt or disbelieve his veracity. Moreover, as Thompson himself says in *The Great Shark Hunt*, however, "the best fiction is far more true than any kind of journalism."[15] By existing somewhere between the real campaign and Thompson's version of the campaign, *Campaign Trail* suggests that reality is too complex and multivarious to be contained within any one text.

Thompson's highly subjective approach suggests that he bears partial responsibility for creating the world in his text. He criticizes conventional journalism's claim merely to report, not to make, the news, and he calls attention to the role conventional journalism plays in creating, and very often distorting, the reality it describes. Thompson demonstrates, for example, that polls influence reality by transforming it into political myth; sometimes, the polls create narratives which bear no absolute relationship to political reality. Early in the campaign, McGovern's chances of claiming the Democratic nomination seem slim: poll results indicate that Edward Kennedy's popularity rating steadily gains ground on Nixon's; if Kennedy chooses not to run, however, the majority of pollsters and party bosses seem to agree that Edmund Muskie, everybody's predicted front-runner, will be given the

---

[13] Caron, 8.
[14] McKeen, *Thompson*, 65.
[15] Bakhtin, 324.

nomination. Virtually nobody regards the McGovern campaign as a threat. According to Thompson, the polls and expert analyses place McGovern in "a frustrated limbo created mainly by the gross cynicism of the Washington Press Corps" (33). Placed in a marginal position, in "limbo," by the press corps, McGovern gains the sympathy and support of Thompson's narrator. Throughout *Campaign Trail*, Thompson expresses virtually unqualified praise for McGovern's grass roots campaign strategy, through which the candidate wins primary after primary despite contrary media predictions. McGovern's ability to defy poll results contributes to his growing reputation as an anti-establishment candidate, an image Thompson himself helps to foster in the belief that McGovern might actually emerge as a champion of the left.

While Thompson frequently questions the veracity and integrity of the dominant media, he nevertheless incorporates fragments of its discourse into his own text. In Bakhtinian terms, *Campaign Trail* is heteroglossic.[16] In some cases, Thompson incorporates fragments of newspaper stories into his own text to assist him in telling the story: the disastrous "Eagleton affair," for example, which many believe wrecked McGovern's campaign (326-336). Thompson generally allows other voices to speak without much interference from the narrator. Nevertheless, by incorporating the dominant media's discourse into his own text, where the rules of conventional journalism are consistently violated, Thompson parodies that discourse, thus undermining its authority. Ironically, the juxtaposition of various voices in *Campaign Trail* symbolizes Thompson's concern for democracy; the colloquy of voices produces an effect of harmonious discord. His use of numerous voices also acknowledges the multiplicity, even the relativity, of truth. Referring to other texts, other versions

---

[16] Thompson, *Shark Hunt*, 106.

of events, Thompson implies that neither the dominant culture's version of events nor his own interpretations are in any way definitive. In this way, *Campaign Trail* remains an open text.

In contrast to Thompson's method, conventional journalists attempt to provide their readers with definitive accounts of current events, and the structure of their discourse reflects a belief that they can define situations objectively. As we have seen, conventional journalists conceive and write their stories according to the standard model: the 5 Ws and the inverted pyramid structure. The model presumes a stable, rational society. Thompson's world view is one of chaos, however, and of a dominant culture manipulating public opinion to suit its own sinister purposes. He therefore finds the conventional journalistic model unsatisfactory. Bruce-Novoa argues that, from Thompson's perspective, "When the world is falling apart, journalistic order is a farce."[17] Hellmann adds that Thompson "has had to replace the detective role of the conventional reporter (based on the assumption of a rational, cause and effect world) with the artist role of the new journalist (based on a realization that the evidence of the macrocosm has already been artificially distorted and invented)."[18] Unlike the conventional journalist, whose deductions are based on the assumption of universal principles of order, Thompson approaches his subject inductively, trusting his perceptions of actual events to determine the form his text will assume. Thompson generally trusts conventional journalists to provide accurate factual details, but for analysis, he relies on his own perceptions and insights. Much of *Campaign Trail* dramatizes his attempt to make sense of the tangled details and complexity of the story. Faced with a bewildering array of poll results, news reports, and campaign

---

[17] Bruce-Novoa, 40.
[18] Hellmann, 99-100.

statements, not to mention rumors and theories, Thompson finds it necessary to place himself in the center of his account, emphasizing the need to decode the political rhetoric and base his report on first-hand experience. He adopts the sort of approach to his assignment Tom Wolfe calls "saturation reporting," the idea being to spend as much time as possible in close proximity and direct contact with the subject in order to record its reality in depth.[19] By traveling with the campaign workers from state to state, Thompson can record "behind the scenes" information unavailable to reporters who spend less time on the campaign trail. Although he considers himself a marginalized figure, Thompson's familiarity with the inner working of a campaign, and of American politics in general, allows him a certain depth of insight. Having participated in a mayoral campaign in Aspen, Colorado, and having run for sheriff of Pitkin County, Colorado on the Freak Power ticket two years before, Thompson considers that his degree of identification with his subject reaches a level unattained by most journalists: "There is no way," he says, "for even the best and most talented journalist to know what is really going on inside a political campaign unless he has been there himself" (267). Direct participation becomes for Thompson and end in itself. As he says, further developing a key analogy between politics and drug addiction, "the High is in the participation" (496). In fact, Thompson considers personal involvement with his subject a prerequisite to writing anything at all. He confesses that he was unable to write about the 1968 Democratic Convention precisely because he had no personal stake in the outcome (46).

Again, however, Thompson cannot wholly assimilate into either the journalistic or the political establishment. After explaining that the press generally considers politicians

---

[19] Wolfe, 52.

"congenital liars and thieves," and that most politicians regard the press as "swine," Thompson agrees with both sides (100). As a concomitant to his emphasis on direct involvement in the campaign, Thompson is sensitive to the emotional or psychical overtones of a particular place, factors that only personal experience can provide access to, and he sometimes sets scenes to convey a certain mood. The "Fear and Loathing" of his title describes the country's mood, or at least Thompson's reaction to what he sees and feels. From the very beginning, on arrival in Washington, D.C., Thompson compares living in the nation's capital to "living in an armed camp" and describes sections of the city as "hellishly paranoid Fear Zones" (24). His hyperbolic description establishes the tone for much of the action that follows. Generally, though, Thompson sets scenes that are more contained within a specific time and place. Reflecting on the time he spent aboard Muskie's "Sunshine Special" campaign train, Thompson remembers, "It was a very oppressive atmosphere—very tense and guarded" (114). In response, Thompson loans his press credentials to a drunken, obnoxious radical named "Peter Sheridan" who runs amok on the train (103-115). By becoming directly involved in the campaign to the degree that he becomes a disruptive influence, Thompson enhances his role as "outlaw" journalist.

As the protagonist of his own campaign narrative, Thompson plays several roles, some of which have been identified by Hellmann: "A descendent of the trickster character of folklore, the Vice of medieval drama, the picaro of early prose narratives, [Thompson] is a self-portrait of the journalist as rogue. Like his literary ancestors, he is a shape-shifter who uses cunning and agility to survive the dangers of his environment."[20] Again, one of the roles Thompson plays is that of the loner, a marginal figure

---

[20] Hellmann, 71.

existing on the fringes of the campaign and of American society in general. A Francios Villon quote, "In my own country I am in a far-off land," serves as an epigraph to the June chapter, and informs our understanding of the narrator's self-image (219). One of the most radical features of Thompson's outlaw journalism is his open acknowledgement that many of his reports were written and filed not only under extreme pressure but also while he was under the influence of a variety of legal and illegal mind- and mood-altering substances. Hartsock writes that "Thompson remains America's bad boy, not only symbolically defecating on traditional American values but also, in his drug-induced narratives, challenging the very notion of what qualifies as the correct state of consciousness (sobriety) in reporting on the world."[21] Thompson asks the reader to identify with his status as an outsider. He observes, "A political campaign is a very narrow ritual, where anything weird," like his drug use and unusual dress, "is unwelcome" (64). As a representative of the emergent counterculture, Thompson finds himself at odds with virtually everyone he meets on the campaign trail. There are exceptions, however, like McGovern and fellow *Rolling Stone* correspondent Tim Crouse, who wrote his own account of the campaign, *The Boys on the Bus*.[22] Ironically, Thompson even finds some common ground between himself and Richard Nixon: both share an appreciation of professional football. At one point, watching a game on TV while musing on the campaign, Thompson uses what he calls "Rhythm Logic," reasoning that the rhythms of the football game will sound the rhythms of Nixon's psyche (344). Sports analogies permeate *Campaign Trail*, suggesting that Thompson sees the world in terms of competition and struggle,

---

[21] Harstock, 201.
[22] Crouse, *The Boys on the Bus.*

172

most often between the dominant culture and emergent subculture, but also between the narrator and his own environment.

Despite their mutual antagonism, however, reporters and politicians share an addiction to political campaigns. Developing an analogy that runs throughout the text, Thompson claims, "the politics junkie is not much different […] than a smack junkie…." (266). He argues that "anybody who has ever tried to live with a smack junkie will tell you it can't be done without coming to grips with the spike and shooting up, yourself. Politics is no different. There is a fantastic adrenaline high that comes with total involvement in almost any kind of fast-moving political campaign" (267). The "high" is what Thompson often attempts to dramatize, and he bets on the outcome of various primaries with the same fervor and enthusiasm with which he bets on sporting events. On one hand, addiction to "junk" or heroin is a sickness, and Thompson again suggests that politics produces the same effect:

> There is something seriously bent, when you think on it, in the notion that a man with good sense would race out of his peaceful mountain home in Colorado and fly off in a frenzy like some kind of electrified turkey buzzard to spend three or four days being carried around the foulest sections of New England like a piece of meat, to watch another man, who says he wants to be President, embarrassing a lot of people by making them shake his hand outside factory gates at sunrise. (65)

Thompson's sentence ends with a rounded period, which dramatizes his awareness of his own condition. The metaphors "electrified turkey buzzard" and "piece of meat" suggest the depths of his degradation. If covering a political campaign is a "sickness," however, writing becomes for Thompson a kind of "stylistic

173

medicine," to borrow Kenneth Burke's term.[23] Burke suggests that literature can serve a therapeutic function, allowing the writer to nullify a perceived threat by laughing it out of existence. This strategy, Burke says, requires a "structural assertion (a form, a public matter that symbolically enrolls us with allies who will share our burden with us)."[24] *Campaign Trail* assumes such a form, and Thompson asks us to share his burden. The degree to which the reader engages emotionally and intellectually with the artistic form determines the degree of his own unburdening or cure. Thompson chooses a playful, digressive stream of conscious style as his own "stylistic medicine." Laughter, again, is an integral part of the cure for Thompson, and he exaggerates both the horror and the tedium of his experience for comic effect:

> I am growing extremely weary of writing constantly about politics. My brain has become a steam-vat; my body is turning to wax and bad flab; impotence looms; my fingernails are growing at a fantastic rate of speed—they are turning into claws; my standard-size clippers will no longer cut the growth, so now I carry a set of huge toe-nail clippers and sneak off every night around dusk, regardless of where I am—in any city, hamlet, or plastic hotel room along the campaign trail—to chop another quarter of an inch or so off of all ten fingers.

> People are beginning to notice, I think, but fuck them. I am beginning to notice some of their problems, too. (219-220)

The rhetorical term for a description of body or mind like the one we find above is characterismus. Thompson's comic style, with it

---

[23] Burke, *Philosophy*, 48.
[24] Burke, *Philosophy*, 48.

hyperbolic tone, its curses and short, aggressively rhythmic clauses, grows out his disease even as it offers him the means to affect a cure. If literature, as Burke maintains, performs a "physiological function" according to which the work itself becomes a "corresponding anatomic structure,"[25] then Thompson's description of bodily decay in the passage above allegorizes his own sickness as well as the decay of the body politic. Symbolically, we all share what Kurt Vonnegut Jr. calls "Hunter Thompson's disease."[26] However, Thompson's breakdown at the end of the November chapter (422-457) implies that the cure has not proven completely effective, and in the end, he talks about covering the 1976 campaign and possibly running for senator in Colorado (491-93).

If covering political campaigns is a kind of sickness, the constant pressure under which Thompson finds himself exacerbates his condition. Weingarten notes, "Every story that Thompson filed was an [sic] painful and protracted ritual of false starts and piecemeal construction."[27] Much of the text's dramatic tension results from Thompson's desperate struggle to meet deadlines. He finds himself under constant pressure to satisfy his editor's need for copy, coherent or fragmented, full of well-reasoned analysis or stream of consciousness ramblings. Unlike the standard chronological reconstruction of an event offered by most journalists, *Campaign Trail* contains flashbacks as well as speculation about the future. *Campaign Trail* is not reporting in the conventional sense, but rather free-form summary and analysis. The narrator strays from the subject of the campaign so often that the reader may be lead to wonder whether *Campaign Trail* is journalism with autobiographical digressions or autobiography

---

[25] Burke, *Philosophy*, 90.
[26] Vonnegut, 94.
[27] Weingarten, 262.

with journalistic digressions. The stream of consciousness form *Campaign Trail* assumes results from the narrator's frazzled, disoriented mental and psychological condition, which in turn grows out of his use of mind-altering substances (alcohol, marijuana, and amphetamines), and his fear and paranoia in response to national events. A third crucial factor is the daily tedium of campaign activity, the behind the scenes work that precedes each primary. One of Thompson's rhetorical strategies is a refusal to take his job, or anything else for that matter, very seriously. He turns the campaign into a game by playing the odds on campaign results: "Political analysis was never my game anyway. All I do is wander around and make bets with people" (167). Thompson's frenzied condition sometimes renders him incapable of continuing at all. At one point, he claims to suffer a complete mental and physical breakdown, making it necessary for him to rely on Crouse to narrate the story of McGovern's victory in the Wisconsin primary (169-181). Toward the end of the text a note (in all likelihood, written by Thompson himself) appears under the byline of Thompson's editor, claiming that the reporter's mental and physical condition are near total collapse, thus making it necessary for Thompson to respond in a taped interview to questions from his editor, a transcription of which appears in the text (422-457). As McKeen notes, "Thompson's reports appeared in nearly every biweekly issue of *Rolling Stone* through the spring and summer [of 1972], with a marked tapering off in the fall as McGovern's impending political massacre became apparent."[28] McKeen's observation suggests that the deadline pressure and intense emotional strain reflected in *Campaign Trail* were more than rhetorical devices, but were in fact quite real.

---

[28] McKeen, *Thompson*, 64.

Stylistic Analysis

Given the constant deadline pressure, the tone throughout much of *Campaign Trail* is one of panic. Thompson creates tension and immediacy by allowing the reader to follow his thought processes at crucial moments. By dramatizing his own high-pressure panic, Thompson transforms his dilemma as reporter into the subject of his report:

> Ah yes ... I can hear the Mojo wire humming frantically across the room. Crouse is stuffing page after page of gibberish into it.... The pressure is building up. The copy no longer makes sense. Huge chunks are either missing or too scrambled to follow from one sentence to another.... And now the bastard is beeping ... beeping ... beeping, which means it is hungry for the final page, which means I no longer have time to crank out any final wisdom on the McGovern campaign. (169)

The ellipses in this passage allegorize the narrator's self-conscious awareness of the passage of time. The use of epizeuxis, the repetition of a word with no other words in between, "beeping ... beeping ... beeping," becomes an objective correlative for the constant deadline pressure. The verbs, "humming [...] stuffing [...] building," convey a sense of manic desperation. The isocolons, grammatical phrases of equal length and corresponding structure, create a paratactic or running style which allegorizes the narrator's refusal to rank disparate elements of his experience in order of their importance: "the Mojo Wire is humming [...] Crouse is stuffing [...] which means [...] which means [...]" Thompson repeatedly finds himself in a losing race to catch up with current events. His editors at *Rolling Stone* persist in their demands for "some kind of definitive work on a major subject" (185), but real-life contingencies stand in the way. At these crucial moments,

Thompson once again seems to make his own situation the focus: "There is not time to explain, now, why this is not a profile of George McGovern. That story blew up on us in Omaha, on the morning of the primary, when George and most of his troupe suddenly decided that Nixon's decision to force a showdown with Hanoi made it imperative for the Senator to fly back to Washington at once" (185). Despite his confession of failure, Thompson still manages to report significant events and shift the focus away from himself and back toward the campaign. Booth has exaggerated the extent to which Thompson becomes the subject of his own report. He complains, "The thesis of *Loathing* is that Hunter Thompson is interesting."[29] Thompson's drama is not a one-man show, however; he is a character in an ensemble, a "troupe," as it were.

As his tendency to transform his own predicament into the subject of his report suggests, Thompson frequently responds to the disorientation, paranoia and boredom by digressing from his subject: "We seem to have wandered out on another tangent. But why not? Every now and again you have to get away from that ugly Old Politics trip, or it will drive you kicking the walls and hurling AR 3's into the fireplace" (92). Thompson suggests that the only way to avoid committing real violence is to fly off on another "violent tangent," sublimating the destructive urge by channeling it into a symbolic recreation of violence (227). The narrator's tangents serve other purposes as well: "With the truth so dull and depressing," he says, "the only working alternative is wild bursts of madness and filigree" (93). The preceding quote suggests that he narrator responds to his situation and environment by transforming tension into the release of tension, work into play. In Bakhtinian terms, Thompson's playful style is internally persuasive discourse, not authoritative, and therefore presents a

---

[29] Booth, 8.

fundamental challenge to conventional reporting and political rhetoric.[30] In the passage quoted above, the term "filigree," which describes the ornamental, lace-like designs found in metal work, suggests Thompson's need as literary artist to embroider or embellish his material, to play with words for their own sake: "Vehicle ... vehicle ... vehicle ... a very strange-looking word, if you stare at it for eight or nine minutes.... 'Skulking' is another interesting-looking word" (250). Occasionally, the narrator abandons his subject to return to it later, employing a rhetorical device called reditus ad prospositum (48). Some of the digressions, however, imply that the writer has lost control over his material. In one instance, following a series of lengthy digressions, the speaker begins the next unit of discourse with the following observation: "Which is getting a bit off the point here. Indeed. We are drifting badly—from motorcycles to Mankiewicz to Omaha, Butte, Fresno ... where will it end?" (246). Thompson maintains his position as central consciousness here, but he no longer seems to possess complete freedom in arranging his material. The harsh reality of contemporary events asserts itself, and our protagonist finds himself engaged in a losing battle with the action going on around him.

Thompson's digressive method reveals a sense of constant interaction, often in the form of a struggle, between self and environment. In its record of the conflict between interior and exterior forces, *Campaign Trail* contains a strong heuristic element, which allows the narrator's perceiving consciousness to dramatize events and discover their meaning as they occur. In the introduction to *Campaign Trail*, Thompson claims that the purpose behind his writing was to "record the reality of an incredibly volatile presidential campaign while it was happening" (20).

---

[30] Bakhtin, 342.

Thompson regards his text as "more of a tangled campaign diary than a record or reasoned analysis" of the campaign, and as "a kind of high-speed, cinematic reel-record of what the campaign was like at the time" (21). The digressions, ellipses, abrupt transitions, the gaps, confusion, and emotional outbursts all reflect this sense of an immediate reality spontaneously recorded. Thompson's name for this sense of spontaneity is "Gonzo," a term that has been variously defined. More than anything else, "Gonzo" describes a stylistic method and rhetorical strategy. Bruce-Novoa explains the method as follows: "Gonzo Journalism is a camera-eye technique of reporting in which the writer's notes are published supposedly without editing. Objectivity, however, is not the ideal; the writer is expected to select details and interpret events, including in his notes whatever comes to mind, as if thoughts were also part of the observed happening." [31]

Thompson generally resorts to "Gonzo" when deadline pressure bears down most heavily. Following the May primary, with "No time for long mind-probing interviews," the narrator decides that "The time has come to get full bore in to heavy Gonzo Journalism" (185-186). What follows, then, is a (supposedly) literal transcription of his notes (193-218). Booth objects to the fact that, despite Thompson's claims for spontaneity, the writer nevertheless made changes in between the text's original serial publication in Rolling Stone and its subsequent appearance in book form,[32] but Booth takes the narrator too literally. Through the use of "Gonzo," Thompson merely asks the reader to identify with the frenzied, comic, sometimes horrifying predicament of his narrator as he gropes his way half-blindly toward understanding. What matters is not the revisions but the reader's perception of the text

---

[31] Bruce-Novoa, 41.
[32] Booth, 9.

as a spontaneous creation. "Gonzo" is thus in part a rhetorical strategy. Booth raises the further objection that "direct transcriptions ... do not yield meanings until a mind works them over and generates relationships."[33] However, Thompson's New Journalistic method and rhetorical strategy depend on the reader's active interpretation. McKeen argues in favor of Thompson's methodology that the reporter in *Campaign Trail* "asks the questions the reader might be asking [...] the reader feels like a collaborator in piecing together the facts."[34] Thompson does not want his readers to receive information passively, and he refuses to do all the work for them; rather he asks, through his heuristic, "Gonzo" method, that the reader participate in the process of generating meaning. The absence of one definitive interpretation of events prevents *Campaign Trail* from becoming a closed text.

A close examination of one passage from *Campaign Trail* demonstrates how Thompson brings fictional, digressive and "Gonzo" elements of his text together. Under extreme psychological pressure, the narrator's style most prominently blurs the distinction between reality and fantasy. At the same time, the prose becomes, to borrow Burke's term, most purely persuasive.[35] As the grim reality of another Nixon presidency closes in, Thompson's discourse becomes highly digressive, and he turns to fiction as a means of coping with his "fear and loathing." He sets the mood for the November chapter with the kind of fragmented headlines that preface every chapter:

NOVEMBER

At the Midnight Hour ... Stoned on the Zoo Plane; Stomped in Sioux Falls.... A Rambling

---

[33] Booth, 9.
[34] McKeen, *Thompson*, 64.
[35] Burke, *Rhetoric*, 269.

Manic/Depressive Screed in Triple-Focus on the Last Days of the Doomed McGovern Campaign.... Then Back to America's Heartland for a Savage Beating.... Fear and Loathing at the Holiday Inn.... (419).

The headlines anticipate the action to follow, comment on the action, and place it in context. The passage below is a flashback within another flashback, but it is also a fictionalized recreation of the scene Thompson described in his essay, "The Kentucky Derby is Decadent and Depraved."[36]

Ah, Jesus ... here we go again: another flashback ... the doctors say there's no cure for them; totally unpredictable, like summer lightning in the Rockies or sharks on the Jersey Shore ... unreeling across your brain like a jumble of half-remembered movies all rolling at once. Yesterday I was sitting on my porch in Woody Creek, reading the sports section of the *Denver Post* and wondering how many points to give on the Rams-49ers game, sipping a beer and looking out over the snow-covered fields from time to time ... when suddenly my head rolled back and my eyes glazed over and I felt myself sucked into an irresistible time-warp.

I was standing at the bar in the clubhouse at Churchill Downs on Derby Day with Ralph Steadman [Thompson's illustrator], and we were drinking Mint Juleps at a pretty good pace, watching the cream of Bluegrass Society getting drunker and drunker out into front of us ... It was

---

[36] Thompson, "Kentucky Derby."

between races, as I recall: Ralph was sketching and I was making notes ("3:45, Derby Day, standing at clubhouse bar now, just returned from Mens Room/terrible scene/whole place full of Kentucky Colonels vomiting into urinals & drooling bile down their seersucker pants-legs/Remind Ralph to watch for "distinguished-looking" men in pari-mutuel lines wearing white-polished shoes with fresh vomit stains on the toes...).”

Right. We were standing there at the clubhouse bar, feeling very much on top of that boozy, back-slapping scene ... when I suddenly glanced up from my notes & saw Frank Mankiewicz [McGovern's campaign manager] and Sonny Barger [former leader of the Hell's Angels] across the room, both of them wearing Hell's Angels Costumes and both holding heavy chrome chain-whips ... and yes, it was clear that they'd spotted us. Barger stared, not blinking, but Mankiewicz smiled his cold lizard's smile and they moved slowly through the drunken crowd to put themselves between us and the doorway.

Ralph was still sketching, muttering to himself in some kind of harsh Gaelic singsong & blissfully unaware of the violence about to come down. I nudged him. "Say ... ah ... Ralph, I think maybe you should finish your drink and get that camera strap off your neck real fast.”

"What”

"Don't act nervous, Ralph. Just get that camera strap off your neck and be ready to run like a bastard when I throw this glass at the mirror."

He stared at me, sensing trouble but not understanding. Over his shoulder I could see Frank and Sonny coming towards us, moving slowly down the length of the long whiskey-wet oaken bar, trying to seem casual as they shoved through the crowd of booze-bent Southern Gentlemen who were crowding the aisle ... and when I scanned the room I saw others: Tiny, Zorro, Frenchy, Terry the Tramp, Miles Rubin, Dick Dougherty, Freddy The Torch ... they had us in a bag, and I figured the only way out was a sudden screaming sprint through the clubhouse and up the ramp to the Governor's box, directly across from the Finish Line & surrounded at all times by State Troopers.

Their reaction to a horde of thugs charging through the crowd towards the Governor's Box would be safely predictable, I felt. They would club the bleeding shit out of anybody who looked even halfway weird, and then make mass arrests.... Many innocent people would then suffer; the drunk tank of the Jefferson County Jail would be boiling that night with dozens of drink-maddened Bluebloods who got caught in the Sweep; beaten stupid with truncheons and then hauled off in paddy wagons for no reason at all....

But what the hell? This was certainly acceptable, I felt, and preferable beyond any doubt to the horror

184

of being lashed into hamburger with chain-whips by Mankiewicz and Barger at the clubhouse bar....

Indeed. I have spent some time in the Jefferson County Jail, and on balance it's not a bad place—at least not until your nerves go, but when that happens it doesn't really matter which jail you're in. All blood feels the same in the dark—or back in the shower cell, where the guards can't see. (420-22)

Through style, Thompson's narrator responds symbolically to the threatening environment in which he imaginatively finds himself. The use of parataxis, of short, staccato sentences, hyphens, ellipses, and parentheses, all characterize the stream-of-consciousness style Thompson uses to dramatize his situation. At its most purely persuasive, the tone of Thompson's writing becomes hyperbolic, excessive. The list of names, "Tiny, Zorro, Frenchy [...] Miles Rubin, Dick Dougherty," compiled from Hell's Angels members and presidential campaign staffers, combines two different phases of Thompson's career, and the juxtaposition of these figures allegorizes the collapse of time and resulting sensory disorientation the narrator experiences during his flashback. The intrusion of dialogue in the middle of the passage contributes to our sense of a dramatic scene unfolding before us.

This passage displays a rhetorical strategy called alliosis, the breaking down of a subject into alternatives, neither of which, in this case, is entirely acceptable: either Thompson and Steadman are brutalized by Mankiewicz, Barger, et. al., or by the state troopers. Significantly, given the context of this passage and Thompson's overall relationship to his work, he chooses the alternative (state troopers) furthest removed from the subject of his present assignment, the campaign. The preceding fragment reaches Twain's "snapper" point fairly early on: the notion that Frank

Mankiewicz and Sonny Barger would appear together, "wearing Hell's Angels costumes and [...] holding heavy chrome chain-whips," is so manifestly ridiculous that it becomes impossible for the reader to take the rest of the story seriously.

Thompson's heuristic style is heavily paratactic: he arranges clauses and phrases in a coordinate relationship to suggest a mind in motion, formulating thoughts and impressions spontaneously in the act of writing. Other elements contribute to the sense of spontaneity in this passage. The reporter's notes (a pure "Gonzo" touch), containing fragments, slash marks, an ampersand, ellipses, even a mechanical error ("Mens"), suggest moment by moment composition. Thompson's clauses and phrases tend to fire up in short, quick bursts, as in "here we go again: another flashback," and allegorize the narrator's frantic effort to record the rapid flow of his immediate thoughts and impressions. Connective phrases, "yes," and short transitions at the beginning of certain paragraphs, "Right," "But what the hell?" and "Indeed," allow the narrator to run a constant, self-reflexive check on his narrative as it develops.

Given the constant deadline pressure and disoriented psychological condition of Thompson's narrator, the paratactic style is especially appropriate. Parataxis conveys a strong sense of the present moment, and does not require the writer to arrive at conclusions or to present a coherent picture of the world. In a paratactic sentence, one thing leads to another temporally but not necessarily causally:

> Yesterday I was sitting on my porch in Woody Creek, reading the sports section of the Denver Post and wondering how many points to give on the Rams-49ers game, sipping a beer and looking out over the snow-covered fields from time to time ...

186

when suddenly my head rolled back and my eyes
glazed over and I felt myself sucked into an
irresistible time-warp.

Parataxis requires the reader to establish relationships between
grammatical units representing disparate elements of experience.
In this case, the grammatical units are isocolons, a succession of
phrases of equal length and corresponding structure: "sitting [...]
reading [...] and wondering [...] sipping [...] and looking [...] my
head rolled back and my eyes glazed over [...]." Often the initial
isocolon extends into adjacent participial phrases, movement
generating further movement, all happening in the present: "Over
his shoulder I could see Frank and Sonny coming towards us,
moving [...] trying [...] crowding [...]." Isocolons also allow
Thompson to pile up metaphorical associations spontaneously,
without ranking them: "summer lightning in the Rockies or sharks
on the Jersey shore [...]."

The fragmented syntax of Thompson's prose is another
heuristic device. In the first sentence, Thompson identifies the
subject, flashbacks, only once; he omits the subject in the
fragments following the semi-colon: "totally unpredictable, like
summer lightning [...] unreeling across your brain [...]." The name
for this stylistic feature is zeugma, the use of one word to govern
several congruent words or clauses, or possibly ellipsis, the
omission of a word easily understood. Thompson also uses this
device in the second from the last paragraph, where the missing
subject is "Bluebloods": "beaten stupid [...] hauled off in paddy
wagons [...]." The fragments and the omission of certain words
create the impression that Thompson is composing too quickly to
form complete sentences. Fragments and omissions also allegorize
Thompson's view of the world as violent and chaotic. The tone of
this entire scene is one of violence and chaos. The frequent

absence of conjunctions between clauses or phrases, asyndeton, further allegorizes this chaos. Conjunctions, after all, make connections between things, and the frantic pace of Thompson's prose suggests that there is not time for him to pull the disparate elements of his experience together.

Verbs drive Thompson's narrative style, providing the reader with a sense of forward motion as the narrator plunges head-on into his story. Most commonly, Thompson uses participial phrases and clauses: "Yesterday I was sitting [...] reading the sports section [...] wondering how many points [...] sipping a beer and looking out [...] my head rolled back [...] my eyes glazed [...] and I felt myself sucked into [...]." The shift from present to past participles within the second sentence indicates a rapid shift in consciousness. Accompanying Thompson's verbs is a proliferation of prepositional phrases: "I figured the only way out was a sudden screaming sprint through the clubhouse and up the ramp to the Governor's Box, directly across from the Finish Line & surrounded at all times by State Troopers." Reflecting back on his days as a sports writer, Thompson remembers that "none of the people I wrote about seemed to give a hoot in hell what kind of lunatic gibberish I wrote about them, just so it moved. The wanted action. Color. Speed. Violence [...]." (502). In an interview with William McKeen, Thompson described the effect of his early sports writing experience on his later writing as "Huge," and commented that "You really get those action verbs flowing."[37] If Thompson's primary purpose is to persuade by making his experience both vivid and entertaining, the verb style allows the kind of "Action" etc. needed to do the job. Even Thompson's descriptive adjectives tend to contain verbs: "snow-covered," "white-polished," "back-slapping," "whiskey-wet oaken," "booze-

---

[37] McKeen, *Thompson*, 106.

bent," and "drink-maddened [...]." The violence and mayhem contained within this passage are typical of Thompson's writing and of his world view, and verbs are the vehicle of this violence. Booth derogatorily labels Thompson's style "tough guy gush,"[38] and *Campaign Trail* unquestionably adopts a "hard-boiled" tone, alternately aggressive and stoical. However, Thompson's use of verbs suggests that he's neither as tough nor as in control as Booth thinks Thompson thinks he is. Thompson uses verbs differently to suggest the opposite roles played by victims and victimizers. He tends to use active voice in relation to whichever character or group of characters is in control at any given time: "We were standing [...] feeling very much on top [...] Berger stared [...] Mankiewicz smiled [...] they would club [...] make mass arrests [...]." Passive voice is reserved for the victims: "beaten stupid [...] hauled off in paddy wagons [...] being lashed into hamburger [...]." Through his verb-driven style, Thompson's narrator demonstrates both the aggressiveness of his "loathing" and his "fear" of sinister forces beyond his control.

Thompson's metaphors tend to express violence as well: "club the bleeding shit," "the drunk tank [...] would be boiling," "being lashed into hamburger [...]." Several of the metaphors in this passage, "sharks on the Jersey shore" and "cold lizard's smile," convey an attitude toward human behavior which is essentially atavistic. Thompson suggests that, in a violent world, men must transform themselves into beasts in order to survive. Atavism and violence lurk just below the surface of a seemingly rational, civilized world. By capitalizing "Southern Gentlemen," "Bluegrass Society," "Kentucky Colonels," and "Bluebloods," then describing these same figures "vomiting into urinals and drooling bile down their seersucker pants-legs," Thompson reduces

---

[38] Booth, 8.

189

them to disgusting bodily functions, satirizing them to convey his contempt for class privilege and pretention. At the end of the passage, "Blueblood" becomes "blood," as in "All blood feels the same in the dark." The word "blood" becomes a synecdoche, the substitution of a part, "blood" for the whole human being, another way of deflating social superiority. "All blood [blue or otherwise]," Thompson says, "feels the same in the dark [...]." Through the use of synecdoche, Thompson again reduces humanity to the lowest common denominator.

Thompson's style contains numerous sound devices which contribute to the text's persuasive effect. The phrase, "sudden screaming sprint," for example, is alliterative, while the phrase, "harsh Gaelic singsong," with its s's and hard r and g sounds is assonant, even onomatopoeic. Thompson alternates long, rambling paratactic sentences with short sentences ("it was clear they'd spotted us," and "they had us in a bag") to establish a rhythm which requires both the narrator and his readers to stop occasionally to catch their breath while they reassess the situation. Isocolons also set, at times, a rhythmic pace: "Summer lightning in the Rockies or sharks on the Jersey shore [...]." In its rhythms and sound patterns, Thompson's paratactic style approaches the condition of verse, a quality which accentuates its pure persuasiveness.

This passage tells a story within a story, but it is a story that has no ending. From the sentence beginning "I figured," the action becomes purely speculative and imaginative, an account of what would be "predictable" given the circumstances. The narrator concludes with dark forebodings hinting at prison violence, even homosexual rape, "back in the shower cell, where the guards can't see." The threat of impending violence creates a sense of dramatic open-endedness. *Campaign Trail* contains numerous suggestions

190

that the story is far from over. Late in the campaign, for example, Thompson alludes to the Watergate burglary (417-418, 473-474), a real-life conspiracy that eventually caused Nixon to resign. No hint of scandal threatened his re-nomination, however. The narrator's comments on the implications of the break-in suggest that the nation is still sick, still in a state of denial which threatens to destroy them: "'Ominous' is not quite the right word for a situation where one of the most consistently unpopular politicians in American history suddenly skyrockets to Folk Hero status while his closest advisors are being caught almost daily in nazi-style gigs that would have embarrassed Martin Bormann" (417-418). The reference to "nazi-style gigs" further develops the narrator's running comparison between the Nixon administration and his prophecy of impending Fourth Reich. The readers' knowledge of the Watergate incident affects the way they read *Campaign Trail* every bit as much as their knowledge throughout the book that, eventually, Nixon will win the election. Nevertheless, Thompson dramatizes the doubt and uncertainty of the moment. Up to the end, he continues to assess the meaning of his experience and of McGovern's campaign: "What went wrong? Why had it failed? Who was to blame? And, finally, what next" (395)? By continuing to ask questions without answers, Thompson refuses to impose an artificial sense of closure on his story. Further, he asks the readers to participate in the process of creating meaning, encouraging them to come to their own conclusions. The text also resists closure by the narrator's reference to the "Pendulum Theory" (467). With Nixon's reelection, the pendulum swings not left but further to the right. Thompson's metaphor implies, however, that at some point in the future, the pendulum will swing back to the left, suggesting that he has not given up the fight.

Conclusion

The action and structure of *Campaign Trail* suggest that Thompson's trials and tribulations are never-ending. In this way, the text resembles a Jeremiad, foretelling the destruction of America by the greed, brutality, and stupidity of its leaders. The long passage we examined above begins with an apostrophe, "Ah, Jesus," an invocation and curse expressing the narrator's long-standing suffering, for which there is no relief in sight. Throughout, Dr. Thompson laments his lot as a journalist chained to the shackles of a hellish campaign ordeal, and prays for deliverance: "How long, O Lord, how long? Where will it end" (225)? Certainly, one of Thompson's roles in the campaign drama is that of the prophet whose intuitive insight into the human condition allows him to see into the future:

> This may be the year when we finally come face to face with ourselves; finally just lay back and say it—that we are really just a nation of 220 million used car salesmen with all the money we need to buy guns, and no qualms at all about killing anybody else in the world who tries to make us uncomfortable [...]. Jesus! Where will it end? (413-414)

The phrase "used car salesmen" refers to Nixon. In the late 1960s, a poster appeared featuring Nixon's face, underneath which read: "Would You Buy A Used Car From This Man?" Thompson once again reminds us that Nixon represents the dark, sinister side of the American character from which McGovern hoped to deliver us. However, Thompson prefaces the December chapter, following the national election, with an allusion to the Book of *Jeremiah*: "The harvest is past, the summer is ended, and we are not saved" (459).

The Biblical quote suggests that, although the narrator's participation in the campaign has come to an end, his suffering, and ours, have not, and the historical narrative continues.

Chapter Five:

Joan Didion's *Salvador* and *Miami*: Journalist as Witness and Oracle

History as Drama

In *Salvador* and *Miami*, Joan Didion dramatizes the ideological conflict between residual, emergent, and dominant cultures, both in Central America and in the United States. In *Salvador*, Didion witnesses and reports the violence perpetrated by the U.S.-backed, right-wing El Salvadoran government against its citizens and left-wing guerilla groups. In *Miami*, she identifies with the efforts of Miami Cubans to live in that American city while maintaining national allegiance to pre-revolutionary Cuba, thus creating for themselves an ambivalent national status discouraged by Washington and by Miami's Anglo community. Didion's persona, a finely-tuned, shrewdly observant, deeply skeptical first-hand witness to events, inscribes her own individual narrative into the master sociopolitical narratives of Miami and El Salvador. She dramatizes events and her reaction to events through her ornate, self-conscious style which serves as an implicit counterpoint to the bureaucratic prose and political rhetoric she exposes and condemns. Through her juxtaposition of opposing, sometimes contradictory, versions of events, Didion comments, directly and indirectly, on the ongoing historical narratives. At the same time, Didion's dramatic narrative leaves the conflicts between protagonists and antagonists (and sometimes the difference is not clear) unresolved. As Juan Corradi observes about the narrative structure of *Salvador*, "[Didion] does not give us a plot to unravel, an interpretive key to unlock the horror, a solution."[1] In oracular fashion, Didion merely witnesses and reports, and the final meaning of historical events that occurred before her participation and continue to occur after she leaves both Miami and Salvador is unknown. Didion's narrative achieves a sense of closure in the sense that her direct participation in events comes to an end, the historical narratives continue. Finally, *Miami* and *Salvador* resist narrative as well as ideological closure.

Both *Miami* and *Salvador* presume a considerable amount of historical background on the part of the reader. Didion assumes that her readers have already familiarized themselves with the pertinent background information so that she can focus on her direct participation in events. Further, rather than present the historical narrative in a straightforwardly chronological fashion, Didion's story begins *in medias res*. She selects impressions and events, compressing, synthesizing, and heightening their dramatic impact, so that, in one sense, Didion's historical narrative is interior; and as Chris Anderson argues, "The dramatization of the mind in the act of thought imposes in the end a narrative line."[2] At the same time, Didion foregrounds the discourse of others, allowing various factions to speak for themselves. Like the other texts in this study, *Salvador* and *Miami* are heteroglossic, but they are also polyglossic: they simultaneously present two national

---

[1] Corradi, 162.
[2] Anderson, 2.

languages, English and Spanish, within a single cultural system.[3] To the extent that Didion calls attention to what others have said, she keeps herself in the background, placing her own engagement and responses within the context of an ongoing historical narrative that is both incorporated by and subsumes her own. In a way, her texts are not so much narratives in their own right than running commentaries on narratives that have already been written. Didion takes history as the text—and sometimes the sub-text—that informs her own writing. As narrator, she faces the task of telling a tale which many others have told, very differently of course, before her. Because Didion's object, the political struggle in either Miami or El Salvador, involves so much discourse about that object, her own text must enter into a conversation with the discourse of others. In *Miami* and *Salvador*, verbal expression is very often the focus; in both books, the political struggle is carried on verbally. Anderson too has made the observation that Didion is "concerned not simply with the experience she is trying to describe but with the language of those experiences—with the jargon, the rhetoric, the diction of individuals and how that language reflects a point of view," and that she is therefore a "rhetorical critic."[4] Nevertheless, Anderson devotes very little time to a discussion of how the discourse of others is evaluated or transformed in Didion's texts. At this point, we need to examine Didion's rhetorical criticism of political discourse in detail.

Didion as Rhetorical Critic

More than any New Journalist in this study, Didion interprets her experience textually, that is, as a series of stories. Much of the discourse which informs *Miami* consists of "Miami

---

[3] Bakhtin, 431.
[4] Anderson, 161.

stories" told to the writer by her Cuban interviewees (201).[5] These stories, "intrinsically impossible to corroborate," Didion says, and "of doubtful provenance," often "recall" other "Miami stories" (201). The writer's consciousness of her Miami experience is thus permeated by narrative. Didion refers to "these stories about what people in Miami may or may not have done on the basis of what people in Washington had or had not said" as the "underwater narrative," a phrase which suggests murky details and underground channels (201). The "underwater narratives" create a shifting substrata of unofficial discourse which destabilizes Washington's official discourse on the surface; "Surfaces," Didion says, "tended to dissolve here" (36). The phrase "underwater narrative" becomes appropriate for a city in which events "remained obscure, as if unknowable," a city in which historical certainty becomes an impossibility (90). The difficulty of obtaining reliable information is augmented by the government's use of what Didion calls "Washington phrases" or "words from a language in which deniability was built into the grammar, and as such may or may not have had a different meaning, or any meaning …" (94). Didion's job as reporter is to sort through all the discourse about Miami (much of which falsifies or distorts its object) and to create her own version of truth against the backdrop of conflicting versions. She interrogates texts, breaks their codes, and invites them to contradict one another, thereby deconstructing their claims to authority, adding her own voice to the mixture of voices.

Didion is preoccupied with the meanings of certain words and phrases, meanings which differ according to user, hearer, and context. She is particularly interested in the way meanings are made arbitrary, or the way meanings shift, or disappear entirely: "Sometimes," she says, "words in Miami are believed to be

---

[5] Didion's *Miami*. All subsequent references to Miami are this edition.

without consequence. Other times they are not" (105-106). In order to critique the rhetoric of dominant cultures, Didion offers her readers the worlds of Miami and El Salvador in fragments of quoted discourse. Incorporated within Didion's text, the rhetorical and contextual dimensions of oppositional and alternative discourses are evaluated, or sometimes transformed. Lounsberry makes the point that Didion uses "only those quotations that underscore her vision of her subjects ... she famously allows the subjects to damn themselves with their own words."[6] Like Anderson, however, Lounsberry provides very little in the way of specific examples. In *Miami*, Didion places the phrase "freedom fighters" in quotation marks to suggest the conviction, held by many Miami Cubans, that the U.S. government has "co-opted exile action" in its failure to offer its full support to the anti-Communist Nicaraguan Contras (146), a group whose cause the Cubans view as similar to their own. Mark Winchell offers a useful gloss on Didion's use of the term "freedom fighters":

> The Kennedy and Reagan administrations (and, to a lesser extent, those that came in between) were content to talk tough while stopping short of an actual confrontation with Soviet imperialism ... Unfortunately, the Cuban exiles and their more militant allies insisted on a literal interpretation of Washington's anti-communist rhetoric and felt betrayed when there was no action behind the brave words. (118)

Didion's use of the phrase "freedom fighter" demonstrates the gap between Washington's rhetoric and Miami Cuban's conceptions of political reality. Many Miami Cubans express skepticism, if not scorn, for Washington's claim that it is doing everything it can to

---

[6] Lounsberry, xv.

remove Castro. Their skepticism dates back to the failure of the Bay of Pigs invasion, an event that Didion says offers Cubans an "ideal narrative" (19). Within the context of Didion's narrative, Washington's use of the term "freedom fighters" becomes ironic, a meaningless phrase. When the Reagan administration refers to "freedom fighters," it is merely retelling a familiar tale, as Didion explains: "These exiles saw, when and if this happened, a rekindling of certain familiar frustrations, the unloosing of furies still only provisionally contained; saw, in other words, built into the mirror trick, yet another narrative on which to hang the betrayal, the utilization, the manipulation of *el exilio* by the government of the United States" (147). In the passage quoted above, Didion ranks grammatical elements in a hypotactic or hierarchical relationship. The appositives and dependent clauses build to a climax which dramatizes the Cubans' anger and frustration. By juxtaposing the Cuban narrative with that of the U.S. government, Didion demonstrates that the Cuban population has inscribed its own subtext into Washington's text, thus undermining its authority. In an almost Borgesian display of texts within texts within texts, she quotes from a CIA report "on the matter of Washington language" pertaining to the removal of Castro from Cuba (95). Didion cites words and phrases such as "disposing" of Castro or "doing something about" Castro which are sufficiently ambiguous to denote either a coup or an assassination attempt (95). Through the inclusion of this unusually candid report, Didion uses the government's discourse against itself to disclose an important, de-mythifiying subtext: that the purpose of Washington's language is frequently to distort or obscure its real motives and purposes. U.S. government officials use language symbolically; language becomes an empty gesture which "makes nothing happen" (160). By focusing on language's symbolic function, Didion calls attention to the gap between rhetoric and political myth-making on one hand, social change on the other. In *Salvador*, as well, Didion suggests that the word or phrase, as used by another, is a euphemism for, or ideological distortion of, the historical situation to which it refers. Anderson suggests that Didion's concern for the moral and political values implicit in language echoes George Orwell's. Like Orwell, he explains, Didion "believes in the inextricable relationship between words and ideas, believes, therefore, that the truth or falsity of ideas is directly reflected in the truth or falsity of the language used to express them."[7] To cite just one example, Didion focuses on the numerous political assassinations carried out by the Salvadoran government, then covered up with euphemistic language. The government does not refer to the killings as "murders," but as "disappearances" (14).[8] Didion's use of quotation marks in this context creates a sardonic tone which suggests that she sees through the government's attempts to hide the truth. Lynne T. Hanley argues that, "among officials of [El Salvador], language is appreciated not for its descriptive but for its fictive possibilities."[9] Didion exposes the government's manipulation of the "fictive possibilities" of language, and her own text reveals the horrible reality that the government attempts to fictionalize.

Fragments of the world placed in quotes sometimes become dramatic motifs in Didion's text. In *Miami* she repeats the phrases "el exilio" (13, ff.), the exiles, used by the Cuban population to refer to their status as exiles, and to "la lucha" (18, ff.), the struggle, a phrase the Cubans use to refer to their ongoing political campaign to undermine the government of Fidel Castro. In Didion's text, "el exilio" and "la lucha" become metonymic phrases, principles of organization; because they are filled with a

---

[7] Anderson, 165.
[8] Didion's *Salvdor*. All subsequent references are to this edition.
[9] Hanley, 26.

201

collective historical significance, the phrases allow her to use a kind of thematic shorthand. The significance of "el exilio" resides partly in its indication of the difference between Anglo attitudes toward Miami Cubans, and Miami Cubans' attitudes toward themselves. Winchell points out, "The two principal reactions of Miami's Anglo minority ... to the Cuban exiles have been condescension and nativist rancor."[10] The Anglos regard the Cubans as "immigrants" and assume that they will choose to renounce their country's language and cultural heritage and willingly appropriate Anglo-American values (57). Volosinov argues that "the ruling class," in this case Miami Anglos, "tries to impart a superclass, eternal character to the ideological sign, to extinguish or drive inward the struggle between social value judgments which occur in it, to make the sign *uniaccentual*."[11] By their use of the term "immigrants," the Anglos suppress the notion that there are many Cubans in Miami who would prefer to live their lives not in the United States but in a politically reconstructed Cuba. According to Didion, the Anglos do not appreciate "the humiliation of continuing exile," or *el exilio* (79). "Immigration," the Anglo version of *el exilio*, then becomes a suppression of Cuban attitudes and Cuban history, and Didion's text reveals the subtext beneath this ideological distortion. She structures this conflict between Anglo conceptions of Miami Cubans and the Miami Cubans' conception of themselves through the use of anaphora and parallelism:

> Cubans were perceived as most satisfactory when
> they appeared to most fully share the aspirations
> and manners of middle-class Americans ... Cubans
> were perceived as least satisfactory when they

---

[10] Winchell, 199.
[11] Volosinov, 23.

'acted clannish,' 'kept to themselves,' 'had their own ways,' and two frequent flash points, 'spoke Spanish when they didn't need to' and 'got political'; complaints, each of them, which suggested an Anglo version of what Cubans should be at significant odds with what Cubans were. (61-62)

By placing certain Anglo phrases in quotation marks, Didion refracts their meaning. She thus illuminates a desire on the part of the dominant Anglo community to deny the Cuban Americans their cultural heritage, and therefore to eradicate their difference from the Anglos. Miami Anglos seem disturbed that Cubans "had their own ways," or "spoke Spanish when they didn't need to." The dominant Anglo culture seeks to create the illusion that only one legitimate culture—its own—exists in Miami. As Ruth Walker notes, the conflict between Miami Cubans and Miami Anglos is "a tension between the believers in a passionately embraced 'truth' and the managers of manipulated media 'images.'"[12] Through foregrounding quoted fragments of Anglo discourse, however, Didion calls attention to the dominant culture's motives. In her text, the *uniaccentuality* of each Anglo phrase becomes *multiaccentual*, again to borrow Volosinov's terms, and the Anglo discourse enters into a dialectical relationship with Didion's own.[13] She thus demonstrates the way in which the Anglos feel threatened by Cuban culture, and seek to remove that threat by co-opting and therefore negating it. The irony, as Didion points out, is that Miami culture is predominantly Cuban, not Anglo: "The entire tone of the city," she says, "the way people looked and talked and met one another, was Cuban" (52). The Anglo media, however, create the

---

[12] Walker, 230.
[13] Volosinov 23.

opposite impression: Didion cites a Miami *Herald* article which lists Miami's most prominent citizens, none of whom, according to the editors, are Cuban (51).

The inclusion of Spanish phrases like "el exilio" in Didion's text signifies a major source of conflict between the two communities in Miami: the "question of language" (63). As Winchell notes, "The nativist response to increasing Cuban domination of Miami often manifests itself in a testiness about the ubiquity of Spanish."[14] Spoken Spanish makes the Anglos uneasy, Didion suggests, because "the inability or the disinclination to speak English tended to undermine their conviction that assimilation was an ideal universally shared by those who were to be assimilated" (65). The passive construction, "to be assimilated," suggests that the Anglos, not the Cubans themselves, will try to determine the character Cuban-American culture eventually assumes. Didion points out that in other major cities, Los Angeles for example, Spanish is heard only rarely, and spoken only by people who occupy positions such as gardeners and waiters; on Miami's "socioauditory" scale, however, exiles who felt "isolated or declassed" by the language in other cities—exiles like Miami's mayor, Xavier Suarez—were able to prosper (63). Didion documents the frustrated efforts of Florida legislators to declare English the official state language. As the legislators implicitly acknowledge, language is a powerful ideological tool; by officially imposing their language on the Cuban-American community, they simultaneously assert their cultural hegemony. At the same time, what Didion designates as "the local patois" sometimes mixes Spanish and English, and this mixture undermines the attempt by the Florida legislature to impose their cultural hegemony (64).

---

[14] Winchell, 119.

Through the incorporation of the dominant culture's discourse into her own text, Didion makes her readers aware of the creation of political myths by ruling power structures in Miami and El Salvador. Juan Corradi writes eloquently that

> Didion places the quotations side by side, or next to the brute facts of life and death, so skillfully that, without recourse to commentary, they testify to the mendacious loquacity of a condition where language is called upon, most of the time, not to illuminate truth but to dream it a it ought to be, to improve its appearance, to formulate ramshackle mythologies, to lure us into the realm of shadow-boxing, or pure symbolic action.[15]

In *Salvador*, Didion continually calls attention to a disturbing discrepancy: Washington reports that the Salvadoran government is improving its record on human right abuses, yet government troops continue to "disappear" Salvadoran citizens. Didion learns that in El Salvador, the truth, "la verdad," has become "a degenerated phrase," the truth according to Roberto D'Aubisson" (66). She also comes to understand that "the change of a name is meant to be accepted as a change in the nature of the thing named" (63). In Salvador, as elsewhere, political hegemony depends to a large extent on which competing faction can impose its definitions on the popular consciousness, or, more importantly, on Washington. The right-wing Salvadoran government discovers, for example, that one way to appropriate aid from the U.S. is to label their opponents communists. Didion shrewdly observes that, for the government's purposes, "anyone in the opposition was a communist, along with most of the American press, the Catholic Church, and, as time went by, all Salvadoran citizens not of the

---

[15] Corradi, 163.

right" (94). By ascertaining that "'anti-communism' ... was ... the bait the United States would always take,'" the Salvadoran government asserts its hegemony (95). Didion appropriates the language of the dominant culture, which attempts to coerce allegiance and belief through the creation of political myths like "communism," in order to undermine its authority.

We see the same kind of political myth-making in *Miami*, as the White House staff speaks self-consciously of "'the story line we are tying to develop that week or that month'" suggesting that they view reality as a myth they are free to invent for their own purposes (175). Dominant forces in society, such as the United States government, seek to impose narrative closure via the myths they create; their goal is to make the world appear naturally and necessarily the way they have created it—they mythicize reality. Through her deconstruction of political myths, Didion exposes futile attempts to achieve narrative closure where no closure is possible. She calls Arthur M. Schlesinger, Jr.'s book on the Kennnedy administration, *A Thousand Days*, "an essentially anti-historical work in which the entire matter of the Cuban exiles is seen to have resolved itself ..." (89). Didion suggests here that Schlesinger's book is "anti-historical" because it denies that the historical narrative remains unresolved. Her own text, as we have seen, works against narrative closure.

As direct participant and narrator, Didion attempts to arrive at truth amidst so many conflicting versions of events. In this passage from *Salvador*, Didion dramatizes how difficult it is to distinguish between truth and falsehood: "Every morning COPREFA, the press office at the Ministry Defense, reported many FMLN casualties but few government. Every afternoon Radio Venceremos, the clandestine guerilla radio station, reported many government casualties but few FMLN" (39). In the balance

206

and antithesis of these sentences, varying reports cancel each other out. Based on these reports alone, it would be impossible to determine who was winning, who was losing, and who was primarily responsible for the violence. This passage allegorizes Didion's confusion that, she maintains throughout the text, every traveler to El Salvador experiences, as she tries to arrive at the truth, *la verdad*, of El Salvador's political struggle. The passage quoted above also exposes the deliberate deception practiced on both sides of the conflict, which makes Didion's job as reporter all the more difficult. Despite the obvious advantages of direct participation, Didion finds that much of what happens in Miami and El Salvador remains unknown. Didion's texts suggest that unless a participant bears personal witness to an event, he or she can never be sure exactly what happened.

As Didion realizes that "la verdad," both in El Salvador and Miami, is completely arbitrary, determined by contradictory versions of events, she reaches the point at which observation and interpretation become a game, a form of verbal play. In the following passage, she allegorizes the bewildering complexity of El Salvador's political situation by qualifying definitions with other definitions:

> All numbers in El Salvador tend to materialize and vanish and rematerialize in a different form, as if numbers denoted only the 'use' of numbers, an intonation, a wish, a recognition that someone, somewhere, for whatever reason needed to hear the ineffable expressed as a number ... the use of numbers in this context tends to frustrate people who try to understand them literally, rather than as propositions to be floated, 'heard,' 'mentioned.'
> (61)

207

This passage relies heavily on appositives: "an intonation, a wish" is "'floated,' 'heard,' 'mentioned'." Didion's use of appositives allegorizes her frustrated search for the truth. This passage also displays asyndeton, the absence of conjunctions between words, which in this context suggests Didion's difficulty in making connections between disparate phenomena. Repetition of the word "materialize" with the prefix "re-" conveys a sense of her mystification. In the following passage, based on second-hand reports of a helicopter crash, Didion illustrates the difficulty of ascertaining the truth in El Salvador:

> The crash occurred either near the Honduran border in Morazan or, the speculation went, actually in Honduras. There were or were not four people aboard the helicopter: the pilot, a bodyguard, Colonel Beltran Luna, and the assistant secretary of defense, Colonel Francisco Adolfo Castillo. At first all four were dead. A day later three were dead: Radio Venceremos broadcast news of Colonel Castillo (followed a few days later by a voice resembling that of Colonel Castillo), not dead but a prisoner, or said to be a prisoner, or perhaps only claiming to be a prisoner. A day or so later another of the dead materialized, or appeared to: the pilot was, it seemed, neither dead nor a prisoner but hospitalized, incommunicado. (68)

The passive construction, "said to be," refers to second-hand sources, which Didion realizes she cannot trust. Numerous qualifiers, "the speculation went [...] appeared to [...] it seemed," as well as the appositives, "hospitalized, incommunicado," suggest Didion's frustrated attempts to get the facts. Didion uses isocolon, the repetition of phrases of equal length and roughly corresponding structure, "not dead but a prisoner, or said to be a prisoner, or perhaps only claiming to be a prisoner," to make the point that all reports of the event carry equal weight. In this passage, Didion makes ample use of epiphora, the repetition of a word or words at the end of successive phrases or clauses: "three were dead [...] four were dead [...] Colonel Castillo [...] a voice resembling that of Colonel Castillo [...] a prisoner [...] said to be a prisoner [...] claiming to be a prisoner [...]." Epiphora allows Didion to convey a sense of multiple, rapidly changing versions of events and allegorizes her confusion. The passage begins with an either/or construction and ends with a neither/nor construction which negates previous reports. The phrase, "were or were not," also offers an affirmation followed immediately by a negation. The past tense verb, "materialized," implies what "appeared to" materialize, but Didion's omission of "materialize" suggests another rapid negation. (The use of one verb to govern several congruent words is called zeugma.) The alternation of short and long sentences in this passage heightens the effect of a seemingly reliable, coherent narrative quickly superseded and negated by another narrative.

As we have seen, many of the participants in Didion's texts have their own stories to tell, and the stories often contradict one another. The competing versions of reality produced by rival factions constitute one of the key dramatic conflicts in *Salvador* and *Miami*. However, most of the attention Didion devotes to the discourse of others, even that of residual and emergent cultures with whom she aligns herself, is critical. The Miami Cubans, she suggests, attempt via their own political mythmaking to impose ideological closure where none is possible. "Miami stories," she says, meaning, in this context, Cuban stories, "tend to have endings" (1622). Although Didion sympathizes with the Cubans' effort to maintain their cultural identity in an American city and allows their voices to be heard, she is unable to accept their fierce

209

allegiance to certain right-wing principles. The paradox within the Cuban community is that, although they have become marginalized by the dominant Anglo culture, they embrace many of the same values as the Anglos. Didion narrates an incident in which Alpha 66, a Cuban American political organization, disrupts a demonstration held by the South Florida Peace Coalition to protest U.S. aid to the Nicaraguan Contras. Alpha 66 seems unwilling to allow the voices of the opposition to be heard. Didion concludes "Miami Cubans were not heirs to a tradition in which undue effort had been spent defining the rights and responsibilities of 'good citizenship,' nor to one in which loosely organized democracies on the American model were widely admired" (70). The Cubans, Didion discovers, are as intolerant of oppositional viewpoints as their Anglo counterparts. She thus finds herself in a marginalized position, between two cultures.

The conflict between Cuban and Anglo cultures tends to obscure the fact that there is yet another emergent culture far more marginalized than the Cubans, Miami's African-American community, which has been systematically excluded from economic and political power, and which, consequently, is barely seen at all. Miami's black residents have been banished to the city's worst ghettoes, where neither Anglos nor Cubans are willing to go. Didion decides, however, despite the admonishments of others, to seek out those victims of the region's failed economic policies. In the following passage from Miami, Didion relates some advice she has been given on where to go and not to go in that crime-ridden, tension-filled city:

> I should not walk the block and a half from the Omni to the *Herald* alone after dark. I should lock my car doors when I drove at night. If I hit a red light as I was about to enter I-95 I should not stop

but look both ways, and accelerate. I should not
drive through Liberty City, or walk around
Overtown. If I had occasion to walk through what
was called 'the black Grove,' those several dozen
blocks of project housing which separated the
expensive greenery of Coral Gables from the
expensive greenery of Coconut Grove, I should
rethink my route, avoid at costs the territory of the
disentitled, which in fact was hard to do, since
Miami was a city, like so many to the south of it, in
which it was possible to pass from walled enclaves
to utter desolation while changing stations on the
car radio. (39)

In this passage Didion uses anaphora, "I should not," to dramatize
an atmosphere of repression and fear. She also dramatizes her
experience through the repetition of balanced phrases: "separated
the expensive greenery of Coral Gables from the expensive
greenery of Coconut Grove [...]." In this case, balanced phrases
stress the forbidding uniformity of Miami's affluent districts. By
balancing the phrases, "from walled enclaves to utter desolation,"
Didion places them in an antithetical relationship to allegorize the
contrast between the two Miamis, rich and poor; Didion's
antithetical syntax also suggests her marginal status in between the
two worlds. "In the end," Didion says, "I went without incident to
all of the places I had been told not to go, and did not or did do all
of the things I had been told to do or not to do" (39). Didion's
sentence forms a chiasmus, a reversal of word order, "did not or
did do...to do or not to do," allegorizing her refusal to allow her
perceptions of Miami to be manipulated, and her desire to face the
most unpleasant truths. Lynne Hanley elaborates on this point
when she says that "Didion compels us to share her recognition
that our desire not to see anything at all leads not to moral

211

superiority but moral extinction."[16] Hanley's comment should not be taken to imply that Didion is fearless, however. One evening, sitting with her husband, writer John Gregory Dunne, in a darkened restaurant in El Salvador, Didion notices "two human shadows," one of which carries a gun, watching them silently (26). The episode is presented dramatically, the tension building to Didion's conclusion, at the end of the chapter, that she felt herself "demoralized, undone, humiliated by fear [...]." (26). Strung together asyndetically (without conjunctions), the appositives, "demoralized, undone, humiliated," help the reader understand "the exact mechanism of terror," for which Didion's text becomes an objective correlative (26).

Journalist as Participant

As in Miami, Didion finds herself marginalized in El Salvador, but the difficulties of assimilation there are quite different. While she foregrounds Washington's discourse and that of its satellite, the El Salvadoran government, the voices of the opposition are heard from either rarely or not at all. Didion's task as reporter in El Salvador is frustrated by the fact that she has little to no access to left-wing Salvadoran guerillas, whose need for anonymity is self-evident. Similarly, the Salvadoran peasants must remain silent in order to protect themselves. Another obstacle that Didion encounters is that due to El Salvador's geographical remoteness, with Guatemala to the north and Colombia and Panama to the south, Spanish and Mesoamerican cultures have never taken hold, which makes it difficult for Didion, as cultural anthropologist, to gain insight into El Salvadoran culture. "There is a sense," she says, "in which the place remains marked by the meanness and discontinuity of all frontier history, by a certain frontier proximity to the cultural zero" (73). El Salvador seems to

---

[16] Hanley, 29.

her to have no culture of its own. At an exhibition of native crafts in Nahuizalco, Didion learns that the traditional way of obtaining wicker to make baskets is to import the material from Guatemala (73). Part of the explanation for this apparent lack of cultural heritage, Didion discovers, is that, by the 1960s, most of the indigenous population of this region had been eliminated. Consequently, Didion says, "Indian dress was abandoned by the survivors," and "Nahuatl, the Indian language, was no longer spoken in public" (74). Didion thus finds herself caught between a dominant culture that murders and deceives, and a residual culture which is almost invisible.

Writing of the El Salvador's national history, Didion says that it is "peculiarly resistant to heroic interpretation. There is no *libertor* to particularly remember" (72). No historic figure assumes the role of protagonist. In the absence of a Salvadoran hero, and faced with unreliability and deception on all fronts, Didion enters the narrative as her own protagonist. Hanley points out that Didion wrote *Salvador* after writing a fictional account of Latin American politics, *A Book Of Common Prayer*, and concludes that "to get at the facts [...] Didion had to penetrate both the fictions about El Salvador and her own desire to disassociate, to fictionalize [...] she crosses the line between *la norteamericana* and the war to report from inside the war [...]."[17] Placing herself in the middle of the action obviously required Didion's direct participation. Katherine Usher Henderson examines Didion's "strongly felt need not only to understand the social and political currents that swirl around us all, but also to become immersed in those currents long enough to experience them emotionally as well as intellectually."[18] Didion's search for understanding in Miami and El Salvador becomes an

---

[17] Hanley, 24.
[18] Henderson, 90.

attempt at self-realization as well. Henderson suggests that behind Didion's desire to confront reality directly lies "her conviction that the individual is shaped by society; she must therefore confront the social and political reality of contemporary America in order to understand herself."[19] Didion uses style to bridge the gap between her understanding of the historical drama and her role in that drama. In *Salvador*, for example, Didion describes a trip to the Metrocenter, a Salvadoran shopping mall featuring American-made products where armed guards check for weapons at the entrance to the supermarket:

> This was a shopping center that embodied the future for which El Salvador was presumably being saved, and I wrote it down dutifully, this being the kind of 'color' I knew how to interpret, the kind of inductive irony, the detail that was supposed to illuminate the story. As I wrote it down I realized that I was no longer interested in this kind of irony, that this was a story that would not be illuminated by such details, that his was a story that would perhaps not be illuminated all, that this was perhaps even less story than a true *noche obscura*. As I waited to cross back over the Boulevard de los Heroes to the Camino Real I noticed soldiers herding a young civilian into a van, their guns at the boy's back, and I walked straight ahead, not wanting to see anything at all. (36)

In this passage, Didion makes extensive use of isocolons, the repetition of phrases of equal length and corresponding structure, and, more importantly, parataxis, clauses or phrases arranged independently in a coordinate relationship: "the kind of 'color' I

---

[19] Henderson, 90.

knew how to interpret, the kind of inductive irony […] that this was a story that would not be illuminated […] that this was a story that would perhaps not be illuminated…that this was perhaps even less a story than […]." In this instance, parataxis and isocolons indicate that she has not yet ranked the elements of her experience in terms of their ultimate significance. Whatever meaning the experience possesses emerges only in the process of writing about it. Didion's sentences frequently begin with an introductory phrase like, "As I wrote this down I realized," through which she dramatizes the immediacy of her own thought process as she gropes for the truth. The infinitive, "to illuminate," transforms into the passive "not be illuminated" as Didion reflects on her inability to make sense of her experience. Self-consciously aware of her role as "writer," the recorder and arranger of experience, she places the word "color" in quotation marks, perhaps to imply the uselessness of conventional methods when applied to her present task. Similarly, she places the word "story" in quotation marks to suggest the impossibility of imposing a conventional narrative line on the chaotic reality of El Salvador. The Spanish phrase "*noche obscura*" in effect alienates American readers, forcing them into a cognitive impasse similar to Didion's own. We might translate "*noche obscura*" as "dark night," an allusion to Didion's dark night of the soul, during which she grapples with her own doubts, fears, and anxieties. She concludes this passage with a reference to another murder in progress, juxtaposing her own dilemma with the terrible reality of everyday life in El Salvador.

Stylistic Analysis

Throughout this chapter, I have been arguing that the verbal constructions employed by dominant cultures allegorize their attempt to assert their hegemony over emergent and residual cultures. Didion's style works against hegemony, asserting

215

freedom over repression. We must now turn to a closer examination of Didion's style, something most critics writing on her texts tend to overlook. Chris Anderson is somewhat of an exception here. Like me, he reads Didion's texts through the filter of certain rhetorical principles set forth by Kenneth Burke, one of which is the process of "identification," an attempt on the writer's part to persuade her audience by asking them to identify with the speaker.[20] Didion reports from Miami and El Salvador not only to convey her impressions about the sociopolitical realities of those places, but also to persuade her readers to identify with her attitude toward them. Anderson's discussion of Didion's nonfiction texts focuses primarily on her earlier essays, collected in *Slouching Towards Bethlehem* and *The White Album*, and not on her journalism. He devotes only a few pages to *Salvador*, and none to *Miami*. As I argued in my introductory chapter, Anderson's interpretation of Didion's texts (like his discussion of the work of Mailer, Capote, and Wolfe) attempts unsuccessfully to locate the true subject of her work in the realm of the metaphysical, ineffable, or expressible. In the process, Anderson mystifies historical processes. My analysis, by contrast, finds the meaning of Didion's texts rooted in her direct experience of sociopolitical realties in Miami and El Salvador. Mark Muggli argues that "Didion's rhetoric [...] is best approached through the close analysis practiced by critics interpreting individual literary texts"[21] but again, he seems content to make some general observations about Didion's early style, devoting a few paragraphs to *Salvador* and none at all to *Miami*. To cite one other example, Daniel Lemman refers to Didion's style as "mannered," yet another impressionistic

---

[20] Burke, *Rhetoric*, 19.
[21] Muggli, 21.

216

description that does little to describe the responses Didion's prose invokes in her readers.[22]

In order to persuade readers to adopt an attitude toward contemporary political events, Didion uses a highly self-conscious and implicitly persuasive literary style, achieving what Kenneth Burke calls "pure persuasion," a process by which stylistic patterns assume persuasive properties.[23] Didion juxtaposes what Bakhtin would call her "internally persuasive" style against the "authoritative" discourse of the dominant culture.[24] "Authoritative" discourse refuses to acknowledge its participation in shaping the events it describes; thus, it creates a false impression of an objective realty. By calling attention to style as style, as verbal play, Didion implicitly acknowledges the individual's role in creating social reality. Like the work of the other New Journalists, Didion's style becomes most purely persuasive when the degree of her direct participation in events is at its most intense. Through a close reading of a selected passage, we can see how Didion achieves "pure persuasion" in her texts and allegorizes her direct participation in historical reality. Once again, I have chosen to appropriate terms from classical rhetoric to explicate a key passage. The opening paragraphs to *Salvador* set the mood for the anxiety and fear Didion experiences during her entire stay in that Central American country:

> The three-year-old El Salvador International Airport
> is glassy and white and splendidly isolated,
> conceived during the waning of Molina "National
> Transformation" as convenient less to the capital
> (San Salvador is forty miles away, until recently a

[22] Lehman, 231.
[23] Burke, *Rhetoric*, 269.
[24] Bakhtin, 342.

drive of several hours) than to a central hallucination of the Molina and Romero regimes, the projected beach resorts, the Hyatt, the Pacifica Paradise, tennis, golf, water-skiing, condos, *Costa del Sol*; the visionary invention of a tourist industry in yet another republic where the leading natural cause of death is gastro-intestinal infection. In the general absence of tourists these hotels have since been abandoned, ghost resorts on the empty Pacific beaches, and to land at this airport built to service them is to plunges directly into a state in which no ground is solid, no depth of field reliable, no perception so definite that it might not dissolve into its reverse.

The only logic is that of acquiescence. Immigration is negotiated in a thicket of automatic weapons, but by whose authority the weapons are brandished (Army or National Guard or National Police or Customs Police or Treasury Police or one of a continuing proliferation of shadowy and overlapping forces) is a blurred point. Eye contact is avoided. Documents are scrutinized upside down. Once clear of the airport, on the new highway that slices through green hills rendered phosphorescent by the cloud cover of the tropical rainy season, one sees mainly underfed cattle and mongrel dogs and armored vehicles, vans and trucks and Cherokee Chiefs fitted with reinforced steel and bulletproof Plexiglas an inch thick. Such vehicles are a fixed feature of local life, and are popularly associated with disappearance and death. There was the Cherokee Chief seen following the Dutch television

218

crew killed in Chalatenango province in March, 1982. There was a red Toyota three quarter-ton pickup sighted near the van driven by the four American Catholic workers on the night they were killed in 1980. There were, in the last spring and summer of 1982, the three Toyota panel trucks, one yellow, one blue, and one green, none bearing plates, reported present at each of the mass detentions (a 'detention' is another fixed feature of local life, and often precedes a 'disappearance') in the Amatepec district of San Salvador. These are the details—the models and colors of armored vehicles, the makes and calibers of weapons, the particular methods of dismemberment and decapitation used in particular instances—on which the visitor to Salvador learns immediately to concentrate, to the exclusion of past or future concerns, as in a prolonged amnesiac fugue. (13-14)

Both *Miami* and *Salvador* are composed of chunks or fragments of discourse often, as in the passage quoted above, several paragraphs in length, related to one another thematically and stylistically, but nevertheless discrete. The passage above is one of many which are separated from one another by blank space on the page. Each fragment builds to a dramatic climax, leaving the reader with a dominant impression of the feel of the event narrated or described. Through the use of fragments, Didion asks her readers to identify with her struggle to understand highly complex historical phenomena, and even to participate in the process of making sense of the situations. Anderson similarly argues that Didion's fragmented texts require the "active interpretation" of the reader.[25]

---

[25] Anderson, 137.

Once again, however, because his discussion of Didion's prose lacks the specificity of my own, he is unable to demonstrate how reader participation actually works. The first syntactically complex sentence allegorizes Didion's frustrated attempts to grasp the overwhelming complexity and mystery of El Salvador. The sentence is seemingly periodic, or hypotactic, but the syntactic suspension finally snaps, collapsing into parataxis. In the paratactic, or running style, isocolonic elements develop out of one another as if by a spontaneous process of association, phrase following phrase toward no anticipated end. Didion's sentence ends not with a rounded period (which suggests a mind which had arrived at certain conclusions before it put words on the page), but with a grimly ironic qualification. Again, the effect is heuristic.

A parenthetical remark, "(San Salvador is forty miles away [...])," disorients the reader. Why, we may ask, is the airport so far away from the capital city? The passive construction, beginning with "conceived," modifies "airport" and helps to answer our question. American investors, the missing subject in "conceived," have clearly attempted to remake El Salvador in their own images, as witnessed by the "projected beach resorts," etc.; (Didion places "'National Transformation'" in quotes to suggest that, to the contrary, American efforts have failed, for clearly they have transformed nothing permanently.) Nevertheless, the modifier, "until recently," suggests the rapid changes American investors have brought about. A string of modifiers follow "central hallucination," a key metaphor which conveys the sense of unreality Didion experiences throughout her stay in El Salvador. Through the use of asyndeton, the omission of conjunctions, Didion combines disparate elements in a condensed hallucinatory blur: "the projected beach resorts, the Hyatt, the Pacifica Paradise, tennis, golf, water-skiing, condos, *Costa del Sol* [...]." The metaphor, "ghost resorts," modifying "hotels," creates a resonant

220

image of mystery and death. One final modifier, "the visionary inventions of a tourist industry in yet another republic where the leading natural cause of death is gastrointestinal infection," undermines the grandiose schemes of American expansionism. In contrast to this final image of bodily decay, Didion describes the airport as "glassy and white and splendidly isolated." The polysyndetic construction separates adjectives with conjunctions to emphasize this feeling of sterility and detachment. In the first sentence, then, we see a progression from an image of institutional sterility, "the El Salvador International Airport," to an image of disease, "gastrointestinal infection," which dramatizes the corrupt reality beneath the rhetorical surface of Salvadoran life.

The first paragraph contains one parenthetical element, "(San Salvador [...])," which interrupts the flow of the discourse. The passage we are examining contains other parentheses which achieve the same effect. In the second paragraph, Didion places multiple items in parentheses, "(Army or National Guard or [...])," in between the phrase, "by whose authority the weapons are brandished," and the phrase it modifies, "is a blurred point." The effect is to disrupt the continuity of the narrative, leaving Didion, and the reader, in a state of suspended uncertainty. Clearly, Didion asks the reader to identify with her own sense of confusion. Another parenthetical element, "(a 'detention' is another fixed feature of local life, and often precedes a 'disappearance')," has already been cited as an example of the way Didion exposes euphemisms which distort reality. Considered in context, this aside appears in the middle of a list of documented murders, details which in Didion's text are never merely descriptive. In contrast to the obfuscating rhetoric of the Salvadoran government, details serve stylistic and even political purposes, as Anderson explains: "The effect is to juxtapose words used to describe death and mutilation with the plain fact of mutilated bodies."[26] Enveloping the "disappearance" passage, Didion's details achieve the effect Anderson describes. The final sentence contains further details and yet another parenthetical element, set off this time not by parentheses but dashes:

> These are the details—the models and colors of armored vehicles, the makes and calibers of weapons, the particular methods of dismemberment and decapitation used in particular instances—on which the visitor to Salvador learns immediately to concentrate, to the exclusion of past and future concerns, as in a prolonged amnesiac fugue. (14)

Didion calls attention to the details by breaking off the sentence to list them. The reader must suspend her attention to "concentrate" on them, and the repetition of "particular" helps her to focus. Summarizing much of the information relayed by this paragraph so far, the isocolons, "models and colors of [...] makes and calibers of [...] particular methods of," suggest Didion's effort to make these details cohere. In an earlier passage, Didion creates a polysyndetic construction (numerous conjunctions) to convey a sense of the random incongruity of disparate objects co-existing in an atmosphere of normalcy and terror: "underfed cattle and mongrel dogs and armored vehicles, vans and trucks and Cherokee Chiefs [....]" Faced with the absence of continuity and the presence of incongruity implied by the passage above, Didion sometimes feels the necessity to record the details of her immediate experience in the simplest possible terms, and the conjunctions here come to her aid. The phrase "to the exclusion of past or future concerns" qualifies "to concentrate," and stresses Didion's need to focus on the here and now. The striking metaphor

---

[26] Anderson, 168.

which concludes this passage, "prolonged amnesiac fugue," also qualifies "to concentrate," and suggests the numbing effect of so many diverse details.

As we saw in the first paragraph, Didion creates a sense of disorientation. She achieves this effect throughout the passage. Numerous historical names ("Romero" and "Molina") and events ("National Transformation") appear in Didion's text, often without explanation. Didion's purpose is not to write a history of El Salvador (that information may be obtained elsewhere) but to recreate a sense of her immediate experience of the place. A reader unfamiliar with the historical references consequently feels alienated, or disoriented, and therefore shares, symbolically at least, Didion's own experience. In order to heighten the effect of sensory disorientation, Didion uses a stylistic construction called zeugma, the use of one word to govern several congruent words or phrases, in the last sentence in paragraph one: in this case, the verb "is" governs "no depth of field reliable, no perception so definite that it might not dissolve into its reverse." The omission of a verb in these last two phrases intensifies the writer's feeling (and the reader's) that "no ground is solid [....]" The second paragraph contains several passive constructions which also allegorize the sense of disorientation and uncertainty Didion feels everywhere in El Salvador: "Immigration is negotiated [...] weapons are brandished [...] Eye contact is avoided. Documents are scrutinized upside down." The phrase, "by whose authority," raises a typical question in a country where it is difficult to determine, at any given point, who is in charge. The polysyndetic construction, "(Army or National Guard or National Police or Customs Police or Treasury Police or one of a continuing proliferation of shadowy and overlapping forces)," presents Didion and the reader with a distinct yet bewildering number of choices. The passive construction, "are popularly associated," is an example of pardiegesis, the use of an observation to set up further observations and to provide cohesion. In this case, Didion goes on to enumerate specific historical incidents which explain why certain vehicles "are popularly associated with disappearance and death." The rhetorical term for the list that follows is enumeratio: the division of a subject into its adjuncts, causes into effect, or antecedents into consequence. Didion also uses anaphora here (one of her favorite stylistic devices): "There was the Cherokee Chief seen following the Dutch television crew [...] There was the red Toyota three-quarter-ton pickup [...] There were [...] the three Toyota panel trucks[...]." Didion uses anaphora to impose order on disparate historical facts. The anaphoric structure stresses the regularity of such "disappearances," while the repetitive structure of "In March of 1982," "on the night they were killed in 1980," and "in the late spring and summer of 1982" creates a sinister refrain in this litany of terror. Didion sets up another repetitive pattern with the appositives, "one yellow, one blue, and one green [...]." The passive constructions, "seen," "sighted," and "reported," emphasize that such reports are often vague, and frequently anonymous, because most Salvadorans are afraid to get directly involved.

The passage we are examining offers examples of Didion's feel for rhythm and sound. Such musical effects contribute to the "pure persuasiveness" of Didion's prose. In the passage beginning, "In the general absence of tourists," and ending, "Eye contact is avoided," Didion mixes short and long sentences for persuasive purposes. The complex longer sentences strain the reader's attention until she almost loses her concentration, and the shorter sentences drive home Didion's point with particular emphasis. The metaphor, "thicket of automatic weapons," with the hard assonance of its "k" and "t" sounds, suggests Didion's difficulty in this passage, as well as the threat of violence. The alliterative phrase "fixed feature of local life" occurs twice, allegorizing the mechanical repetitiveness of organized repression.

Conclusion

As I stated at the outset, Didion's decidedly left-wing ideological slant is never dogmatic of doctrinaire. She condemns the murders committed by the U.S.-backed Salvadoran government, yet her indictment does not imply an endorsement of the FMLN or any other Salvadoran guerilla group. She similarly sympathizes with the second-class status granted Miami Cubans by the dominant Anglo community, but she also reports that anti-Castro Miami Cubans systematically terrorize their leftist and moderate counterparts. Finally, Didion offers no solutions to the political problems posed by the Cuban-Anglo conflict, which is why Mark Winchell warns:

> The reader who comes to Didion's *Miami* looking for specific policy recommendations is likely to be disappointed. Despite her sympathy for the Cuban exiles, she is not about to urge Washington to back their counterrevolution and seems to be almost as scornful of the hard-line right-wingers who do so as she is of the cynical pragmatists who simply milk the situation for their partisan advantage.[27]

Further, Winchell maintains that "the foreign policy implicitly endorsed by *Miami* is not different from the one found in *Salvador*—a skeptical isolationism based on the assumption that no good can come from American meddling in the affairs of other countries."[28] Didion's refusal to offer concrete or programmatic solutions to the problems posed by Miami and El Salvador

---

[27] Winchell, 120.
[28] Winchell, 121.

225

indicates that her version of the historical narrative remains unresolved.

Frederick Kiley finds that "Didion's *Salvador* is a terrifying enigma that frustrates each new promising effort to solve it, ironically merging solution and problem into a new dilemma."[29] Similarly, Chris Anderson states that a characteristic feature of all of Didion's nonfiction is its "refusal to come to reconciling conclusion."[30] Anderson maintains that Didion's heuristic approach accounts for her lack of conclusiveness: "in the present moment of these acts of discovery," he says, "Didion's conclusion can only be tentative and qualified."[31] Didion has expressed her own conviction that "the last sentence in a piece is another adventure. It should open the piece up. It should make you go back and start reading again from page one."[32] The style and rhetorical approach of Didion's nonfiction texts are appropriately open-ended because the situations they address are still in the process of historical development. As I have demonstrated, Didion exposes futile attempts to achieve ideological closure where no closure is possible. Hartsock argues that what Didion feels about her experience in Miami and Salvador "must ultimately remain imprecise as she confronts the inconclusive present."[33] In *Miami*, Didion says that "Miami stories tend to have endings," but the historical narrative does not (108). Her role in the drama comes to an end, but the ideological struggle between Miami Cubans and the dominant Anglo community continues. On the final page of *Miami,* Didion hints obscurely at "what has yet to take place" on that particular stage in world history (208). *Salvador* ends more

---

[29] Kiley, 188.
[30] Anderson, 160.
[31] Anderson, 141.
[32] Keuhl, 410.
[33] Harstock, 201.

226

dramatically as Didion describes the nervous tension and anticipated release of her flight out of that country (105-108). Nevertheless, the book's long final sentence lists further "disappearances" and accompanying reports from the Regan administration proclaiming El Salvador's progress on human rights (108). "She does not say it, but her book strongly implies that the American project is inevitably a failure. It still remains to be seen how disastrous the failure will become and when, if ever, the difficult, long, modest, unglamorous task of founding a history proper to the resources and idiosyncrasies of El Salvador will begin."[34] Through the textual incorporation and evaluation of dominant ideology, and the inscribing of its ideological subtext, Didion dismantles the dominant texts. She engages them in a dialectical relationship, refusing to grant them their intended status as absolute truth. She thus undermines the authority of opposing discourse, opening the way for ongoing debate and struggle.

---

[34] Kiley, 165.

Bibliography

Published Primary Sources

Capote, Truman. *In Cold Blood: A True Account of a Multiple Murder and Its Consequences*. New York: Random House, 1965. Print.

Didion, Joan. *Miami*. New York: Simon and Schuster, 1987. Print.

_____. "On Morality." *Slouching Towards Bethlehem*. Paperback ed. New York: Farrar, Straus and Giroux, 1990. 157-63. Print.

_____. *Salvador*. New York: Simon and Schuster, 1982. Print.

_____. *Slouching Towards Bethlehem*. New York: Dell, 1968. Print.

_____. *The White Album*. New York: Simon and Schuster, 1979. Print.

_____. *The Year of Magical Thinking*. 1st ed. New York: A. A. Knopf, 2005. Print.

Herr, Michael. *Dispatches*. New York: Avon, 1978. Print.

Mailer, Norman. *The Armies of the Night : History as a Novel, the Novel as History*. New York: New American Library, 1968. Print.

_____. *Cannibals and Christians*. New York: Dial Press, 1966. Print.

_____. *The Executioner's Song*. Boston: Little, Brown, 1979. Print.

_____. *The Naked and the Dead*. New York: Rinehart, 1948. Print.

Thompson, Hunter S. *Fear and Loathing in Las Vegas: A Savage Journey to the Heart of the American Dream*. New York: Random House, 1971. Print.

_____. *Fear and Loathing: On the Campaign Trail '72*. Straight Arrow Books: San Francisco, 1973. Print.

_____. *Hell's Angels: A Strange and Terrible Saga*. New York: Ballantine, 1995. Print.

_____. "The Kentucky Derby Is Decadent and Depraved." *The Great Shark Hunt: Strange Tales from a Strange Time*. New York: Summit Books, 1979. 24-38. Print.

Wolfe, Tom. *The Electric Kool-Aid Acid Test*. New York: Farrar, Straus and Giroux, 1968. Print.

Secondary Sources

Adams, Laura. *Existential Battles: The Growth of Norman Mailer*. Athens: Ohio UP, 1976. Print.

Anderson, Chris. "Dramatism and Deliberation." *Rhetoric Review* 4.1 (1985): 34-43. Print.

_____. *Literary Nonfiction: Theory, Criticism, Pedagogy*. Carbondale: Southern Illinois UP, 1989. Print.

_____. *Style as Argument: Contemporary American Nonfiction*. Carbondale: Southern Illinois UP, 1987. Print.

Aristotle. *Rhetoric*. Trans. W. Rhys Roberts and Ingram Bywater. The Modern Library of the World's Best Books [246]. Ed. Friedrich Solmsen. New York: Modern Library, 1954. Print.

Arnold, Matthew. "Dover Beach." *The Works of Matthew Arnold*. London: Macmillan, 1903-04. 56-57. Print.

Bakhtin, M. M. *The Dialogic Imagination: Four Essays*. U. of Texas Press Series. Ed. Michael Holquist. Austin, TX: University of Texas, 1981. Print.

Begiebing, Robert J. *Acts of Regeneration: Allegory and Archetype in the Works of Norman Mailer*. Columbia: Univ. of Missouri, 1980. Print.

Beidler, Philip D. *American Literature and the Experience of Vietnam*. Athens, Ga.: Univ. of Georgia, 1982. Print.

Berthoff, Warner. "Witness and Testament: Two Contemporary Classics." Rev. of *The Armies of the Night* by Normal Mailer." *Fiction and Events*. New York: Dutton, 1973.

Print.

Bloom, Harold. "Introduction." *Norman Mailer*. Vol. 1-6. Philadelphia: Chelsea House, 2003. Print.

Booth, Wayne C. "Loathing and Ignorance on the Campaign Trail: Rev. of *Fear and Loathing: On the Campaign Trail '72* by Hunter S. Thompson." *Columbia Journalism Review* 12.4 (1973): 7-12. Print.

Breslin, James E. "Style in Norman Mailer's *The Armies of the Night*." *The Yearbook of English Studies* 8 (1978): 157-70. Print.

Bruce, Novoa. "Fear and Loathing on the Buffalo Trail." *MELUS* 6.4 (1979): 39-50. Print.

Bufithis, Philip H. *Norman Mailer*. Modern Literature Monographs. New York: Ungar, 1978.

Burke, Kenneth. *A Grammar of Motives*. Berkley: Univ. of California, 1969. Print.

_____. *The Philosophy of Literary Form: Studies in Symbolic Action*. 3d ed. Berkeley: University of California Press, 1974. Print.

_____. *A Rhetoric of Motives*. Berkeley: Univ. of California, 1969. Print.

Campbell, Joseph. *The Hero with a Thousand Faces*. Princeton: Princeton UP, 2004. Print.

Caron, James E. "Hunter S. Thompson's 'Gonzo' Journalism and the Tall Tale Tradition in America." *Studies in Popular Culture* 8.1 (1985): 1-16. Print.

Chomsky, Noam and Edward S. Herman. *After the Cataclysm: Postwar Indochina and the Construction of Imperial Ideology*. Boston: South End Press, 1979. Print.

_____. *Manufacturing Consent: the Political Economy of the Mass Media*. NY: Pantheon Books, 1988. Print.

Corbett, P. J. Edward and Robert J Connors. *Classical Rhetoric for the Modern Student*. New York: Oxford UP, 1965. Print.

Corradi, Juan E. "A Culture of Fear." Rev. of *Salvador* by Joan Didion." *Dissent* 30 (1983): 387-89. Print.

Crouse, Timothy. *The Boys on the Bus*. New York: Random House, 2003. Print.

De Saussure, Ferdinand. *Course in General Linguistics*. New York: McGraw-Hill, 1966. Print.

Defoe, Daniel. *A Journal of the Plague Year*. Everyman Library. London: J. M. Dent; New York, Dutton, 1966. Print.

Dickstein, Morris. "How Mailer Became 'Mailer': The Writer as Private and Public Character." *The Mailer Review* (2007): 118-31. Print.

_____. "The Working Press, the Literary Culture, and the New Journalism." *The Georgia Review* XXX.4 (1976): 855-77. Print.

Dillon, George L. "Fiction in Persuasion: Personal Experience as Evidence and as Art." *Literary Nonfiction: Theory, Criticism, Pedagogy*. Ed. Chris Anderson. Carbondale: Southern Illinois UP, 1989. 197-210. Print.

Dowling, William C. *Jameson, Althusser, Marx: An Introduction to the Political Unconscious*. Ithaca: Cornell UP, 1984. Print.

Eason, David L. "The New Journalism and the Image-World." *Literary Journalism in the Twentieth Century*. Ed. Norman Sims. New York: Oxford UP, 1990. 191-206. Republished Evanston, IL: Northwestern University Press, 2008. Print.

_____. "New Journalism, Metaphor and Culture." *Journal of Popular Culture* 15.4 (1982): 142-50. Print.

Ehrlich, Robert *Norman Mailer: The Radical as Hipster*. Metuchen: Scarecrow Press, 1978. Print.

Epstein, Edward J. *Between Fact and Fiction: The Problem of Journalism*. New York: Vintage, 1975. Print.

Filloy, Richard. "Orwell's Political Persuasion: A Rhetoric of Personality." *Literary Nonfiction: Theory, Criticism, Pedagogy.* Ed. Chris Anderson. Carbondale: Southern Illinois UP, 1989. 51-69. Print.

Frus, Phyllis. *The Politics and Poetics of Journalistic Narrative: The Timely and the Timeless.* Cambridge: Cambridge UP, 1994. Print.

Frye, Northrop. *Anatomy of Criticism: Four Essays.* Princeton: Princeton UP, 1957. Print.

Geertz, Clifford. *The Interpretation of Cultures: Selected Essays.* New York: Basic Books, 1973. Print.

Gutman, Stanley T. *Mankind in Barbary: The Individual and Society in the Novels of Norman Mailer.* Hanover: Univ. Press of New England, 1975. Print.

Hanley, Lynne T. "To El Salvador." *The Massachusetts Review: A Journal of Literature the Arts and Public Affairs* 24.1 (1983): 13-29. Print.

Hartsock, John C. *A History of American Literary Journalism: The Emergence of a Modern Narrative Form.* Amherst: U of Massachusetts P, 2000. Print.

Hayakawa, S. I. Hayakawa Alan R., ed. *Language in Thought and Action.* 5th ed. San Diego: Harcourt Brace & Co., 1992. Print.

Hebdige, Dick. *Subculture: The Meaning of Style.* New York: Routledge, 1979. Print.

Hellmann, John. *Fables of Fact: The New Journalism as New Fiction.* Urbana: Univ. of Illinois, 1981. Print.

Henderson, Katherine U. *Joan Didion.* Modern Literature Series. New York: Ungar, 1981. Print.

Hentoff, Nat. "Journalism Old, New, and Corporate." *The Reporter as Artist: A New Look at the New Journalism Controversy.* Ed. Ronald Weber. New York: Hastings House, 1974. 49-

233

53. Print.

Herman. Edward S. and Noam Chomsky. *Manufacturing Consent: The Political Economy of the Mass Media*. New York: Pantheon Books, 1988. Print.

Hersey, John. "The Legend on the License." *Yale Review* 70.1 (1980): 1-25. Print.

Herzog, Tobey C. *Vietnam War Stories: Innocence Lost*. New York: Routledge, 1992. Print.

Heyne, Eric. "Toward a Theory of Literary Nonfiction." *Modern Fiction Studies* 33.3 (1987): 479-490. Print.

Hollowell, John. *Fact and Fiction: The New Journalism and the Nonfiction Novel*. Chapel Hill: Univ. of North Carolina, 1977. Print.

Humphries, David T. *Different Dispatches: Journalism in American Modernist Prose*. New York: Routledge, 2006. Print.

Jameson, Fredric. *Marxism and Form: Twentieth-Century Dialectical Theories of Literature*. Princeton, New Jersey: Princeton UP, 1971. Print.

Jeffords, Susan. *The Remasculinization of America: Gender and the Vietnam War*. Theories of Contemporary Culture. Bloomington: Indiana UP, 1989. Print.

Johnson, Michael. "Journalist." *Will the Real Norman Mailer Please Stand Up*. Ed. Laura Adams. Port Washington: Kennikat, 1974. 173-94. Print.

Joyce, James. *Ulysses* 1st ed. New York: Vintage Books, 1986. Print.

Kennedy, William. "Normal Mailer as Occasional Commentator in a Self-Interview and Memoir." *The Mailer Review* (2007): 183-91. Print.

Kenner, Hugh. "The Politics of the Plain Style." *Literary Journalism in the Twentieth Century*. Ed. Norman Sims.

234

New York: Oxford UP, 1990. 183-91. Print.

Kiley, Frederick. "Beyond Words." *Joan Didion: Essays and Conversations*. Ed. Friedman Ellen G. Princeton, NJ: Ontario Review Press, 1984. 181-88. Print.

Kuehl, Linda. "Joan Didion." *Women Writers at Work: The Paris Review Interviews*. Ed. George Plimpton. New York: Modern Library, 1998. 319-36. Print.

Lanham, Richard A. *Analyzing Prose*. Scribner English Series. New York: Scribner, 1983. Print.

_____. *A Handlist of Rhetorical Terms*. 2nd ed. Berkeley: U. of California, 1991. Print.

Lehman, Daniel W. *Matters of Fact Reading Nonfiction over the Edge*. Columbus: Ohio State UP, 1997. Print.

Lennon, J. Michael. "Norman Mailer: Novelist, Journalist, or Historian?" *Journal of Modern Literature* 30.1 (2006): 91-103. Print.

_____. "Introduction." *Norman Mailer : Works and Days*. Ed. Michael Lennon Donna Pedro Lennon. Shavertown: Sligo Press, 2000. xi-xiii. Print.

Lentricchia, Frank. *Criticism and Social Change*. Chicago: U. of Chicago, 1983. Print.

Lindemann, Erika. *A Rhetoric for Writing Teachers*. 3rd ed.: Oxford UP, 1995. Print.

Locke, Richard. "Field Reports: Alaska and Vietnam." Rev. of *Dispatches* by Michael Herr. *New York Times Book Review* 3 (1977): 26-27. Print.

Lounsberry, Barbara. *The Art of Fact: Contemporary Artists of Nonfiction*. New York: Greenwood Press, 1990. Print.

McKeen, William. *Hunter S. Thompson*. Twayne's United States Authors Series. Boston: Twayne Publishers, 1991. Print.

_____. *Outlaw Journalist: The Life and Times of Hunter S. Thompson*. New York: W.W. Norton, 2008. Print.

235

Meisenhelder, Thomas. "Sociology and New Journalism." *Journal of Popular Culture* 11.2 (1977): 467-78. Print.

Merideth, Robert. "The 45-Second Piss: A Left Critique of Norman Mailer and *The Armies of the Night.*" *Modern Fiction Studies* 17.3 (1971): 433-50. Print.

Meyers, Thomas. *Walking Point: American Narratives of Vietnam.* New York: Oxford UP, 1988. Print.

Muggli, Mark Z. "The Poetics of Joan Didion's Journalism." *American Literature* 59.3 (1987): 402-21. Print.

Murphy, James E. "The New Journalism: A Critical Perspective." *Journalism Monographs* 34 (1974). Print.

Neilson, Jim. *Warring Fictions American Literary Culture and the Vietnam War Narrative*: Jackson, MS: U. Press of Mississippi, 1998. Print.

Newfield, Jack. "Behold the New Journalism--It's Coming after You!" *The Reporter as Artist: A Look at the New Journalism Controversy.* Ed. Ronald Weber. New York: Hastings House, 1974. 49-54. Print.

Orwell, George. "Politics and the English Language." *A Collection of Essays.* New York: Harcourt, Brace & Co., 1981. 156-171. Print.

_____. "Why I Write." *A Collection of Essays.* New York: Harcourt, Brace & Co., 1981. 309-316. Print.

Pauly, John J. "The Politics of the New Journalism." *Literary Journalism in the Twentieth Century.* Ed. Norman Sims. New York: Oxford UP, 1990. 110-129. Republished Evanston, IL: Northwestern University Press, 2008. Print.

Petigny, Alan. "Norman Mailer, 'the White Negro,' and New Conceptions of the Self in Postwar America." *The Mailer Review* (2007): 184-93. Print.

Plimpton, George. "Truman Capote: An Interview." *The Reporter as Artist : A Look at the New Journalism Controversy.* Ed.

Ronald Weber. New York: Hastings House, 1974. 188-206. Print.

Poirier, Richard. *Norman Mailer*. New York: Viking Press, 1972. Print.

Postman, Neil. *Amusing Ourselves to Death: Public Discourse in the Age of Show Business*. New York: Penguin Books, 1986. Print.

Ringnalda, Don. *Fighting and Writing the Vietnam War*. Jackson: Univ. Press of Mississippi, 1994. Print.

Roszak, Theodore. *The Making of a Counter Culture: Reflections on the Technocratic Society and Its Youthful Opposition*. Garden City: Doubleday, 1969. Print.

Rygiel, Dennis. "Stylistics and the Study of Twentieth-Century Literary Nonfiction." *Literary Nonfiction: Theory, Criticism, and Pedagogy*. Ed. Chris Anderson. Carbondale: Southern Illinois UP, 1989. 29-50. Print.

Schiller, Dan. *Objectivity and the News: The Public and the Rise of Commercial Journalism*. Philadelphia: U. of Pennsylvania, 1981. Print.

Schroeder, Eric James. *Vietnam, We've All Been There: Interviews with American Writers*. Westport: Praeger, 1992. Print.

Searle, John. "The Logical Status of Fictional Discourse." *New Literary History* 6 (1975): 319-332. Print.

Seib, Kenneth A. "Mailer's March: The Epic Structure of *The Armies of the Night*." *Essays in Literature* 1 (1974): 89-95. Print.

Sheed, Wilfrid. "A Fun-House Mirror." *The Reporter as Artist: A New Look at the New Journalism Controversy*. Ed. Ronald Weber. New York: Hastings House, 1974. 312-24. Print.

Smith, Kathy. "Norman Mailer and the Radical Text." *Norman Mailer*. Ed. Harold Bloom. Philadelphia: Chelsea House Publishers, 2003. 181-97. Print.

Stevens, Wallace. "The Anecdote of the Jar." *The Collected Poems of Wallace Stevens.* New York: Vintage Books, 1982. 76. Print.

Stewart, Matthew C. "Styles in *Dispatches*: Heteroglossia and Michael Herr's Break with Conventional Journalism." *America Rediscovered: Critical Essays on Literature and Film of the Vietnam War.* Ed. Owen W. Smith Lorrie Gilman. New York: Garland, 1990. 189-204. Print.

Taylor, Gordon O. *Chapters of Experience: Studies in 20th Century American Autobiography.* New York: St. Martin's Press, 1983. Print.

Taylor, Mark J. *The Vietnam War in History, Literature and Film.* Edinburgh: Edinburgh UP, 2003. Print.

Trachtenberg, Alan. "Mailer on the Steps of the Pentagon." Rev. of *The Armies of the Night* by Norman Mailer." *The Nation* (1968): 701-02. Print.

Tuchman, Gaye. "Making the News by Doing Work: Routinizing the Unexpected." *American Journal of Sociology.* 79 (1979): 110-31. Print.

Voloshinov, V. N., Matejka Ladislav, et al. *Marxism and the Philosophy of Language.* New York: Seminar Press, 1973. Print.

Vonnegut, Kurt., Jr. "A Political Disease." *Harper's Magazine,* July (1973): 92-94. Print.

Walker, Ruth. "Didion's *Miami* and Multiple Realities." *Christian Science Monitor* 24 (1987) 24. Print.

Weber, Ronald. *The Literature of Fact: Literary Nonfiction in American Writing.* Athens: Ohio UP, 1980. Print.

_____. *The Reporter as Artist: A Look at the New Journalism Controversy.* New York: Hastings House, 1974. Print.

Weingarten, Marc. *The Gang That Wouldn't Write Straight: Wolfe, Thompson, Didion, and the New Journalism Revolution.*

New York: Crown Publishers, 2005. Print.

Williams, Raymond. *Marxism and Literature.* Marxist Introductions. New York: Oxford UP, 1977. Print.

Winterowd, W. Ross. *The Rhetoric of the 'Other' Literature.* Carbondale: Southern Illinois UP, 1990. Print.

Wolfe, Tom and E. W. Johnson, ed. *The New Journalism.* New York: Harper & Row, 1973. Print.

Zavarzadeh, Masud. *The Mythopoeic Reality: The Postwar American Nonfiction Novel.* Urbana, IL: U. of Illinois, 1976. Print.

Index

Gutman, Stanley T., 115,
116, 120, 152

H
Hanley, Lynne T., 201, 211-
213
Hartsock, John, 2, 9, 21, 45,
47, 52, 53, 226
Hayakawa, S.I., 34
Hebdige, Dick, 19, 20, 26
Hellmann, John, 19, 20, 33-
35, 37-39, 42, 47, 54, 64-
66, 77, 81, 89, 99, 100,
111, 112, 136
Hell's Angels, 6, 12, 183,
185, 186
Hemingway, Ernest, 1, 65
"A Way You'll Never
Be", 65
Henderson, Katharine U.,
213, 214
Hentoff, Nat, 6
Herman, Edward, 45, 47,
116, 130
Herr, Michael, 1, 10, 25, 26,
28, 29, 33, 37, 41, 44, 48,
51, 54, 56, 63-66, 68-72,
74-80, 88-94, 96-105, 107,
108, 118, 119
Dispatches, 8, 10, 25, 37,
41, 48, 56, 63-65, 69, 72,
73, 75-77, 80, 88-90, 99,
101, 103-105, 107, 108
Hersey, John, 1, 3
Herzog, Tobey C., 10
Hipster, 63

Hollowell, John, 17, 48, 49,
53, 150-152
Howells, William Dean, 35
Humphrey, Hubert H., 157,
159, 164, 165

J
Jameson, Fredric, 24
Jeffords, Susan, 67
Jeremiah, Book of, 13
Johnson, Lyndon B., 1, 109,
115, 128, 132
Journalism, 2, 3, 45, 49
Joyce, James, 37
Ulysses, 37

K
Kennedy, Edward, 167
Kennedy, John F, 199
Kennedy, Robert F, 158
Kennedy, William, 50
Kenner, Hugh, 39, 58
Keuhl, Linda, 36
Kiley, Frederick, 226, 227
Kupferburg, Tuli, 141

L
Lanham, Richard, 39-43, 55,
56, 58-60, 69, 77, 81, 82,
88
Lehman, Daniel, 5-7, 28, 36,
133, 140
Lennon, Michael, 11, 13, 71,
117, 118
Lentricchia, Frank, 22-25
Liebling, A.J., 1
London, Jack, 1, 26, 44

245

Jason Mosser

Dr. Jason Mosser is an Associate Professor at Georgia Gwinnett College. He received his Ph.D. in English from the University of Georgia. Dr. Mosser has taught English at the Georgia Institute of Technology, where he was a Marion L. Brittain Fellow in Writing, the Atlanta College of Art, Rockford College, and Gainesville State College.